Real Angels
Guiding Spirits, Benevolent Beings,
and Heavenly Hosts

About the Authors

For more than five decades, the award-winning writer **Brad Steiger** has been devoted to exploring and examining unusual, hidden, secret, and otherwise miraculous occurrences. A former high school teacher and college instructor, Brad published his first articles about supernatural phenomena in 1956. Since then he has written more than two thousand articles with spiritual or paranormal themes. He is author or coauthor of more than 150 titles, including *Revelation: The Divine Fire*; *Real Ghosts, Restless Spirits, and Haunted Places*; *Atlantis Rising*; *Conspiracies and Secret Societies*; *The Werewolf Book*; and *Mysteries of Time and Space*.

An expert on health and healing, spirituality, and the paranormal, **Sherry Steiger** has numerous magazine articles to her credit and has authored or coauthored more than forty books, including *The Power of Prayer to Heal and Transform Your Life*; *Indian Wisdom and Its Guiding Power*; and the best-selling "Miracles" series. An ordained minister, Sherry has served as counselor to troubled youth, the homeless, migrant workers, and families in need of crisis intervention. With her background in nursing and theology, Sherry began researching alternative health issues and mysteries of the unknown in the 1960s, and she cofounded and produced the highly acclaimed Celebrate Life, a multimedia experiential presentation and workshop program.

Brad and Sherry Steiger live in Iowa, and can be found on the Internet at www.bradandsherry.com.

About the Artist

A rtist, musician, songwriter, and composer Bill Oliver resides in Vancouver, B.C. Oliver has had a life long interest in the paranormal and all things esoteric, stemming from many personal experiences. This keen interest brought him into personal contact and interview opportunities with experiencers in all aspects of the paranormal. These encounters have had significant influences on much of Bill's work. He won the Christmas Art contest on the Jeff Rense site in 2005, as well as honorable mention Halloween 2006. Bill's web design was an award winner in 2005 for his workplace website. His music is reflective and moody and has caught the attention of MTV. Bill's songs, like his art, act as photographs capturing a moment of life and freezing it in time for further contemplation.

"I am humbled being asked to contribute to this book," Oliver said. "Brad Steiger was one my boyhood heroes with his great work on the paranormal, the esoteric, and things that go bump in the night. To be reading Revelation: The Divine Fire one day and being asked to do some art for Brad's and Sherry's new book *Real Angels* the next, tells me one thing—*there must be angels.*"

Bill Oliver would love to hear from you. Contact him at eastender@shaw.ca.

Real Angels

Guiding Spirits, Benevolent Beings, and Heavenly Hosts

BRAD STEIGER AND SHERRY HANSEN STEIGER

DETROIT, MICHIGAN

Real Angels

Guiding Spirits, Benevolent Beings, and Heavenly Hosts

Copyright 2009 by Benjamin Street Press™

Benjamin Street Press™
benjaminstreet.com

Front and Back Cover Art: Bill Oliver
Interior Art: Bill Oliver

Art Director: Mary Claire Krzewinski

Typesetting: Marco Di Vita

ISBN 978-0-9817261-0-6

CIP on file with the Library of Congress

Printed in the United States of America
All rights reserved
10 9 8 7 6 5 4 3 2 1

Real Angels: Book Two, Christmas 2009

Contents

Introduction ... ix
Acknowledgments ... xiii

1. Powers and Principalities from the Unseen World 1

2. Angels in the World's Religions 13

3. The Sound and Sight of Angel Wings 20

4. Guardian Angels Never Sleep 30

5. Invisible Defenders 36

6. Angels Who Left Evidence of Their Visits 45

7. Benevolent Beings Who Intervened in
    Crisis Situations 55

8. Encountering Angels Unaware 69

9. Meeting Spirit Guardians during
    Near-Death Journeys 82

10. Angelic Love and Guidance Are Always Present 94

11. Shamanic and Totem Guides 102

12. Sacred Places Where Miracles Happen 113

13. Grandmother Is My Guardian Angel 123

14. Light Beings from Etheric Vehicles 135

15. An Ancient Order of Spirit Teachers and Healers 146

16. There Is a Timeless Garden of Love within
    Each of Us 156

17. Angels Do So Want to Help 163

18. Benevolent Healing Visitors 168

19. Angelic Yentas Who Bring People Together 181

20. A Very Special Night School Taught by Spirit Guides..... 196

21. The Watchers and the Nephilim....................... 203

22. Majestic, but Not Magical: Spiritual Hazards of
    Seeking to Command Angels 214

Angelic and Other Heavenly Resources ... 227
Index ... 239

Introduction

As early as the third millennium B.C.E., the written records of ancient Egypt and Mesopotamia recognized a hierarchy of supernatural beings that ruled over various parts of the earth, the universe, and the lives of human beings. All the great world religions have some kind of tradition of a guardian angel or a spiritual guide assigned to each individual human soul. The ancient teachings also agree that angels are an earlier and separate order of creation from that of humans, who were sculpted from the dust of the earth and were brought into being (according to Psalm 8) "a little lower than the angels."

On December 12, 2000, the London *Times* reported on the first academic research conducted into the subject of guardian angels. During the course of a two-year study, Emma Heathcote of Birmingham University examined the stories of more than 800 Britons who claimed encounters with heavenly beings. Almost a third of those who contacted the researcher reported seeing a traditional angel with white gown and wings. About 21 percent saw their guardian angel in human form. Others experienced the sensation of a force around them or being engulfed in light.

In many accounts, the angelic beings appear to be paraphysical; that is, they seem to be both material and nonmaterial entities. Although they originate in some invisible and nonphysical dimension, they seem completely capable of shaping reality in our three-dimensional world to suit their heavenly purposes.

There is no question that in both the Old and New Testaments, angels are considered fully capable of becoming physical and material, at least long enough to accomplish their appointed mission of rescue, healing, or guidance. Throughout the Bible there are accounts of angels who wrestled with stubborn shepherds, guided people lost in the wilderness, and freed persecuted prophets from fiery furnaces and dank prisons. Jesus himself was fed by angels, defended by angels, and strengthened by angels.

The scriptures of all faiths state firmly that angels are not to be worshipped or held as objects of veneration. Even though humans are "lower than the angels" and made of material, physical substance in comparison with the heavenly spirits' ethereal energy, the angels are not omnipresent, omnipotent, or omniscient—and they are not immune from falling into temptation or into error.

Ms. Heathcote said in her Birmingham University study that although humans have been preoccupied with angels for centuries, we may now be going through an increased period of interest in the heavenly beings because "people are feeling a spiritual shortage and angels fill the gap."

Here are a few more statistics that indicate how well angels are "filling the gap":

The Leger Marketing Survey of Canadians of October 21, 2001, indicated that 57.1 percent of the population of Canada believes in angels.

On December 20, 2001, Scripps Howard News Service released its findings that one out of every five Americans believes that he or she has seen an angel or knows someone who has.

A 2002 Gallup Poll stated that 72 percent of Americans believe in angels, compared to 96 percent who believed in God and 90 percent in heaven. A recent survey of the nation's religious beliefs and practices finds 55 percent of all adults, including one in five of those who say they have no religion, believe they have been protected from harm by a guardian angel.

"I would never have expected these numbers. It was the biggest surprise to me in our findings, says sociologist Christopher Bader of Baylor University in Waco, Texas. The survey, based on interviews with nearly 1,700 adults in fall 2007, found that members of almost every major religious group sensed angels running heavenly interference: Evangelical Protestant, 66 percent; black Protestant, 81 percent; mainline Protestant, 55 percent; Catholic, 57 percent; Jewish, 10 percent; other religions, 49 percent; no religion, 20 percent.

"People's sense of the divine is remarkably widespread and tangible, even if they don't call it God. Clearly, there's a sense of the sacred prevalent throughout society," says Matthew Gilbert of The Institute of Noetic Sciences in Petaluma, California, which studies subjective experiences using scientific techniques.

Randall Balmer, chairman of the religion department at New York's Barnard College, says that the Baylor angel figures are one in a periodic series of indications that "Americans live in an enchanted world," and engage in a kind of casual mysticism independent of established religious ritual, doctrine or theology. "There is," he says, a "much broader uncharted range of religious experience among the populace than we expect."

The *Evening News* of Edinburgh, Scotland, on October 14, 2004, quoted a poll that found that while membership in organized religions had been plummeting in Britain for decades, one in three people still believed strongly in angels, and one in six claimed they personally had been helped by one. In Ireland, *The Sunday Times* reports that the country is in the midst of an angelic boom, which includes shops opening across the country to meet the demand for paraphernalia, and angel books on top of the bestseller lists. As Ireland balances on the cusp of economic crisis, spiritualism and the promise of hope is selling like never before.

Theologians and historians have observed that accounts of angels and spiritual beings are always very popular in apocalyptic writings and in periods of wars, catastrophes, and political unrest, which indicate to members of certain religious faiths that the "end times" are near. The devout say that this is so because angels were placed in charge of the cosmic order of the universe, and times of crisis summon angels to help set things right. The skeptic will dismiss such explanations of the current reports of angels as the externalized projections of men and women whose own fearful imaginations create the images of benevolent beings to assuage the terror of existence in terrible times.

It is often a bit difficult amidst the technology, science, and cynicism of our contemporary culture to find patient and tolerant audiences for the reports from those who claim to have received visitations or guidance from angels or benevolent beings. However, we assert in *Real Angels: Guiding Spirits, Benevolent Beings, and Heavenly Hosts* that we have recounted stories of guidance, rescue, illumination, healing, and teaching from spiritual beings who were quite separate from the men and women who received their wisdom and divine intervention.

The voluminous mail we have received from respondents to our Steiger Questionnaire of Mystical, Paranormal, and UFO Experiences has demonstrated to our satisfaction that thousands of contemporary men and women are unashamedly interacting with their guardian angels and spiritual guides. What is more, these men and women come from every conceivable walk of life. We have heard from scientists, educators, military officers, concert musicians, members of the clergy, law enforcement personnel, journalists, medical doctors and nurses, psychiatrists, truck drivers, cowboys, stevedores, farmers, housewives, students, and commercial fishermen—all of whom have profited spiritually and sometimes materially from contact with a source of strength and guidance external to themselves.

For many of us there has never been any question whether or not angels exist. However, the theologian and Roman Catholic scholar Matthew Fox has observed that the number-one cosmological question in the Mediterranean area in the first century C.E. was not whether angels existed but whether the angels were friends or foes. We recognize that there are angels of darkness who frequently provide the undiscerning with false prophecies and shallow promises, but in this book we shall explore a very large population of benevolent beings who exist in unseen dimensions all around us.

We shall examine the role and the extensive participation in the spiritual, mental, and physical evolution of humankind of such ethereal entities as God's heavenly messengers, guardian angels, spirit guides, Devas, elves, spirit teachers, the Watchers, Space Brothers and Sisters, Star Beings, and the Sons of God. Perhaps through our determined quest, we shall gain a better understanding of the true identity of these benevolent beings. Are they all the same entities with different names? Are they all different beings with the same cosmic mission?

We can promise you that if you join us on this path of discovery, you will meet an angel or a spirit guide face-to-face—if not in person, then vicariously through the eyes of an individual who is sharing his or her angelic encounter with us.

Acknowledgments

The authors consider the communication of truths about the unseen worlds and the reality of the powers and principalities who interact with humans to be one of their most important earthly missions. The concept of a book about benevolent beings received early encouragement from Mary Beth Perrot, Benjamin Street marketing director, and from our wonderful editor Christa Gainor at Benjamin Street, and we are grateful for their unfailing support throughout this project. Publisher Martin Connors and editor Roger Matuz were quick to declare their confidence in a concept for a book about "real angels," using definitions broad and cross-cultural. Special thanks are extended to art director Mary Claire Krzewinski, whose book design reached for an ethereal essence that meshed perfectly with the text; indexer Lawrence W. Baker and his alphabetic alchemy; Bill Oliver, for his dazzling artwork; Terri Schell, for her support and good cheer; and typesetter Marco Di Vita of the Graphix Group, without whom we would be lost. We also wish to thank our agent, Agnes Birnbaum, whose friendship and encouragement is so much appreciated.

In an undertaking such as this, the authors owe a debt of gratitude to many individuals who contributed accounts of their personal interaction with benevolent beings. There were many men and women who submitted their stories of personal inspiration and transformation through the conduit of our Steiger Questionnaire of Mystical, Paranormal, and UFO Experiences (www.bradandsherry.com) who wish to remain anonymous. Our thanks to them.

A number of individuals generously contributed angelic stories, messages, revelations, and art work and would welcome interaction with readers of this book:

AngelReam.com: David R. Van Slyke, webmaster: webmaster@angelrealm.com

P.M.H. Atwater, L.H.D: Author of Beyond the Light; We Live Forever: The Real Truth About Death www.pmhatwater.com; pmhatwater.blogspot.com

Clarisa Bernhardt: www.ClarisaBernhardt.com; (Clarisa's monthly astrology column) www.shirleymaclaine.com; ClarisaBernhardt@hotmail.com

Bettye B. Binder: betty binder@earthlink.net; www.pastlives.cc

M. Bryant: mbryant@wavecable.com

Mary Crotts: www.marytrogden.atspace.com

Lori Jean Flory: www.namastecafe.com/lori/; mountainflow@msn.com mountainflow.blogspot.com

Ariane Glon: artofariane@yahoo.com; www.ariane.artistportfolio.net

Steven Halpern, music of Inner Peace: www.innerpeacemusic.com

John Harricharan: www.insight2000.com

Susan Helene: Old Souls Station www.osstation.com

Iasos, Celestial Music Creator: www.iasos.com

Norma Joiner: www.carissas.homestead.com

Janice Kolb: Author of Solace of Solitude: Afterlife Visits—A Journey; Jan@janicegraykolb.com

Dr. Jimmy and Heather Lowery: APRS Paranormal Talk Radio Show Hosts and Investigators, www.apsrradion.com

Ed Monroe: quatrefoil@email.com; www.pastlives.cc

Tom T. Moore: www.ReelMediaintl.com; www.TheGentleWayBook.com

Lee Moorhead, Medium and Psychic: www.stargaze.com

Darlene Phares: www.somanyangels.com

Michael Richard, Paranormal Photography: P.O. Box 715, Durango, CO 81302 www.paranormalphotography.com

Douglas Stingley: OR8997@hotmail.com; HoodedEntityResearch-owner@yahoogroups.com

Julian West: Julianwest.upwinger@gmail.com; www.upwinger.blogspot.com

Priscilla Garduno Wolf (Little Butterfly), Storyteller, artist, Apache-Spanish Medicine woman: threespiritwolf@netzero.net; threespiritwolf@aol.com

    Wolfman Dan: Plan9motorsports@cs.com

1

Powers and Principalities from the Unseen World

Humankind has been aware that it is a part of a larger community of powers and principalities, seen and unseen, physical and nonphysical, since at least the Paleolithic Age (c. 50,000 B.C.E.), when primitive artists painted images of supernatural beings on the walls of their caves. As early as the third millennium B.C.E., the written records of ancient Egypt and Mesopotamia recognized a hierarchy of supernatural beings that ruled over various parts of the earth, the universe, and the lives of human beings. They also believed in lower levels of entities that might be either hostile or benign in their actions toward humans. Every known culture has its accounts of benevolent and malevolent beings who manifest from an unseen world, and in recent years there has been a tremendous surge of interest in guardian angels and guiding spirits who transcend everyday existence.

Fifty-year-old Earl recently told us that he had been visited by three angels in August 2005, just a few days after his father died. The taller angel, attired in a white robe with blue and gold cuffs, had "deep-blue, beautiful eyes," and he let Earl know that all would be well. "He did not have to use his mouth to talk to me," Earl said. The angel appeared to be about thirty years of age with blondish, "pushing gold-colored hair that was wavy and about shoulder length." The tall angel emanated great physical beauty and strength. "But I knew that his strength would only be used against things that were bad," Earl added.

Earl felt that the two shorter angels were subservient to the taller being. "I received the impression that the tall one was an angel from Heaven, who goes to people in their time of need. I did not feel that he was my guardian angel, but a special angel who manifested to people in sorrow and grief," Earl said, then concluded his account by admonishing us: "I hope you share the experience that I have shared with you. I am letting you know about something real that I have witnessed."

Sincere men and women have been sending us their personal stories of angelic encounters for more than four decades and beseeching us to share their witness of benevolent beings from the unseen world. Since 1968 we have been distributing various versions of the Steiger Questionnaire of Mystical, Paranormal, and UFO Experiences to our readers and lecture audiences. Of the more than 30,000 respondents, 78 percent claim to have witnessed angelic activity; 89 percent believe they have a guardian angel or spirit guide; and 77 percent say they have had an encounter with a benevolent being of light. These percipients generally describe the beings as appearing youthful, commanding, beautiful of countenance, and often majestic and awesome. Manifestations of light often accompany them, which adds to the grandeur of their appearance and the feeling of profound reverence that suffuses those who encounter the beings. In many accounts, the angelic beings appear to be paraphysical—that is, they seem to be both material and nonmaterial entities. Although they originate in some invisible and nonphysical dimension, they seem completely capable of shaping reality in our three-dimensional world to suit their heavenly purposes.

"At age five," according to Sondra, a psychotherapist from New York, "an ethereal female figure appeared at the foot of my bed. This entity frightened me into leaving my bedroom. A few minutes later, there were gunshots outside the house that ricocheted into my bed. Had the angel not appeared and had I remained in my bed, I would have been killed." Sondra continued: "Since my teenaged years, I have regularly made contact with this entity through meditation, but she has also appeared spontaneously. Sometimes I can hear her voice. She guides me, scolds me, corrects me. She sometimes appears as a very bright light in my room."

Dr. G.H., a clinical and child psychologist from Texas, stated in her questionnaire: "I saw my first angel at about age six. I had one experience with a blinding white light when I was twenty, and I have had many clairvoyant and precognitive experiences."

Ralph, a businessman from Missouri, has retained very clear impressions of himself as a child around the age of four or five staring with wonder and delight at a white, vibrant sphere of light that had materialized near him when he was outside playing in the family's apple orchard. He has also recalled the presence of four entities observing him as he discovered the glowing ball of light. From his present understanding, Ralph perceives that these beings originate from a dimension that is of a vibration that is much higher than ours and that they maintain a kind of guiding, teaching role in his life.

Some contemporary scientists suggest that such mystical experiences can be explained in terms of neural transmitters, neural networks, and brain chemistry. The feeling of transcendence that mystics describe could be the result of decreased activity in the brain's parietal lobe, which helps regulate the sense of self and physical orientation. Perhaps the human brain is wired for mystical experiences.

While the physical activity of the brain and its psychological state may sometimes serve as a conduit to a transcendent world, we believe that the appearance of the benevolent beings most often recognized as angels is far more than a manifestation of a belief in the unknown, a blending of brain chemistry, or a personification of our hope in a spiritual comforter. We believe there is some spiritual reality that exists outside of us, that is interested in our human condition, and with which we may somehow communicate.

Many Types of Angels

In this book, we are expanding the definition of "angels" beyond the boundaries of those with which many readers will be accustomed, and we shall include experiences and encounters with each of the following kinds of benevolent beings:

1. God's Heavenly Messengers

All religions have some kind of tradition of a guardian angel or some type of spirit guide assigned to each individual human soul. In the ancient Hindu texts of the Vedas, written in Sanskrit, the word for angel is *angira*; in Hebrew, *malakh*, meaning "messenger," or *bene elohim*, for "God's children"; in Arabic, *malakah*; and in India, multiwinged angels or beings are called *garudas*.

The broadest definition of an angel is simply one who serves as a messenger of God. In this sense, a living person could serve in such a capacity and fulfill God's purpose by delivering a particular thought, knowledge, or counsel that an individual might require at a certain crisis point in his or her life. Many of us have been privileged to have had a good friend or family member become an "angel" when we really needed the unconditional love and assistance of another, and some of us may even have had such a person assume a protective, "guardian angel" role for a time.

Strictly speaking, however, in the three monotheistic religions of Judaism, Christianity, and Islam, angels are a species apart from us who are directed to a human by the Supreme Being for the purpose of delivering a message of guidance, offering spiritual counsel, or, in some extreme instances, providing miraculous healing of physical illness or accomplishing rescue from threatening circumstances.

Adhering strictly to the traditional definition of an angel as interpreted by the three monotheistic religions, humans do not die and become angels. Judeo-Christian scriptures declare that mortals were created a "little lower than the angels," and the two are different energy forms. The Qur'an states that there are three distinct kinds of intelligent beings in the universe: first, the angels (*malak*), a high order of beings created of light; second, the *al-jinn*, ethereal, perhaps even multidimensional beings; and third, humans, molded of the stuff of Earth and born into material bodies.

2. Guardian Angels

When we speak of our "guardian angels," we are referring to those unseen, benevolent entities who, according to many traditions, have been assigned to us at birth to guide, direct, and on occasion, protect us.

Throughout the years of our research, we have continued to be impressed by the remarkable adaptability of the angel guardians. In one instance, they are the fireman who carries victims of smoke inhalation to safety and who later cannot be found to be thanked by grateful survivors. In another, they become the traffic cop who prevents a fender-bender during rush hour from becoming a twelve-car pileup with inevitable casualties and fatalities—and who then literally disappears before the real officers arrive on the scene. Sometimes they appear as ordinary men and women who just happen to be there at the right time to listen with an attentive ear and relay just the necessary words of advice to prevent a troubled soul from taking his or her life—before they vanish from sight.

Many contemporary spiritual seekers have begun to wonder if the differences between a spirit guide and a guardian angel are just a matter of semantics. Guardian angels and spirit guides are both nonphysical, multidimensional beings whose mission it is to provide important guidance, direction, and protection for their human wards on the physical plane. Nearly all traditions assign the guardian angel or guide to watch over their human from the time of the soul's birth into the physical earthly body until the soul leaves its corporeal shell for the Other Side. Today, more and more spiritual seekers prefer to avoid issues of religious, shamanic, or spiritualist dogma and have begun to refer to any benevolent, compassionate, otherworldly entity as a Light Being.

3. Spirit Guides

When spirit mediums or channelers speak of their guide, they are referring to an entity from the Other Side who assists them in establishing contact with the spiritual essence of deceased humans. The spirit guides of mediums usually claim to have lived as humans on Earth before the time of their physical death and their graduation to higher realms of being.

In shamanic traditions, the spirit guide serves as an ambassador from the world of spirits to the world of humans and often manifests to the shaman to serve as a chaperone during visits to other dimensions of reality. It seems quite likely that today's mediums and channels are contemporary expressions of ancient shamanic traditions.

For the more contemporary spirit mediums, who often prefer to call themselves "channels," the guide may represent itself as a being who once lived as a human on Earth or as a Light Being, an extraterrestrial, or even an angel. Regardless of the semantics involved, today's mediums and channels follow the basic procedures of ancient shamanic traditions.

Native American traditionalists and others who follow the old teachings embark on vision quests to learn the identity of their spirit guide and their symbolic totem animal manifestation. These men and women trust that their guides are concerned about them and observe their earthly activities. While mediums and most shamanic traditions believe spirit guides may be summoned during altered states of consciousness and that one may pray for their intervention or assistance, there is general agreement that one must never pray to spirits guides or worship them.

4. Spirits of the Dead Who Earn Their Wings as Angels

For centuries, popular culture has perpetuated the belief that people become angels when they die. Movie audiences shed a collective tear along with James Stewart when his daughter hears the ringing of the bell on the Christmas tree in the final scene of *It's a Wonderful Life* and recites the oft-repeated folk wisdom that the sounding of such a bell signals another angel receiving its wings. "Atta boy, Clarence," Stewart winks knowingly, and the audience delights in the knowledge that the awkward neophyte angel Clarence, once a human, has earned his wings and has advanced a bit in the angelic hierarchy.

In the traditions of the three great monotheistic religions— Judaism, Christianity, and Islam—humans and angels were created as separate and distinct beings. Humans do not become apprentice angels awaiting their advancement in the heavenly hierarchy. However, because we have received so many accounts from individuals who claim that a deceased relative or friend is their guardian angel, we have decided to cast religious dogma aside and allow the possibility that humans may ascend to angelic status—or at least assume the role of guardian angels for reasons beyond mortal knowing.

5. Nature Spirits: Devas, Elves, Fairies

Certain activities once attributed to such entities as fairies in so-called pagan times often became elevated to manifestations of angels with the advent of Christianity. Good deeds, which were an important element of the repertoire of the fairy folk, became the province of heavenly beings, and kind nature spirits were replaced in the mass consciousness with benevolent angels. Local gods and goddesses as well often became transformed into saintly humans with extraordinary powers, while mischievous entities were transmogrified into imps.

6. Benevolent Spirit Teachers from Other Dimensions

Some recipients of angelic phenomena have come to believe that they were visited by benevolent beings from another dimension of time and space. Perhaps, some have theorized, these spirit teachers manifest from another plane of reality, another dimension of being. They may be members of an ancient teaching order from the past, a spiritual brotherhood or sisterhood from the future, or a fellowship that exists in the Eternal Now.

7. The Sons of God

In recent years, the theory that the angels themselves may have created humankind has become increasingly popular. The seed of life may have been planted by superior beings who had the knowledge, the science, and the technology to fashion planets that could support life and the evolution of intelligent species. Paraphysical entities or beings of pure mind, these "angels" shepherd the planet and monitor its progress.

8. The Mysterious Watchers

Mentioned in the apocryphal texts as well as the accepted books of the Bible, the mysterious angelic beings known as the Watchers or the Holy Ones observe humankind and make certain the inhabitants of Earth never forget that "the Most High rules the kingdom of men and gives to whomsoever He wills ..." (Daniel 4:17).

9. Space Brothers and Sisters

In 1963, when we first began seriously investigating the claims of UFO contactees—those individuals who claimed contact with beautiful, blue-eyed, blond benevolent beings who piloted the flying saucers arriving on Earth from other worlds—we drew immediate parallels between those who channeled outer space beings and the spirit mediums who relayed inspirational messages from their guides. In our opinion, the phenomenon of the Space Brothers and Sisters has nothing to do with the question of whether extraterrestrial biological entities have visited Earth. In our assessment, the Space Brothers and Sisters are the familiar supernatural intelligences—angels, guides, Light Beings—cloaking themselves in more contemporary, and thereby to some humans, more acceptable, personae.

10. The Fallen Angels

We believe that every sincere seeker who is willing to practice discernment, discipline, and devoted study may receive inspiration and guidance from angelic beings. However, if you believe that you have made contact with a heavenly being or a spirit guide, remember the admonition of scripture to test the spirits. Don't forget the astral masqueraders who take great delight in deceiving humans. Those malevolent beings, the fallen angels, are always out there, waiting patiently to ensnare the innocent, the unwary, and the unprepared.

True angels never become magical servants who will carry out the bidding of those humans who learn the proper spells to command them. Some individuals have been deceived into believing that angels can be made to reveal winning lottery tickets and the names of the fastest horses at the racetrack. Some who claim angelic encounters imply that these beings can even be commanded to carry out acts of personal revenge. The men and women who make such claims have been seduced into accepting the dangers and hazards of bargaining with dark-side entities. A true angelic being would never permit itself to be transformed into a money machine or a thug, but the fallen angels would gleefully appear to obey would-be dark magicians long enough to ensnare their souls.

One Commonality:
How They Come and How They Go

The Reverend B. W. Palmer, a retired Methodist clergyman from Haines City, Florida, spent many years collecting hundreds of accounts from around the world of contemporary visions of supernatural figures, such as Mother Mary, angels, or Jesus. His exhaustive research on the subject, which he kindly shared with us more than forty years ago, indicates that there are at least twenty-four methods these spiritual entities use to manifest their images. Such a list of the advent of religious and angelic figures might also apply to the materialization of ghosts, spirit entities, and multidimensional beings.

1. The skies appear to open up, and the supernatural figure is seen to descend to Earth.

2. In the presence of a human witness, the figure appears to descend in a shaft of light.

3. The holy being appears or disappears through a solid object, such as a door or a wall.

4. Witnesses may hear footsteps outside the house. When they hear a knock at the door, they open it to behold the religious/angelic figure.

5. The figure can also appear as though he or she is a picture on the wall.

6. Witnesses may awaken because they feel a spiritual presence in the room or feel someone's touch. When they open their eyes, they see the spiritual being bending over them.

7. An angel may first appear to the witnesses and lead them to the materialization of the holy figure of Mother Mary, Jesus, Moses, and so forth.

8. A witness may see the face of the religious figure appear above a person who is desperately in need of help.

9. Witnesses may hear a voice that tells them to go to a certain place and to do a certain thing. When they comply, they encounter the Holy Mother, Jesus, or angelic figures.

10. The image of the religious figure may appear in the sky, greatly magnified.

11. Witnesses may be awakened by what they at first suppose is the light of a very bright moon. In the next few moments they see the image of the religious personage.

12. The Virgin Mary and angels have often been seen appearing out of a cloud and moving toward witnesses. These spiritual beings have also often used clouds to make their departure.

13. A cloud or a heavy mist may materialize in a witness's room. Out of that mist, an image of the religious figure will appear.

14. During the miracle in Fatima, Portugal, in 1917, the Holy Mother appeared to the three children in exactly the same way. As often as they were interrogated, all three consistently gave the same description of what they had seen. In many cases, however, Mother Mary or another religious figure appears to several witnesses at the same time and is seen in different ways by the individual percipients. To one witness at the scene, the figure may appear as a ball of light; to another, a flash of lightning; to yet another as a disembodied voice.

15. On some occasions, the being may appear in a room occupied by many people and yet is seen by only one or two witnesses.

16. The image of the holy figure may appear in the dreams of witnesses. Many times such a manifestation will bring about a healing.

17. After the figure has manifested, it may vanish suddenly, or it may fade away slowly, moving into a cloud or the ceiling, doors, or floors. The figure may also walk away from the witnesses, fading from view as it moves farther and farther away from them.

18. In most manifestations of angels or holy figures, only the witnesses singled out for communications may see or hear them, even though there may be thousands of people present, such as occurred with Mother Mary during the Fatima appearances.

19. The religious figure often manifests in a strange light that illumines both it and the witnesses.

20. In a number of visionary appearances, the witnesses said that they did not see the holy figure, but they were aware of its presence through the manifestation of a supernatural light or through a voice that came to them.

21. Numerous men and women have experienced out-of-body phenomena in which they claimed to have seen the holy figure looking after them.

22. In other out-of-body experiences, people claimed to have seen the holy figure together with deceased friends or relatives.

23. In still other out-of-body experiences, witnesses have said they perceived the lower-spirit worlds where good spirits attempt to assist lower-level entities and where the holy figure and attending angels seek to give solace and comfort.

24. During near-death experiences, men and women have returned to consciousness stating they journeyed to Heaven, where they saw the holy figure together with deceased friends or relatives and attending hosts of angels.

The Bible records many awesome appearances of angelic beings that indicate that at least some of the heavenly messengers are not the beautiful entities depicted in common accounts of angelic encounters. The entities described by Ezekiel and identified as cherubim certainly border on the grotesque. As the Old Testament prophet beheld the "Living Creatures," their outstretched wings touching the corners of the square that encased them, he perceived that each cherub appeared to have four faces: that of a man, a lion, an ox, and an eagle. Regardless of whether Ezekiel actually saw four separate visages on a single head or was simply using figurative language to describe a single face combining the attributes of human, lion, ox, and eagle, the beings who delivered this particular prophetic vision would have had most people trembling in fear and revulsion.

The figures seen by Ezekiel are suggestive of the manner in which the ancient Mesopotamians depicted their spiritual guardians, the *lamassu*, as rather grotesque creatures that often appeared as lions or bulls with human faces and large wings. Such monstrous images were often placed at the entrances of temples to ward off evil, and the common people of Mesopotamia cherished them as very accessible guardian spirits.

After he was spared from a royal death sentence in a lions' den by a heavenly being who sealed the big cats' mouths, the prophet Daniel probably felt that he was in no position to complain about the angel's physical appearance. Later, when Daniel perceived a heaven-sent messenger beside him at the Tigris River, he beheld an entity who was dressed in linen, wearing a solid gold belt, and had a face like lightning, eyes like flaming fires, and a voice like the roar of a crowd.

Perhaps there are certain kinds of angels who do have a countenance that some humans would consider frightening—or awe inspiring at the least. Perhaps that is why the majority of their heavenly assignments are carried out while they are invisible to the human eye.

We personally wonder if any human has ever seen angelic beings or spirit guides as they appear to one another in their otherworldly dimensions. For one thing, angels and guides are spiritual, rather than physical, entities. Throughout our many years of research and our interviews with hundreds of men and women from cultures and countries around the world who have claimed angelic or spirit contact, it has seemed to us that the benevolent beings have always manifested to each individual witness in a form that is most acceptable to him or her.

In the many cases we have investigated, we long ago came to believe that the physical appearance of the manifesting angel or spirit guide depends almost completely upon the witness's personal cosmology— that is, his or her religious background, cultural biases, and level of spiritual evolution. Therefore, even in this technological, scientific age, a person of a conservative or fundamental religious persuasion may tend to behold angels in their traditional winged and robed persona while a member of a more liberal religious expression may be more likely to perceive an angel minus the wings and other sacerdotal trappings.

Of one thing we are quite certain. If an angel or spirit guide should appear to you, you will perceive the benevolent being in an image and demeanor that will be most acceptable and understandable to you.

2

Angels in the World's Religions

Although strictly orthodox religionists are somehow able to dissociate their doc-
trinally approved concept of guardian angels and archangels from the more mys-
tical spirit guides, spirit teachers, and benevolent beings of other faiths, it seems to
us that it is a matter of semantics and personal religious-cultural background that
determines the name or title that one assigns to other-dimensional entities who,
for some reason, concern themselves with the activities of mortals. While every-
one knows that benevolent beings are a part of every religion, many may not be
aware that these otherworldly missionaries actually imparted the teachings of
various religions to spiritually receptive prophets. From a certain perspective, one
might even say that the angels were responsible for founding Earth's religions.

Angels stopped Father Abraham from sacrificing his son, wrestled
with Jacob (who lost the match, but was renamed Israel), and

intervened frequently to further the teachings of the God of Abraham, the one true God, throughout the Pentateuch, the first five books of the Bible.

In Christianity, it was angels who announced the coming of Jesus' birth to a young, betrothed virgin named Mary and who later shielded her son from angry mobs in the villages, protected him from Satan in the wilderness, and announced his resurrection to Mary Magdalene. Angels also prompted the apocalyptic visions of John the Revelator, which led to the book of Revelation with its accounts of the final struggle between good and evil at Armageddon.

Muslims believe that the Qur'an was dictated to the Prophet Muhammad by the archangel Gabriel (Jibril), and angels continue to serve as the agents of revelation in Islam.

In Islam, Judaism, and Christianity, angels have the ability to appear in a variety of forms. In certain cases, they may even reveal themselves as beings of pure light. Angels seem capable of influencing our three-dimensional world to suit heavenly purposes, but they cannot affect our free will—something that they themselves do not possess.

Although angels are frequently described as being strong, swift, and majestic, they are not to be worshipped or held as objects of veneration. True heavenly beings will immediately discourage humans who attempt to bend their knees to them. The fallen angels, or demons, however, are motivated by their own selfish goals and delight in corrupting humans. They encourage mortals to express greed and the acquisition of material treasures rather than spiritual ones. As a general spiritual law, these negative entities cannot achieve power over humans unless they are somehow invited in a person's private space or are attracted to an individual by that person's negativity or vulnerability.

The English word *angel* originated from the Latin *angelus*, which is derived from the Greek *angelos*, meaning "messenger." Although many readers first became familiar with angels in the Bible stories of the Old and New Testaments, the nearest Hebrew word for such beings is *mal'ach*, which also means messenger. English translators of the Old Testament have used the familiar "angel" in those passages where the original Hebrew uses *abir* or *abbir* ("mighty"), *Elohim* ("powers"), or *bne Elohim* ("sons of God," members of a class of divine beings).

Buddhism

Buddhism acknowledges celestial beings known as Devas, who manifest primarily as beings of light, hence their title in Hinduism as "the Shining Ones." In the western world, Devas are primarily considered nature spirits, and while they do not interfere in human affairs, they often reward humans for their good deeds. Buddhists also recognize the existence of compassionate beings known as bodhisattva, epitomized in the spirit of Kwan Yin or Chenrezing, as she is known in Tibet.

Christianity

Christianity recognizes angels as God's messengers, who may also serve as intermediaries for humans. Roman Catholicism divides nine choirs of angels into three groups: The first are Seraphim, Cherubim, and Thrones; the second are Dominations, Virtues, and Powers; the third are Principalities, Archangels, and Angels. Roman Catholics believe that each person has a guardian angel that is pure spirit and cannot manifest in corporeal forms. This guardian spirit joins a human child at the time of birth and remains with that individual throughout the cycle of life, even joining the soul in Heaven.

Gabriel, Raphael, and Michael are recognized as archangels, and Roman Catholics may pray to the angels, as they do the saints, for assistance in human affairs. Generally speaking, angels have the power to influence the senses and thoughts of human, but not their free will.

Eastern Orthodox Christians believe that angels are assigned by God to help and to guide humans. The archangel Michael is the most powerful of the angels, and his lieutenants include Gabriel, Raphael, Uriel, Selaphiel, Jehudiel, Barachiel, and Jeremial.

Christian mystics and alchemists during the Middle Ages recognized a rather lengthy roster of angels and archangels to whom the supplicant might make entreaties: Azrael, Barachiel, Chamuel, Gabriel, Haniel, Israfel, Jegudiel, Jophiel, Malik, Michael, Munkar, Nakir, Obbieuth, Phanuel, Raguel, Raphael, Raziel, Remiel, Sandalphon, Shamsiel, Sariel, Uriel, and Zadkiel.

While Protestant Christians acknowledge the power and majesty of angels, most consider the act of praying to them as treading dangerously close to angel worship. Protestant theologians are likely to make a point of reminding their congregations that Satan, the leader of the rebellion against God in Heaven, was also an Angel of Light.

Angels, Protestants believe, were created as a race apart from humans; humans do not become angels when they die. Angels are spirit beings who can assume corporeal form while performing earthly missions.

Both Roman Catholic and Protestant Christians will cite the admonitions in the New Testament to be cautious of any manifesting entity and to test it to determine its true motives. "Beloved, do not believe every spirit, but test the spirits to see whether they are of God" (1 John 4:1). While such a passage is easily quoted, its admonition is much more difficult to put in to practice when Christians are warned in 2 Corinthians 11:14: "Even Satan disguises himself as an angel of light."

According to some theologians, such a "test," that is, an evaluation, of alleged heavenly beings might contain these elements for serious consideration:

1. Did the being tell you that it has appeared because you are a chosen person from a special group of evolved humans?

2. Did the being encourage you to pray to it or to worship it?

3. Did it promise to reward you with material wealth in exchange for your devotion?

4. Did it issue short-term prophecies that all came true?

5. Did it perform apparent miracles for your benefit?

6. Did it issue revelations that upon closer scrutiny are filled with half-truths, lies, or bigotry?

A general admonition mentioned by several spiritual teachers is never to enter meditation or prayer with the sole thought of obtaining ego aggrandizement or material gain. Selfish motivation may put one at risk for becoming easily affected by those spirit beings who rebelled against the Light and became ensnared in their own selfish lust for power.

Hinduism

The followers of Hinduism have many different categories of spirit beings who can help or hinder humans. Devas, the "shining ones," play a more significant role in Hinduism than they do in Buddhism, and they correlate more closely to the Christian, Islamic, and Judaic concept of angels. Devas reside in the higher astral plane and are regarded by many Hindus as minor gods. The Devas, together with ancestral spirits and other minor gods, can work with one's guru on the earthly plane to provide protection and guidance. The Devas who have fallen off the shining path are demoted to the lower astral plane, the mental plane of existence, where they become *asuras*, or evil spirits. While Islam, Christianity, and Judaism consider demonic entities as forever in Satan's dominion, Hindus believe that the *asuras* can redeem themselves by performing good deeds.

There are many nature spirits in Hinduism, such as the lovely nymphs called *apsaras*; the *angiris*, who preside over the sacrifices of the devout; the *lipika*, who oversee karmic payments and debts; and the marvelous winged *garudas*, who often play a role similar to the angels of the three monotheistic religions.

Islam

The teachings of Islam state that there are three distinct species of intelligent beings in the universe. First are the angels that are a high order of beings created of Light, the *malaikah*; second, the *al-jinn*, which are ethereal, perhaps even multidimensional entities; finally, human beings, fashioned out of the stuff of Earth and born into physical bodies. On occasion, the *al-jinn* can serve as helpful guides or guardians, but they can also be tricksters.

Muslims believe that every person is given two guardian angels who oversee and record every action, good and bad, performed throughout the person's lifetime. Although angels may assume various forms, especially in dreams or visions, their true appearance can never be comprehensible to humans.

Gabriel is the most revered of the angelic messengers, for it was he who brought the revelation of the Qur'an from Allah to Mohammad. Other archangels important to Islam are Israfil, who will sound the trumpet on the last day; Iza'il, the angel of death; and Munkar and Nakir, who visit graveyards to test the faith of those recently deceased.

Iblis, also known as Shaitan, is the sworn enemy of humankind who scatters evil throughout the world. Although Shaitan has vowed to continue a ceaseless campaign to tempt humans into sin, he is not considered a fallen angel but a *jinn* who chose to be evil.

Judaism

Prior to the emergence of Judaic monotheism, the children of Abraham were guided by the Angel of the Lord or Angel of God (*Mal'akh Yahweh* or *Mal'akh Elohim*). Elohim is most often used to refer to the one true God, but in certain instances *bne Elohim* was applied to divine beings or beings of great power, "sons of God (gods)." Although these super beings were mighty, they were always distinct from Yahweh and not to be confused with him. YHWH was, in fact, very jealous of any confusion between himself and other gods or the angels, and Moses emphasized that it was forbidden to worship any member of the heavenly host.

By the time of the Babylonian Captivity, the prophet Daniel hears the great Nebuchadnezzar recounting a troubling vision (Daniel 4:5, 10–15, 17) in which the monarch describes a Watcher, a Holy One, coming down from Heaven: "This matter is by decree of the Watchers, and the demand by the world of the Holy Ones to the intent that the living may know that the Most High ruleth in the kingdom of men." After the years spent in Babylon, the scriptures begin to refer to angelic beings as "holy ones" and "watchers," thus provoking contemporary debates about whether the hierarchy of the Babylonian religion and the angelology of Zoroastrianism influenced Judaism's view of angels. Some immediate responses to the argument are that one of the essential points of the Book of Daniel is how the Hebrews resisted the religion of Babylon, and it is uncertain whether Zoroastrianism was even developed by so early a date.

When the doctrine of monotheism was firmly established in the period immediately before and during the exile in Babylon, angels become prominent in the books of Ezekiel and Zechariah. Ezekiel has his great visions of the wheel within the wheel and the seven angels who execute the judgment of God upon Jerusalem. Angels are mentioned occasionally in Psalms, and in Job "the sons of God" manifest as the attendants of God. Included in their number is Satan, who appears not as the embodiment of evil but to serve as a kind of public prosecutor of Job.

Generally speaking, contemporary Judaism regards angels as beings of pure spirit who are messengers of God and who carry out his will.

Although the angels of the Bible were said to have appeared at times in human form, most modern scholars regard those descriptions of physical beings to have been metaphorical.

Still heeding the admonitions of Moses, Jews do not pray to angels and are careful not to employ any procedures that might edge close to angel worship. Micha'el is the guardian angel of the people of Israel. Gabriel is the angel of strength and eventual judgment. Raphael visits the faithful as an angel healing. Uriel shines God's light brightest on the right path to guide the soul through the dark forest of life.

The Episcopal bishop Philip Brooks once observed that there is nothing clearer or more striking in the Bible than "the calm, familiar way with which from end to end it assumes the present existence of a world of spiritual beings always close to and acting on this world of flesh and blood.... From creation to judgment, the spiritual beings are forever present. They act as truly in the drama as the men and women who, with their unmistakable humanity, walk the sacred stage in successive scenes. There is nothing of hesitation about the Bible's treatment of the spiritual world. There is no reserve, no vagueness which would leave a chance for the whole system to be explained away in dreams and metaphors. The spiritual word, with all its multitudinous existence, is just as real as the crowded cities and the fragrant fields and the loud battlegrounds of the visible, palpable Judea, in which the writers of the sacred books were living."

3

The Sound and Sight of Angel Wings

Angels may come upon us in many ways. A glimpse, a sound, a small sign to let us know they are there.

The Sound of Angel Wings

On January 10, 2006, Nancy Candler was driving home from work in a Colorado suburb.

"I was on Clarkson and had just passed Craig Hospital and Swedish Hospital heading toward Hampden," she told us. "I was the second car stopped at a red light. The person in front of me was an older woman who had been driving slowly and really far over to the right. When the light turned green, she didn't go right away, and for some reason (I think it was my guides or angels looking out for me) I didn't follow her into the intersection as I normally would."

Then, as Nancy waited behind the vehicle in front of her to enter the intersection, she heard "the strangest sound." Nancy said that she could not describe the sound or even attempt to compare it to any sound that she had ever before experienced, but she felt right away that she had heard "the sound of angel wings."

All of a sudden, Nancy continued, "either an SUV or a truck (it was going so fast I couldn't tell) ran the red light going at least 65 mph. The elderly lady was already in the intersection, and I thought for sure that she was going to get hit in her rear bumper—but the speeding vehicle missed her by no more than an inch!"

Nancy still hadn't started across the street. She sat for a moment, realizing that if the lady in the car in front of her hadn't remained at the light and hadn't waited before she started across the intersection, she would have been hit in the driver's door by the speeding vehicle that had run the light.

"I'm sure that I would have been killed!" Nancy said. "The thought hit me like a ton of bricks. I could have died that day. But I am also sure that my guides or angels or somebody in spirit prevented the accident. I have never heard a sound like that before, the angel's wing sound. It was sort of like wind, but it is impossible to describe.

"I am just very, very grateful," Nancy said. "It was very hard to drive the rest of the way home. I was a little shaky. I'm not certain if the lady in front of me even knew what happened—or maybe she was an angel herself."

Nancy concluded, "This is the closest I've ever come to being killed. The experience is helping me to clarify how I want to spent the minutes, hours, and days that I have available to me. We really are protected and watched over by angels or guiding spirits all the time."

Backed Up by an Angel with a Flaming Sword

At one time, Peggy said, she lived in a very dangerous neighborhood in a run-down apartment building. The managers ran the building like overbearing tyrants and extended their thug-like behavior to harassing some of the women in the building and even destroying some of their belongings. In one instance, they broke into a young woman's apartment, loaded all of her clothes on top of her brand-new bed, set the clothing on fire, and extinguished the flames before they got out of control and threatened the building. The rowdy managers became outright thieves when they broke into another woman's apartment and stole her most valuable electronics, then wantonly smashed what they didn't want. In Peggy's opinion, the managers were behaving as if they were possessed by demons.

A male friend of Peggy's, who lived elsewhere, was worried about her residing in such a lawless building, so he helped Peggy's son put a security gate on her apartment door. The gate was put up none too soon, Peggy said, for the next day when she came back from work she found that the hoodlums had broken the door but had not been able to get past the sturdy security gate.

Because Peggy felt close to God and had a lot of spunk, she gathered the whole female population of the building together to protest the way the building was being managed. "We went to court and filed a suit against the owner as well as the managers," Peggy said, "and we put our rent into escrow. We were willing to fight this through."

The brutish managers retaliated by cutting the female residents' telephone lines and turning off their water and their heat.

"These thugs were determined to do all sorts of evil to these young ladies and me," Peggy recalled. "We got together in my apartment, and I led them in prayer. I let them store their valuables in my apartment."

One evening during a rain storm, Peggy had to leave her apartment to get her children milk for the morning. As she was coming back into the building and walking up the stairs to her apartment, she noticed that all the lights were off in the hallway.

As Petty entered the hallway, the largest of the managers met her and blocked her passage to her apartment. He told her that she was a troublemaker and that he was going to rape her and leave her for dead.

"Now mind you," Peggy said, "this creep was more than a foot taller than me and weighed at least 300 ponds. I am only 5 feet 1 inches tall and weighed maybe 150 pounds. You would think I would be frightened out of my mind, but I was not. A spirit came over me and spoke through me and said in a loud booming voice, *"I fear no one but God almighty. You can do no harm to me, for I denounce your demon and send it back to the pit!"*

"As I spoke these words," Peggy stated, "I began to rise off the hallway floor and I met him eye to eye. The hood's eyes became wide in disbelief, and he ran off screaming."

As Peggy hovered above the hallway floor, she noticed that the shadows spread across the hallway walls were of large angel wings. Then, as she was being gently lowered, the angel wings slowly folded inward and disappeared.

One of the young women, who had been watching the incident fearfully through the peephole in her apartment door, pulled Peggy aside and said, "You have an angel who sits on your balcony and holds a flaming sword. I was coming home late one night, and I saw a huge angel standing in your balcony's doorway."

The manager who fled as he watched in fear as Peggy rose to his height must also have seen the large angel with the flaming sword standing before him. The managers' attitude toward the female residents in the apartment building underwent a dramatic readjustment after the terrified thug told the others of his encounter with Peggy's guardian angel.

"I have never doubted my Lord and Savior," Peggy concluded. "He has sent my guardian angel to me on several occasions."

An Angel Appeared to Pray with Them after an Accident

Bill was in the U.S. Army playing basketball for Fort Benning, and the team had to go to Florida for a game. Bill drove down with three friends, and because he got injured during the game, he couldn't drive back. One of his friends said that she would assume the duty of driver, and the four of them started back to the base.

"About an hour into the trip," Bill said, "we had an accident. The car spun around and dropped into a ditch. The impact was so forceful that the car then bounced out of the ditch, rolled twice, and proceeded to skid even farther. We found out later that if we'd gone another foot or so, we would have gone over a cliff."

The road they had taken was totally deserted, so they had to wait a while for medical attention. The friend who had been driving was holding Bill's head steady because he had hit it when they flipped over.

"While we were waiting, a gentleman appeared beside me and the driver," Bill recalled. "He asked us if we believed in God. We said yes, and he asked us to pray with him. We closed our eyes and he prayed for us. When we opened our eyes, he was gone."

Bill said that there were three other members of the basketball team with them, yet when he and the driver asked if anyone had seen where the stranger had gone, "everyone thought we were crazy, because no one else saw him—and we described him in great detail."

Although the accident occurred nine years ago, Bill still vividly remembers what his guardian angel looks like. "God's grace and mercy was with us," Bill said, "because other than one person receiving six stitches and a little bruising for the rest of us, there were no other injuries. My car was completely totaled, and the paramedics could not believe we had made it out alive. Thank you, Lord!"

Her Dying Friend Saw Angel Wings

At age thirty-nine, Linda suddenly developed serious heart problems. The emergency room doctors could not determine what was happening to her, and after five hours in ER, she ended up in an intensive care unit. She was given a shot to help her sleep, but after all the trauma she had undergone, Linda recalled that she was too wound up to sleep.

"I remember looking at the clock," Linda said. "It said 12:43 then everything went white. I saw a tunnel ahead of me—then I was in it! I was skyrocketing toward the light—a beautiful, radiant, warm, loving light. I knew what it was, and I couldn't get there fast enough!"

But it seemed that the faster Linda soared toward the light, the farther away it appeared. She was told by "someone" that it wasn't her time, that she had to go back and finish her work on Earth. Then Linda heard her mother, who had been deceased for many years, tell her the same thing: She had to go back.

Linda heard someone asking, "Time?" and another voice responded, "Eight twelve."

"I had died, literally, at 12:43, and I had been gone for eight minutes and 12 seconds," Linda said. "I was born on 8/12 at 12:43 a.m.! I found this to be a bizarre coincidence, but I didn't discuss this with anyone."

After this dramatic event, it seemed as though Linda was always there for people when they needed help the most. She said that she would never forget the last conversation she had with a friend who died of ovarian cancer. "She told me that I had such beautiful wings!" Linda recalled.

Linda smiled and asked her friend if she could see her angel's wings.

"Yes, they're so beautiful!" Linda's friend told her. And then she asked, "How come I don't have any wings?"

Linda told her that her wings weren't ready yet, but she would be getting a special set of wings when it was time. Her friend lapsed back into sleep.

She awoke shortly after and said, "Do I have my wings yet?"

Linda said, "Yes, and they are absolutely gorgeous."

"Well, if we both have our wings," her friend wondered, "why are we still here?"

Gently, reverently, Linda told her friend that they could leave whenever she was ready.

"She said 'I love you,' and I told her I loved her, too," Linda recalled with emotion. "She asked if it was okay if we left, and I told her whenever she was ready, it was okay. Then she drew her last breath.

"I will always remember this incident as special, because she didn't see *my* wings, she saw my *guardian angel's wings*," Linda said. "I had prayed to God to send someone to help get me through this. I know He answered my prayers—and I know my guardian angel was there."

Visualizing Your Guardian Angel or Spirit Guide to Reach Higher Awareness

We would like to share a visualization exercise that we have employed with great success in numerous seminars and workshops throughout the United States and overseas. If followed correctly, the visualization can elevate you to a state of consciousness wherein you will be able to establish a spiritual link with a more aware aspect of yourself. By making such a mystical connection, you may also be able to prompt an increased perception of contact between you and your guardian angel or spirit guide. Your success will depend upon your willingness to permit such an experience to manifest itself in your individual spiritual essence.

The first step in this process is to become as relaxed as possible in your mind and body. To achieve this state of relaxation, have a trusted friend or family member read the text below. Some students have found it very powerful to record their own voice reading this exercise and to allow their own voice to guide them. We would recommend some soft, ethereal background music, classical or New Age, to help you to fashion a mood of tranquility. Be certain that the music you choose contains no lyrics to distract you.

The Text for the Relaxation Technique

Imagine that you are lying on a blanket on a beautiful stretch of beach. You are lying in the sun or in the shade—whichever you prefer. You are listening to the sounds of Mother Ocean, listening to the rhythmic sounds of the waves as they lap against the shore. You are listening to the same soothing, restful lullaby that Mother Ocean has been singing to men and to women for thousands and thousands of years.

As you relax, you know that nothing will disturb you, nothing will distress you, nothing will trouble you or bother you in any way.

Even now you are becoming aware of a golden light of love, wisdom, and knowledge that is moving over you and protecting you from all negativity.

You know that this golden light of love from the God Force of the Universe protects you from all evil and negativity.

You have nothing to fear. Nothing can harm you on any level—body, mind, or spirit.

As you listen to the sound of the ocean waves, you feel all tension leaving your body. The very sound of the waves helps you to become more and more relaxed.

With every breath you take, you find yourself feeling better, more positive in body, mind, and spirit. With every breath that you take, you find yourself becoming more and more relaxed, relaxed.

You know that your body must relax so the real you may rise higher and higher to greater states of awareness.

And now you are feeling a beautiful, soothing energy of tranquility, peace, and love entering your feet, and you feel every muscle in your feet relaxing.

That beautiful, soothing energy of tranquility, peace, and love moves up your legs, into your ankles, your calves, your knees, your thighs, and you feel every muscle in your ankles, your calves, your knees, your thighs relaxing, relaxing, relaxing.

If you should hear any sound at all other than the sound of my voice, you will relax even more. If you should hear any sound at all—a slamming door, a honking horn, a shouting voice—that sound will not disturb you in any way. That sound will only help you to relax even more.

Nothing will disturb you. Nothing will distress you in any way.

And now that beautiful energy of tranquility, peace, and love is moving up to your hips, your stomach, your back, and you feel every muscle in your hips, your stomach, your back relaxing, relaxing, relaxing.

With every breath that you take, you find that your body is becoming more and more relaxed.

And now the beautiful energy of tranquility, peace, and love enters your chest, your shoulders, your arms, your palms, your fingers, and you feel every muscle in your chest, your shoulders, your arms, your palms, and your fingers relaxing, relaxing, relaxing.

With every breath you take, you find that you are becoming more and more relaxed. Every part of your body is becoming free of tension.

And now that beautiful energy of tranquility, peace, and love moves into your neck, your face, the very top of your head, and you feel every muscle in your neck, your face, and the very top of your head relaxing, relaxing, relaxing, relaxing.

Your body is now relaxing, but your *inner self*, your *true self*, is very much aware.

The Exercise to Visualize Your Guardian Angel or Spirit Guide

[Once you are as relaxed as possible in body and mind, you may proceed to the exercise of visualizing your guardian angel or spirit guide. As with the relax-

ation text, these techniques are to be read aloud, perhaps pausing occasionally to contemplate the significance of the inner journey and to permit its full meaning to permeate your mental and spiritual essence.]

And now a beautiful golden light is moving all around you. You are not afraid. You feel only love. You know that the golden light signals the presence of your guide, your guardian spirit.

Feel the love as this presence moves over you. Feel the vibrations of love moving over you—warm, peaceful, tranquil.

You know that within the essence of this golden light is a spirit being who has always loved you just as you are.

You have been aware of this loving, guiding presence ever since you were a child, a very small child.

You have been aware that this spiritual intelligence has always loved you just as you are—no facades, no charades, no pretenses.

This spiritual presence loves you unconditionally. This spiritual being loves you with love that accepts you just as you are.

You feel unconditional love moving all around you. Feel the love that flows to you from your angel guide.

And now *look!* Two eyes are beginning to form in the midst of the golden light. You are beholding the eyes of your spirit guide. Feel the love flowing to you from your spirit guide, your angelic guardian.

Now a face is forming. Oh, look at the smile on the lips of your angelic guide. Feel the love that flows from your guardian to your inner being.

Now a body is forming. Behold the beauty of form, structure, and stature of your spiritual guide. *Feel* the love that flows to you from the very essence of your angelic guide.

Your guide is now stretching forth a loving hand to you. Take that hand in yours. Feel that spirit hand in your own. Feel the love flowing through you. Feel the love as your spiritual essence blends with that of your angel guide.

Now, hand in hand, you feel your spirit being lifted higher and higher. Your guide is taking your spiritual essence to a higher dimension of awareness and love. You are moving higher, higher, higher.

Colors and lights are moving around you ... red, orange, yellow, green, blue, violet, purple, gold.

Stars seem to be moving around you. It seems as though you are moving through the universe.

It seems as though you are moving into another dimension of time and space.

You are moving into a higher vibration of reality.

You are moving to a higher level of awareness, a higher level of consciousness.

Understand that you have within you the ability to rise to higher levels of awareness and to make contact with higher aspects of your inner being and the love of your spirit guide and guardian.

Understand that you never walk alone, that you are never friendless, that you are never unloved.

Understand that you have the ability to travel with your spirit guide to a higher level of awareness where you can experience love as you have never felt it on Earth. Love as you have yearned for all of your life.

Feel that love now; feel it all around you. *[Pause for two or three minutes to experience this beautiful, tranquil unconditional love from the spirit guide and a higher level of awareness.]*

And now you are returning from this beautiful, tranquil state of love and relaxation, feeling better than you have felt in weeks and weeks, months and months.

At the count of five, you will be fully awake and filled with the wonderful feelings of love, wisdom, and knowledge from your spirit guide and guardian.

One, coming awake. *Two*, coming more and more awake, filled with love. *Three*, coming more and more awake, filled with unconditional love from your spirit guide and guardian. *Four*, coming awake, opening and closing your hands. *Five*, wide awake, opening your eyes—and feeling wonderful.

4

Guardian Angels Never Sleep

Guardian angels must be ever vigilant, as divine protection may be needed at any time.

A Mother Requests Angelic Assistance

Mollie's husband Dan and oldest son Jim work at the same place in a small town in California. Jim no longer lives at home with his parents, but both he and his father work early hours.

One morning after her husband left for work, Mollie could not sleep. She looked at the clock and saw that it was 4:45 a.m. Jim was on her mind and heavy on her heart, she said. "I just thought I was being overprotective, and I tried to close my eyes to go back to sleep."

But her concern grew so strong that she could no longer stay in bed. Mollie called Dan at work and asked if Jim had arrived. She felt a cold chill when Dan said that he had not.

"By this time it was 5:20, and he was to start at 5:30," Mollie said. "I started praying and asking God to please put his angels around Jim and get him safely to work. I was still praying when about 20 minutes later I heard a car outside. As I opened the front door, I saw Jim walking to the door. His car was still running, driver's door open, and he held his head in his hands as he walked toward me. Jim was crying, and he said, 'Mom, I almost died.'"

Jim had fallen asleep at the wheel as he was crossing a bridge. As the road curved, his car went straight into the other lane and hit the cement wall. Jim awakened upon impact, and he struggled to back the car off the wall, scrapping the passenger side of the vehicle for at least 10 feet.

Mollie hugged her son and told him about her feelings of dread concerning him and how she had prayed for God's angels to protect him.

"We both cried," Mollie said, "and we thanked God for giving Jim his guardian angel."

"So when you feel that tugging on your heart," she said, passing along a word of advice, "get on your knees and start praying, because it was only by the grace of God that our son is still with us."

The Good Samaritan Stopped Traffic . . . then Disappeared

One rainy morning, Bridget was driving to work on a busy expressway when a car swerved into her.

"I applied the brake to keep from hitting the oncoming vehicle," she said. "When I did so, my vehicle skidded out of control. A pickup truck hit my car as I slid toward the median. When the 'demolition' was over, I saw the front of the truck. It was distorted, and broken glass was scattered on the black top."

Bridget's first fear was that the driver of the truck might have been killed. Remarkably, she could get out of her own battered vehicle. She ran to the truck and saw that the driver, a young man, was not seriously injured. As she stood in the road, trying to pull herself together, a middle-aged good Samaritan said to her, "I saw the accident. I stopped the traffic so you and the other driver would not be hit again."

The man pointed to his white car, which signaled the other drivers to slow down.

Bridget immediately walked toward the truck driver and commented, "Wasn't it nice of that man to stop and help us like that? He risked his own vehicle and his safety to help us."

The pickup driver looked confused and asked her, "What man?"

"I whirled around and saw that the good Samaritan had vanished," Bridget said. "Where his car had been just moment before, a police car with flashing lights now warned motorists of the accident scene."

Bridget is convinced that a guardian angel was there on the highway that day and that God had prevented a fatality. "The middle-aged 'man's' face was pleasant and his smile reassuring," she said. "I thought later about the white car and remembered the Bible's association of the color white with purity."

Bridget said that she is thankful to God—the Great Spirit, as her Native American ancestors would have said—for sending an angel to keep her safe that rainy morning when the accident occurred.

Snowball Got Gina to the Hospital in Time to Deliver Her Daughter

On December 1, 1985, the ten o'clock evening news announced that, due to the intense snowstorm, people should only attempt to drive in the event of an emergency. Gina remembered that the snow was so deep that even the snow plows were getting stuck in the drifts.

That was when her water broke.

"I was nine months pregnant," Gina said, "and even though the hospital was just 10 minutes away, the ambulance could not get to us." She and her husband Ray decided to go in their truck, which was not four-wheel drive.

"The drifts of snow were well over three feet," Gina said, "but all I could think of was getting to the hospital. My contractions were becoming faster and more frequent. The fear of getting stuck and having the baby in the truck was becoming a reality."

Finally, through the blinding snowstorm, they could see the hospital ahead. Gina knew she could hang on just a little big longer. Then they got stuck in a large drift.

The pain was unbearable, and the goal of reaching the hospital in time seemed impossible.

"As painful as it was," Gina said, "I tried to walk the rest of the way to the hospital, but the snow was up to the top of my legs and I had to go back to the truck." She remembered thinking: "I am going to die! My baby and I are going to die here!"

Her husband was growing increasingly distraught with the hopelessness of their situation and with his helplessness to do anything about it. Gina closed her eyes and started to cry.

"All of a sudden the brightest light was shining into the cab of our truck," she said. "For a moment I could not tell where it was coming from. That's when my husband's door opened and there stood the tallest man I had ever seen. He looked like Moses, and he was driving the biggest four-wheel-drive truck I could ever imagine. Written in large letters on his truck was its name, SNOWBALL."

It took the two men to get Gina in the big truck, and the whole time she thanked him and asked how he had known they were there and needed help. A few minutes later, they were at the door of the hospital and just about to go inside.

"I had to know his name," Gina said. "I turned to ask and he was gone. Neither my husband nor I saw him now, but he had been there with us—and then was gone in the blink of an eye."

Gina believes with all her heart and soul that God sent an angel in a four-wheel-drive pickup to get them to the hospital that night.

"After my daughter was born, the doctors said that had we not made it to the hospital when we did, both of us could have died," Gina said. "The umbilical cord was wrapped around my daughter's neck three times and, during the delivery, I had a grand mal seizure. I thank God every day, and I still look for SNOWBALL every winter."

Angels Were with Him

Ed is a full-time deputy sheriff in North Carolina who decided one afternoon to take a day off to attend a going-away party for a coworker. It was such a pleasant and sunny day that he decided to ride his Harley-Davidson motorcycle to the event.

"When I left the luncheon, I began cruising down a four-lane city roadway where the traffic was heavy," Ed said. "I was riding at the posted speed of 35 miles per hour when I approached a road defect, a dip in the road. My motorcycle struck the dip with such force that the frame bottomed out and gouged into the pavement. The rear of the bike bounced up, and I began to fall off of the seat. I could not get my foot onto the rear brakes, so I applied the front."

As Ed began to skid, the handle bars turned to the left, striking him in the chest. The bike flipped over onto the left side, and Ed's body was slammed onto the pavement.

"My ride to hell began," Ed recalled. "I remained on the seat of the bike for a short distance. The crash bar around the engine kept my legs from being pinned and crushed. I felt pain, and I curled up to avoid extensive road rash."

Then his bike jerked out from under him, and he began to slide on the roadway. Ed managed to look up, and he saw a large sport utility vehicle closing down on him. He knew that he was about to be run over.

"I tumbled, flipped, and rolled over and over," Ed said. "My vision began to blur. I was not sure if I was still in my lane or rolling across the open opposing lanes. Suddenly I stopped sliding, right next to my motorcycle."

Ed stood up in a daze, walked over to the sidewalk, and sat down. He later learned that he had been dragged a total distance of 92 feet. "I suffered road abrasions to my left arm and knee, but no broken bones," he said. "Although I received extensive internal bruising to my ribs and internal organs, I was alive.

"How did I avoid the SUV or being run over by the opposing traffic? I was spared serious injury or death by the grace of God. I indeed was shielded by heavenly angels. My motorcycle received scratches only to its left side and was completely functional."

Ed said that before going on the job or driving off duty, he is always certain to pray for divine protection from God's angels.

"Everyone who hears my story is amazed and exclaims, 'Angels were with you!' And I always answer that there is no doubt about it. I was truly blessed."

Blessings Are Packets of Light from the Heavenly Realms

This is a message from Archangel Michael given to mystic Lori Jean Flory:

Blessings are packets of light radiating from the doorways that exist within the heart.

Blessings of light flow from the heavenly realms and from the God light itself.

Blessings are the beauty of love personified, touching many hearts—or one heart at a time—to bring forth peace from within.

The greatest miracle of all is love in all its multifaceted expressions, large or small, noticeable or quiet. Love is a waterfall of light that flows in inexhaustible measure from the heavens and can be seen in all people, places, and things. It is the light of the soul that flows from the heart and can be seen in the light of others' eyes and in their smiles.

Even within the difficulties and challenges of the lessons that life may present, there is always a blessing present. Always is there something, someone, somewhere for which to be grateful. Always is there someone needing your love and your help. Be open to giving and to receiving both.

The greatest blessings come in the love shared with others. The greatest enrichment comes from having been touched with a loving heart.

Love yourself first, heal yourself first, and then love and heal others as an open vessel for love and healing from the One, from God. Real love comes through the helping of another's heart. Let the light of your heart be a blessing for others today.

Archangel Michael

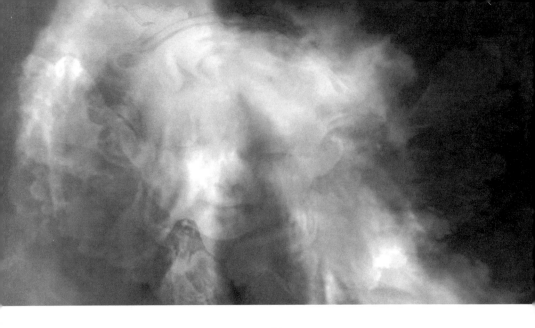

5

Invisible Defenders

Warnings from angelic beings take many forms and are often fleeting, whether a burst of light or a voice or an equally ethereal sign.

You See Me Only with Your Heart

Sondra, a psychotherapist from New York whose story we related in Chapter 1, saw an ethereal female figure appear at the foot of her bed when she was five.

"This entity frightened me into leaving my room," she said. "A few minutes later, there were gunshots outside the house that ricocheted into my bed. Had I remained in my bed, I would have been killed."

Sondra explained that contact with her spiritual guide is now made mostly through meditation, but the ethereal being has also appeared to her spontaneously: "I can hear her voice. She guides me, scolds me, corrects me. Recently I have felt her massage my face and neck when I get very tired. She sometimes appears as a very bright light outside my room."

Once when Sondra asked her guide to manifest in a more substantial form, the entity replied that she was of none of the things of the flesh: "You see me only with your heart, which has no form."

Abused by Her Family, Nurtured by an Angel

Laura, a schoolteacher from Kansas City, recalled a very difficult childhood during which she was abused physically and mentally by her parents and by her brother and sister. She was able to endure the torture done to her body and mind only because of the angel who first appeared to her when she was a child.

"I couldn't have been more than four or five when the beautiful angel appeared to comfort me one night after my parents had spanked me and sent me to bed for fidgeting when my older sister was practicing the piano. My parents had decided that she was a child prodigy at eight years of age. Regretfully, they woefully overestimated her talent. I had not lain in my bed in complete darkness for very long when my brother, who was ten, entered the room and whispered in my ear that I was evil and that the devil would come to take me that very night for his very own child. My brother added that all of the family would be happy when the devil took me, because they all hated me and thought I was ugly."

A few minutes after her brother had left her sobbing in pain and rejection, Laura recoiled in terror at the bright light that hovered over her bed. She thought it was the devil come to take her to hell, but when she tried to scream in fear, no sound came.

"It was my guardian angel, who hushed me and told me not to be afraid," Laura said. "She said that I was loved, that I was precious in God's sight, and that I had chosen this family and this path in order to make me a stronger person. I didn't understand all of what she said and meant, but I realized that I had a very special friend who cared for me."

Laura said that she could never begin to comprehend why her family seemed to despise her very existence. Her parents would beat her with a leather belt for the most minor of infractions, and her siblings felt somehow authorized to mete out their own forms of physical punishment whenever they decided that Laura was annoying them.

"Throughout my abusive childhood," she said, "my guardian angel would speak to me mentally and appear to me physically. He would tell me that I was worthwhile, that I was loved by God, that I had talents and abilities that my family could never understand and would never appreciate. As a result of this regular angelic love and communication, I grew up with a great deal of self-awareness. I was a straight-A student in high school, then I put myself through college and earned straight-A grades there as well. I received my teaching degree and began teaching school. I married a wonderful man, a fellow teacher, who would not dream of abusing me, and we have a young child."

"There's a Rattlesnake in the Berry Bushes!"

Elizabeth recalled the time when she was a girl of around seven helping her father, mother, two older brothers, and some neighbors pick blackberries on their farm in Arkansas. The berries were plentiful that year, and she had been given a small bucket to carry the succulent fruit to a larger basket that would be hauled to the house by an adult.

"Don't you lollygag none, Liz," her mother warned her. "There's lots of chores to do yet today, so we want to finish up this job in a hurry."

Since Elizabeth was smaller and had to take her time to avoid the stab of the prickly briers, she decided to find a patch of her own where the older berry pickers wouldn't rush her.

"I had just started to push my way into the thicket where the berries were most plentiful when I heard a voice shout at me, 'Don't go in there, Liz! Back away!'" Elizabeth recalled. "I was really startled, because the voice sounded a lot like Grandma Hankins, who had died that winter at the age of eighty-six. But I looked around and saw nobody near me."

She continued, "I knew it couldn't be Grandma Hankins, but it sounded like a woman's voice. After I thought about it a bit, I figured it might be Chaw, my younger brother, disguising his voice to tease me, to scare me, so I wouldn't pick as many berries as he could and then he could make fun of me. So just to be ornery and show him, I started to push into the briers to go after the blackberries."

This time the voice was louder and sterner: "*Elizabeth*, you get away from there. There's a big rattlesnake in there, and it will bite you!"

Elizabeth said that the second time the voice really got her attention with its talk of a rattlesnake, "plus the fact that when I was a little kid, no one ever called me Elizabeth except Mom or Grandma Hankins when they got really cross with me."

Elizabeth ran toward her parents and brothers and told them to come quick with their hoes. "I told them that there was a big, really big rattlesnake in my berry patch, and they had better come and take care of it good and proper," she said. "At first Mom just scolded me for telling a tale, thinking that I was making up a story to get out of picking berries, but Dad told my brothers to go check it out.

"Pretty soon the boys were yelling and chopping away like mad in the midst of my berry patch," Elizabeth continued. "When they came back out, they dragged a dead rattlesnake behind them. It had fifteen rattles on its tail. That is a *big* rattlesnake! The voice had saved my life. It had told the truth. There really was a big rattlesnake just waiting for me in the berry patch."

Elizabeth said that after she told her parents about the voice that had warned her not to go into the berry bushes, they both agreed that the alert had come from her guardian angel.

"I've heard that same voice a couple more times," Elizabeth said. "It is definitely a woman's voice, and sometimes it truly does sound like Grandma Hankins. One time, my guardian angel warned me not to take a bus that later had a crash with a big truck. Three folks were killed and eight were badly injured. I wouldn't have wanted to have been included in either category—especially the 'killed.' Another time, the voice told me not to let my daughter Lucy go with this fellow to a dance. The young man got himself liquored up and rolled his car that Saturday night. My Lucy would have been killed or badly hurt."

A Warning Voice Told Them to Jump in the Ditch

An account of a warning voice that saved a husband and wife from fatal injury was told to us not long ago when a group of friends shared their experiences of unusual events in their lives.

George Hansen remembered the Christmas holidays in 1956, when he and his wife, Eleanor, were visiting his mother on the old home place in southern Wisconsin.

"Dad had passed away the preceding Christmas," George said, "and Mom lived alone in the farmhouse. Her brother, my uncle Leonard, farmed the land. Eleanor and I were joining my sisters, Klara and Sal, and their husbands on the family farm for the traditional holiday feast and gift exchange, with the ulterior motive of convincing our mother to leave the farm and move into an apartment in town.

"We still had the '48 Ford coupe at that time, and the old bucket of bolts was notorious for dying and stalling at the most inopportune moments. We were driving toward the family farm on a cold, starless night when the Ford's motor died about a mile and a half from our destination."

George managed to glide the car a bit closer to the side of the two-lane blacktop before it came to a complete halt.

"Wonderful!" Eleanor groused, shaking her head bitterly. "This is just wonderful. Now we have to carry our luggage over a mile to the farm house. And I'm in high heels besides!"

George knew his wife could get frostbitten toes hiking through the snow on such a cold night. He told her to stay in the car. He would walk to the farm, get a tractor from the machine shed, and pull the Ford to the house.

"Be careful. Don't slip on the icy spots, honey," Eleanor warned him as he got out of the coupe.

George acknowledged her concern, but he knew by the way that she draped the travel blanket around her exposed toes that he had responded in the gallant manner that she had hoped.

When he got out of the coupe, he saw that there was a slight downward incline just a few yards ahead of him. It might not be necessary for either one of them to walk to the farmhouse.

"Sweetie," he said, "if I can push the car just a few yards to an incline up ahead, I think we can jump-start the engine. So you steer while I push."

Eleanor slid over behind the steering wheel and pushed in the clutch. She was to keep the clutch to the floorboard until the Ford picked up speed, then take her foot off the clutch and hope that the coupe would jump back to life. She was quite familiar with the procedure from the countless prior occasions when the car's engine had died.

George got the Ford rolling, and he just had stepped to the rear to give it his solid shoulder from behind. He was pushing against the rear of the coupe with all his strength when he heard a loud voice shout at him to jump in the ditch.

"The voice was clear as it could be," George recalled. "I thought that it sounded like my father's voice. It even seemed to have the slight Swedish accent that he had never managed to lose. 'George,' the voice shouted, 'Get out of the way! Jump in the ditch ... now!'"

George was in the process of obeying the voice when, seemingly from out of nowhere on that lonely country blacktop, a car, speeding so fast that neither he nor Eleanor had seen its approach from the rear, slammed into the back of the '48 Ford coupe.

"I was not quite fast enough," George said. "The Plymouth sedan struck my hip a glancing blow and tossed me into the ditch, where I lapsed into unconsciousness."

When he awakened in the hospital, George was informed that he had suffered a broken leg, a fractured hip, and numerous bruises. Although he spent a couple of weeks in the hospital and it took months for all of his injuries to heal, George knew that if it had not been for the warning shout that sounded so much like his father's voice, he would have been crushed and almost certainly killed by the force of the Plymouth sedan smashing him against the rear of their Ford coupe.

Eleanor had suffered only a few cuts and bruises, but she, too, had heard the warning voice.

Startled into instant obedience by the sound of an unseen voice, she had begun to slide from the front seat of the coup and head for the ditch. The impact of the sedan striking the rear of their Ford had served as an additional impetus to project her free of the violent crash.

Fortunately, the teenaged couple driving the Plymouth also survived the accident with minor concussions, breaks, and bruises.

"Eleanor and I both heard quite clearly the warning voice," George said. "Although we could never decide for certain if the shout had come from a guardian angel or my father, we both felt that we recognized the distinctive voice as likely belonging to my dad."

In addition to the warning voice having saved their lives, it was reassuring to them to contemplate that George's father's spiritual presence was still with them and looking after them. And if it had been an angel's voice, that was certainly reassuring as well.

"My mother joined Dad two years later," George concluded. "Eleanor passed on in 1987, and now that I am seventy-eight years old, I know that it may not be long before we will all be together again."

Sometimes God Has to Lend the Angels a Helping Hand

Joey is an epileptic who has seizures if he doesn't get enough rest.

"I was going to work one morning," he said. "I thought I'd had enough sleep, but I guess I hadn't. I was about 20 minutes away from work, so I turned on my CD player and started singing one of my favorite songs, 'Awesome God.'

"I had just passed a very busy part of the highway, filled with stop lights and a lot of morning traffic. Then I don't remember anything except waking up and a paramedic telling me that I could look for my glasses later. She told me that I had to go to the hospital."

Later, Joey learned that one of his buddy's coworkers had seen the crash. "He said that my little '89 Escort GT had passed him like he was sitting still. After passing him at 75 or 80 miles an hour, I drove straight into the median and took out a construction sign. Then I drove into oncoming traffic all the way over to the emergency lane. Next I cut back to the median and flipped my car on its side, then on the roof. After sliding to the other side of the road, I flipped again, this time doing a complete end-over-end. I landed on my wheels, pointing toward the road in a field beside the road.

"Just before I had my seizure," Joey said, "something told me to put my shoulder belt on. My injuries were two bumps on my head. I spent an hour at the hospital. No one else was injured, and no other cars were damaged.

"Yes, we do have guardian angels," he concluded, "but God sometimes has to shield us with his hands."

The Mysterious Nun Was a "Godincidence"

When Steve was a teenager and an apprentice mechanic near Manchester, England, he loved to drive.

"One week it was my intention to set off on Friday night and go to Cornwall for the weekend," he wrote. "When I mentioned this to my fellow apprentice, he asked me if he could come with me. He also asked me if we could stop at his aunt's house in Margate on the way. At the time I didn't realize that it was several hundred miles in the opposite direction, so I agreed."

The two young men traveled through Friday night with about two hours'sleep in the car somewhere in Kent, then spent Saturday morning at his friend's aunt's house. They set off for Cornwall after lunch.

Late on Saturday night somewhere near Stonehenge, they grabbed another couple of hours'sleep in the car and ended up at Mevagissey on the South Cornish coast on Sunday morning. Later, when they arrived home, Steve calculated the mileage covered that weekend at 1,165 miles.

"On the way back several hours later," Steve said, "we were on the M6 near Birmingham, about 80 miles from home, and I was struggling to stay awake. Then I saw a nun on the hard shoulder walking northwards. There were no turnoffs for miles, no service areas for over 20 miles in either direction, nor any sign of a broken-down vehicle. All the way back home all I could think about was solving the mystery. Where had the nun come from, where had she been going, what was she doing out all alone in the middle of nowhere?"

For twenty-five years, Steve has kept coming back to the enigma of the mysterious nun, trying to work it out.

"One day quite recently," he said, "I related it to a good friend of mine who is very spiritual. He was with his pastor at the time, and they both said it must have been an angel sent to keep me awake. My friend and his pastor call this kind of event a 'Godincidence.'

"At that moment, it was as if I received a message from Heaven. I felt something so strong inside both spiritually and physically that I just absolutely know beyond a shadow of doubt that they had solved the puzzle for me. I have never once again wondered about that nun walking along the side of the motorway. She was my guardian angel."

6

Angels Who Left Evidence of Their Visits

In their life-changing or life-saving endeavors, angels occasionally leave physical proof of their visit.

An Angel Brought Him Water

A few years ago, Brad Steiger met a man (who wishes only to be known as Mac) who had a reputation for honesty, truthfulness, and great generosity in his local business community. After we had enjoyed lunch together at the invitation of Glenn, a longtime friend of Brad's and another businessman of fine reputation, Mac was encouraged to tell a most remarkable account of the time an angel saved his life.

In 1942 Mac had been a member of the First Ranger Battalion that was trained in Scotland by the British Commandos and, together with the Third and Fourth Ranger Battalions, served in North Africa and Italy in the early days of World War II.

As Mac told the story, he had become separated from his men after a vicious encounter with the German general Erwin Rommel's Afrika Korps in the desert region of North Africa. "They didn't call him *der Wüstenfuchs*, the Desert Fox, for nothing," Mac said. "Erwin Johannes Eugen Rommel was a brilliant strategist and a courageous officer, and his men were far from pussycats. They were tough, seasoned veterans, and it was our job to push them out of the African desert, where they had enjoyed some spectacular victories, and knock them to their knees."

Battered from constant fighting and more than a bit the worse for wear, Mac knew that he had to keep going in the merciless heat and do his utmost to avoid walking right into the German army and be killed or captured. He also knew that he had to go sparingly on the little bit of water that he had left in his canteen, but the scorching sun seemed to be sucking every drop of moisture from his body. He knew that he was dehydrating quickly, and he did his best to conserve his energy. At the same time, Mac realized that to remain stationary was absolutely no guarantee of survival with German patrols in the area.

"I had been in tight spots before," Mac said, "but I thought maybe this time my luck had run out. I figured some day some desert tribesman would find my bleached bones drying in the sand."

When Mac was finally found several days later, his rescuers brought in a man in need of medical attention, but a man very much alive and not at all dehydrated. In fact, his canteen was still more than half full.

How had Mac survived? How could he possibly have lasted days in the desert on only a few sips of water at most a day?

Mac had a reputation among his men as being the toughest of the tough, always rugged and always ready, but nobody was that tough! No one could survive the broiling sun of the African desert without water. How could he have lasted on only half a canteen?

Although he was essentially an unchurched man whose father was an avowed atheist, Mac told his rescuers that he would tell his story of survival only to Father Tony, a Roman Catholic chaplain.

"An angel brought me water on the desert," Mac told the astonished clergyman. "Each day the angel would appear to me and fill my canteen with water. I could never have made it without that angel's help, Father. I guess I must not be all bad. I guess someone up there is looking out for me."

Mac had somehow managed to keep his canteen with him, and he handed it to the priest, sloshing it around as he did. Father Tony knew that Mac had not had a chance to refill the canteen after his retrieval from the desert—and yet the container was nearly full of clear water.

"See for yourself, Father Tony," Mac invited. "Take a drink of pure angel water."

Father Tony smiled and declined the offer, but having heard such remarkable testimony from so tough and no-nonsense a soldier as Mac, he was intrigued to the extent that he asked to have the water in Mac's canteen analyzed.

Later, the chaplain told Mac, the chemists had said that the water was extremely pure, that it contained none of the minerals or other substances which were indigenous to that area of the desert and of that region of Africa. Father Tony was tempted to call it holy water. And he definitely agreed with Mac that it had been brought to him by an angel.

After he had survived the campaign in the African desert, the invasion of Italy, and the fall of Berlin, Mac returned home with the inspiration that he would help young boys such as those he saw orphaned by the terrible war. When Brad Steiger met the tough former Ranger who had been saved by an angel for a greater mission than fighting in a war, he learned that Mac, together with his wife, had served as foster parents to more than one hundred homeless boys.

He Thought He Was Giving His Last Dollars to a Starving Man

Darlene will always remember the story that her father told her brothers and sisters when they were younger. As she related:

When Dad was eighteen years old, he was getting ready to leave his hometown, a small town nestled deep in the hills of eastern Kentucky. Upstate New York was his destination. My dad was a hellion in those days—booze, women, and barroom fights. You name it; he did it. This trip would be an experience that would eventually prove to change his life forever.

As he waited for his bus he met a man sitting alone in the near-empty station. The man wore filthy, tattered clothes, and he looked like he had not eaten for a few days. After talking to the man for a few minutes, my dad learned this man had no particular destination. Dad found this interesting, yet odd, given the fact that they were sitting in the middle of a bus station.

After chatting with the stranger for about an hour, my dad said he felt an overpowering conviction. There was no mention of religion in their conversation, yet he felt this heaviness in his heart that he could not understand. Before leaving the bus station my dad said he dropped two of his last three dollars in the man's hand and said, "Here, go get yourself something to eat."

He bid the man farewell, and he turned to pick up his luggage. He had barely made it a few feet down the aisle before he heard a female voice behind him calling out to him, "Sir, sir. You must have dropped this, it was on the floor in front of the bench where you were sitting."

He turned and glanced in the direction of the voice to see a lady hurrying toward him. He looked over the lady's shoulder, and there was no sign of the old man in the tattered clothing.

The lady placed the two dollars in his hand and walked away.

It would be many years before he'd be able to explain the incident, but my father came to believe that the man he met at the bus station that night was an angel. One of my dad's favorite Bible quotes was Hebrew 13:2: "For thereby some have entertained angels unawares."

In my eyes, Dad became a great spiritual figure. He labored almost alone to build a church with his bare hands. When times were tough for the church, he took money from his own pocket to pay for whatever was needed, leaving God the responsibility of feeding his family. We never did without. Amazingly, there was always plenty. My father never met a stranger. He welcomed all into his home and his heart. He willingly gave the shirt off his back, the money in his pocket, and the time allotted to him on this earth to anyone in need. What a wonderful role model he was in the Christian faith.

A Golden Stranger Came to Their Aid on a Cold Winter's Day

Julia recalled the extraordinary stranger who visited their family at a time when they suffered from great poverty and depression after their mother's death and who left gifts and money on the kitchen table of their Nebraska farm home. Although Julia did not see the benefactor herself, her younger sister Merry did, and she swore that he was an angel.

Julia remember the incident well as occurring just after Thanksgiving in 1964. Their mother, Opal, had died in March, so it had been the first holiday without her warm and loving presence.

Four days later, Merry came down with a terrible fever. The three children—Julia, Merry, and Jake—had but one blanket apiece, but Julia and Jake piled the covers on Merry when they were doing their chores or their homework. Normally they walked around the old farmhouse with blankets wrapped around them to ward off the cold, but they wanted Merry to get warm enough to break her fever.

Since late October, their father, Gus, had been working at the grain elevator in town. During planting and harvest, he had been a hired man for an elderly farmer, but the man had no need for help during the winter months. Gus' family, however, still had need for food, regardless of the season, so he worked at the elevator.

Julia remembered that their father was really depressed. It would soon be Christmas, the first one without Mama. They had always had really nice Christmases. They were never rich, but they were well enough off until their father had a run of bad luck.

All the children noticed the deep melancholy that had darkened their father, so Merry had not wanted to concern him with her illness. She knew that he had enough on his mind, so one day when Julia and Jake were at school, Merry had prayed that they could have some more blankets and just a little extra money so that they could have a nice Christmas.

Merry told the story often, how she was lying next to the oil burner that afternoon when she saw the angel. At first she was startled to hear the door open, for she knew that Julia had locked it behind her when she and Jake left for school that morning. Then she saw a "beautiful man" walk into the house. He was fairly tall and well-built, with long blond hair and bright blue eyes.

Merry let out a small cry of surprise and concern at a stranger boldly entering their home, but the man smiled and lifted a hand in a friendly way that seemed to say he wouldn't hurt her.

He had four thick blankets under his arm, and he set them down on the kitchen table. For the first time, Merry noticed that he wore hardly anything at all against the terrible November cold. He wore no coat, just a thin white shirt and blue jeans.

Merry knew that he intended to give them the blankets, so she spoke up and said, "You had better keep those for yourself, mister. You'll freeze to death in this cold country." Julia and Merry have since found it interesting that Merry had somehow felt that he had come from some warmer place.

The stranger smiled again and spoke for the first time in a voice that Merry described as sounding as though he were singing and talking at the same time. "I won't need the blankets, Merry," he said, calling her by name. "They are for you and your family."

Just before the blond stranger left, he took five twenty-dollar bills from inside his shirt and set them on top of the blankets. He smiled, told Merry that she would soon be feeling better, and walked out the door. After he had gone, Merry was convinced that she had been visited by an angel—the one she had prayed for to come and help them.

Julia said in her account of the incident that when she and Jake got home from school they found the front door locked just as she had left it, so they were really surprised when Merry told them that someone had walked in on her that afternoon. And when she said that an *angel* had brought them new blankets and some money for their father, Julia remembered that she felt Merry's forehead and feared that she must be running a really high fever. Julia covered her with the new blankets and gave her some steaming hot tea until the fever broke.

Their father felt that some nice young man in town or on one of the neighboring farms had learned of the family's plight and had given them the blankets and the money.

Julia pointed out that while $100 might not seem like much today, in 1964 it was just enough to give the buffer their dad needed to get caught up with some bills, and he was even able to afford some Christmas presents for the kids. One hundred dollars would also be quite a bit of money for some anonymous donor to lay on a stranger's kitchen table.

Jake and Julia always believed Merry. An added bit of proof, Julia said, was the fact that Merry was a good artist even then, and she was able to draw what she said was a good likeness of the benevolent stranger. They had lived in that community all of their lives, and they lived there another eight years after the incident, and none of them had ever seen anyone who looked like the image in Merry's drawing. Jake, Julia, and Merry agree that it was angel who helped them survive that terrible winter after their mother's death.

Money from Heaven

In his always interesting Web site (http://paranormal.about.com), Stephen Wagner wrote an article on mysterious manifestations of "money from Heaven."

In the experience of Mary, an unwed mother of an eleven-month-old son who had fallen on very hard times, the needed money materialized when she had only twenty dollars left to her name. The small sum would cover diapers and baby formula but was not enough to buy the food that she and her son needed to survive.

On a very cold, damp, windy night, Mary got out of her car in the grocery store parking lot and placed her son in a shopping cart. No one else was in sight. "Then," she said, "three twenty-dollar bills blew up to me. Then the wind suddenly stopped. I looked right and left ... there was no one else in the parking lot. I knew that God saw and heard my plight and sent money from Heaven."

Another account offered by Wagner told of a woman who was struggling to complete college while raising her small daughter. Although money was extremely tight, the woman kept finding dimes that would materialize out of the air in the bathroom of her tiny one-bedroom apartment.

Throughout the eighteen months that she and her daughter lived in the apartment, enough dimes came out of the ether to help them get by financially. She said that at all hours of the day or night, she would "hear the distinct sound of coins dropping" in the bathroom. "Sometimes there would be several, always in the same place near the tub."

It so pleased her, she said, to believe that the falling dimes were "a sign of caring from loving beings."

One final story from the many that Wagner collected from the readers of his website:

Helen Q. had reached such a financially desperate time in her life that she didn't have enough money for her three sons' lunch the next day at school. Although she only needed three dollars, Helen was so embarrassed by her complete lack of funds that she decided to keep the boys home from school. Her twelve-year-old son, who had perfect attendance, protested and said that he absolutely could not miss school the next day, lunch money or not.

There was a strange noise from the kitchen, and when Helen and her older son investigated, they saw some quarters scattered on the floor. In her account, Helen admitted that she was frightened and wanted to run out of the house. However, her son entered the kitchen, picked up the quarters, and placed them on the table, declaring them to be icy cold. There were exactly three dollars in quarters.

"They're from Grandma," her son said, referring to Helen's deceased mother. "She always gave me quarters."

Even better than providing enough money for her sons' lunch money the next day in school, Helen concluded, was the good news that the quarters from Grandma in Heaven signified that things were going to get better for the family. Life just seemed to come together for them that night, and they never had to go without again.

The Case of the Fireplace Angel

It was during the early spring of 2004 when the phenomenon began, one that still baffles us and those involved. There is no doubt that miracles occur and that we are given divine messages in very subtle ways, but it is the non-subtle manifestation that gets your attention. "The Case of the Fireplace Angel," from the files of Dr. Jimmy Lowery, paranormal researcher, demonologist, and exorcist, is no exception. As Dr. Lowery tells it:

I was just wrapping up doing a very interesting interview with a guest on our paranormal talk-radio show when I received an urgent call on my cell phone. It was my mother-in-law, Carla. She was very excited, sadness and joy all wrapped into one. She began telling me that there was an angel on the fire brick of the fireplace in her home and that it just mysteriously appeared sometime between 9 p.m. the night before and that afternoon. She is not unfamiliar with the paranormal nor with the type of work that Heather, my wife and her daughter, and I do concerning the paranormal. After speaking with Carla, I immediately knew that I had to see this "miracle" for myself. I hurriedly finished up the evening's work and darted off to Carla's home.

After arriving at the home I immediately went to the fireplace, and she told me again why she believed there was an angel on the fireplace. As I examined the seven- to eight-inch-tall, bluish figure, it did appear to be that of a angel, the kind that you would see in old drawings. I will have to admit that my first thought was that it was drawn by someone. Even though Carla was my relative, I still had to be an objective investigator and treat the case just as I would any other—perhaps especially since she was a relative.

According to Carla, the previous evening she had been lying on the couch watching the flames burn down in the fireplace and was in heavy meditation to God. For several months her mother had been ill and the prognosis was very grim, and she knew this. Carla was very close to her mother and was trying to deal with the idea of losing her very soon. She prayed hard and asked for a comforting sign that would let her know everything was going to be all right.

One of the subjects that Carla and her mother would discuss was angels, so much so that her mother would buy angel figurines for her all the time. The mantel was covered with angel figurines, as was every nook and cranny in the home.

After meditating for some time, Carla finally fell asleep for the night. When she woke up the next morning she got up and went about her usual routine. Later that morning she noticed something odd in the fireplace. The more she looked at the back wall of the fireplace, the more she was convinced that she was seeing a picture of an angel. God had given her a comforting sign.

For months we studied the figure on the fireplace wall. We even went as far as to try to scrub it off. But to no avail; the angel remained. Carla was so convinced of the angel's image that for almost a year she would not burn a fire in the fireplace.

The next summer, she did lose her mother, which made it even more important to her for the angel in the fireplace to remain untouched. It became almost a shrine of sorts to Carla—which bothered me somewhat, because I felt the angelic image was placed there as a message of comfort, not to become a shrine.

Eventually, we convinced Carla to let us conduct some more studies on the figure. We even used acid and other strong cleansing solutions to try to take it off, but the image would not come off. It remained as bright and solid as it did when it first appeared.

We finally persuaded her to let us burn a fire to see if that would have any effect on the angel figure, and reluctantly she allowed it. Still it remained. But then after about a week of burning a fire in the fireplace, the angel finally disappeared as quickly as it had appeared.

Was this angelic image a miracle or a message from God? It is unclear as to exactly what put the figure there, but all of us believe it was a divine message from God and sent as an answer to prayer for comfort. And there is no way that Carla will believe any different, nor do I expect her to do so.

As a side note: During some of the investigations we acquired some very clear electronic voice phenomena (EVPs) from Carla's home that we believe to be that of human spirits. Could they be the ones who put the angel figure on the fireplace as a message of reassurance that life continues beyond the grave?

7

Benevolent Beings Who Intervened in Crisis Situations

There are many stories of guardian angels and other benevolent beings coming to the rescue of people in great distress.

Protected by an Angel Behind Enemy Lines

Pilot Scott O'Grady has said that he began asking his guardian angel for help the instant his F-16 fighter was struck by a missile fired by Serbian troops on June 2, 1995. As he plummeted to the ground in a parachute, he placed his fate in God's hands.

Scott found a hiding place in some brush as soon as he reached ground, but he knew the Serbs had seen him parachute from the F-16 and had a good idea where he was. He hugged the earth as the Serbs sprayed the area with machine gun fire.

While bullets were gouging the leaves, branches, and dirt all around him, Scott said he heard his guardian angel assure him not to worry. The angelic voice told him that he was with him, that he would protect him, and that it was his job to get him home safely to his family.

As the bullets ripped through the area where he was hiding, Scott said that he felt that his angel was actually deflecting the slugs from striking him. A Serbian soldier who investigated the area to check whether or not they had killed the pilot nearly stepped directly on Scott in his hiding place. There was no way the Serb could not have seen him, Scott said later, unless his angel had cloaked him and made him invisible to enemy eyes.

On the third day of his ordeal, Scott again felt that he was certain to be discovered by a farmer herding his cattle. He readied his knife, certain that he would be forced to kill the man to avoid discovery. But once again, Scott's angel told him to relax and to lie still. Incredibly, the farmer walked on his way, totally oblivious to the U.S. airman, who was almost in plain sight.

After successfully evading the Serbian troops for six days, two Marine Corps helicopters that had managed to track the fugitive airman landed in a clearing to remove Scott from enemy territory. Although it had been a nightmarish six days of hiding out and narrowly evading capture, Scott suddenly froze when he saw the means of his rescue so near at hand. A wave of fear swept over him, convincing him that Serbian troops were just waiting for him to expose himself so they could mow him down.

Then he once again heard the reassuring voice of his angel, telling him to go for it. It was time for him to go home to his family. Scott later said that it was as if his angel lifted him to his feet and carried him to the waiting helicopter, where a Marine reached out and pulled him into the vehicle.

When Serbian troops began to fire at the helicopter, Scott wasn't worried. His angel had assured him that he was going to go home.

As soon as the rescue helicopter and its escort had made it safely out to sea, Scott said that he gave thanks to God for the miracle of his six-day survival and managing to evade the enemy. Then he gave special thanks for the Lord sending him an angel to guide him through the ordeal.

An Angel Forced an Abusive Father to Change His Ways

After one of the Steigers'seminars in a large Pacific Coast city, Jenny, a twenty-one-year-old college student, told them that she had endured an abusive childhood that had eventually progressed to her father's crude attempts at incest. And then one incredibly wonderful evening, a miracle occurred and an angel intervened.

Jenny told us that to say that her childhood home life was imbalanced would be putting it mildly. As early as she could remember, her father drank too much. When the family was lucky, he fell asleep in front of the television set. When they were unlucky, he would first beat Jenny's mother, then her brother, Billy, then Jenny. She described the system of the beatings as kind of terrible ritual her father would perform.

When Jenny reached the age of eleven, however, her abusive father began to look at her with a perverse awareness that she might be able to provide a new outlet for his hostilities than a simple beating. One night after he had finished beating his wife and son, he suddenly grabbed Jenny by the arm and pulled her after him into a bedroom. Jenny figured that she was going to get a really terrible beating all alone in the room, but then she saw her father fumbling with the fly of his trousers.

Thankfully, he was too drunk to finish what he started that night, but the intended act of incest was very ugly and upsetting to Jenny. She got sick to her stomach when she feared that this act would probably be a terrible new aspect of the ritual of abuse.

Although Jenny got pulled into the bedroom by her father on many other occasions, each time her prayers were answered when he either fell asleep or was unable to complete the act due to the effects of the alcohol.

One night, as soon as she had twisted free of her father's drunken grasp, Jenny ran from the house and took refuge in the Baptist church a few blocks away from their home. She sat in the back pew, all alone in the church, and she knew that she had to pray and ask God for strength. She wanted to run away from home, but she knew that she was really too young to survive in the streets, and she couldn't leave her mother and Billy to face the drunken rages of her father all by themselves.

After a few moments of prayer, Jenny was startled to see an angel appear in the aisle, then move into the pew and sit down beside her.

"When he looked at me, all fear just melted away," Jenny said. "Then he began to talk to me. Not with his mouth, but with his mind. He spoke of many things that I cannot remember, but I just rejoiced in the love that I felt emanating from him. And I clearly remember that he told me to go home and not to be afraid anymore."

Three nights later, Jenny's father was again wholly devoted to the ugly process of becoming drunk and increasingly mean. On this night of miracles, however, there were no more beatings.

"Dad started toward Mama, and I remember that I shouted at him to stop," Jenny said. "He turned to me with that same awful look that came over him. He started to stagger toward me and that was when this brilliant ball of blinding light came right through the window and hovered over me. Believe me, that light was so bright that none of us could more than glance at it for a few seconds at a time.

"Then we all heard this deep voice speaking from the light: 'Jacob, change your life tonight. Change your life or lose your soul!'"

Jenny said that her father fell to the floor in a dead faint. The brilliant light spun around the room three times, then disappeared. When her father regained consciousness, he began to cry like a baby. Jenny's mother hugged him, and they all started to cry.

After a few minutes, her father wiped his tears, got to his feet, and poured a six-pack of beer and two bottles of whiskey down the kitchen sink. Their mother kissed the children and told them that an angel had just brought back the man that she had married.

"She was right," Jenny said, concluding her remarkable story. "To my knowledge, Pa never took another drink, and I know that he never raised a hand to Mama and us kids again. He died in his sleep four years later, and we all felt that he went to Heaven with his soul intact."

A Beam of Light from Heaven Led to Her Rescue

Stephanie Grana was driving along Bingo Lake Road around 10 p.m. on December 27, 1996, when her auto hit a tree, skidded more than 50 feet off the road, and buried itself in a thick growth of bushes. When twenty-four-year-old Stephanie regained consciousness, she awoke to terrible pain and the awful realization that her left arm and leg were smashed and a broken bone from her leg was embedded in the door panel.

It was 25 degrees that night. She was certain to become hypothermic if she lived that long. She knew that she had many broken bones and was bleeding badly.

With her one movable arm, she tried to beep her car horn, but no sound came. The headlights were out and there was no interior lights, and Stephanie understood then that the battery must have been ripped loose during the skidding crash into the thick brush.

Stephanie knew that she was too far off the road to be seen by any passing cars on that cold, foggy night. As she began to lose consciousness, she prayed that God would help her.

Dave Kaul had driven past the intersection where Stephanie had skidded off the road, but he hadn't noticed anything out of the ordinary. He had driven about 100 yards when his attention was drawn to his rearview mirror and the remarkable sight of a bright beam of light shining down from the sky and illuming a patch of brush off the road.

Intrigued by the mysterious light, Kaul turned back to the intersection and flashed his lights on high to the place where the brilliant beam of light was pinpointing. Startled, he saw the crumpled car in the brush. Once Kaul had identified the scene of the accident, the strange light from Heaven went out.

Kaul rushed to a nearby gas station to call for help, then rushed back to the accident scene to see what he could do to help anyone who might be alive in the vehicle. As he walked to the crash, he found the car battery lying about ten feet away from the automobile. Whatever had caused the mysterious beacon in the sky could not have come from the car hidden in the brush.

Kaul comforted Stephanie until a twenty-member rescue crew arrived with the "jaws of life" to free her from her terrible metal prison. While the two of them sat in the darkness awaiting help, Kaul was overcome with the wonderful sensation that he had been touched by an angel and privileged to witness a miracle.

Without knowing why, Kaul told Stephanie that it must have been her grandmother turning on the light in Heaven so that he could find her in the dark. He felt a shiver run through his body when Stephanie told him that her grandmother had only recently passed on.

Later, Stephanie told journalist Esmond Choueke that an angel sent down a light from Heaven to save her life. "My grandmother is my guardian angel," she said. "She helped me in my time of greatest need."

Police Sergeant Mike Fryzel told Choueke that it was truly a miracle that Stephanie's life was saved that night. "If that strange light hadn't pinpointed her location," he said, "she would have been dead in less than 45 minutes. It was only 25 degrees, and she had hypothermia, loss of blood, and many broken bones."

A Violin-Playing Angel Saved His Life

Sandor (Shony) Alex Draun was born to religious Jewish parents in 1930 in the small city of Cristuru-Secuiesc, Romania. He began violin lessons when he was five, and it was decided that he had musical talent. Shony continued his lessons when his town was occupied by Hungary in 1940 but had ceased practicing by the time Cristuru-Secuiesc was invaded by Germany in 1944. In May 1944 his family was deported to the Auschwitz camp in Poland.

One evening an officer came into the barracks where the starving fourteen-year-old Shony was housed and announced that if anyone could play the violin for the commandant, that person would be given food. Although he hadn't touched a violin for years, Shony quickly raised his hand at the thought of getting some food as a reward for playing a tune on a violin. Two older men also raised their hands, and the three prisoners were marched to the commandant's dining room.

As they were rushed along in the cold night, Shony thought that he would play something he had learned when he had taken lessons as a boy of seven or eight. Perhaps a sonata by Antonin Dvorak or a composition by Fritz Kreisler.

When they entered the dining room, the succulent aroma of exquisitely prepared food almost made Shony faint with hunger, and the pangs in his stomach tightened all the more painfully.

The commandant sat expectantly, arms folded across his chest. His eyes narrowed, appearing almost lupine. An attack dog, a massive German shepherd, lay at his side, and he was flanked on either side by ranking officers who stared coldly at the three prisoners.

The oldest prisoner took the violin that a guard handed him. Shony recalled that the violinist, obviously very accomplished, expertly tuned the instrument and began to play a beautiful sonata.

The violinist had just finished the final note of his accomplished professional performance when the commandant put his hands over his ears. "Awful! Terrible!" he shouted. "Kill him!"

Guards rushed forward and beat the unfortunate musician to death with iron pipes. The unfortunate violinist died a painful death in a matter of a few minutes.

The bloody death seemed to mean no more to the officers and the commandant than if he had ordered a fly killed whose annoying buzz had disturbed his dining.

Shony said that the second violinist was so frightened that he could not manage a single note. He smiled, shrugged nervously, and asked for a few moments to compose himself. At a signal from the commandant, the guards beat him to death with the iron rods. The man died without having had a chance to play the violin.

The instrument was thrust into Shony's trembling hands. He had never even held an adult-sized violin before. All of his lessons as a child were played on a little violin.

One of the guards approached him with a bloody iron pipe. "Play *The Blue Danube*," he whispered in a coarse, rasping voice. "If you play it, he might let you live."

In an interview given in 1990, Shony said that he thought his death was inevitable and very imminent. He had never before played *The Blue*

Danube. He couldn't even remember what the piece sounded like. He knew that he had many times heard Gypsies playing it and recalled that his brother, an accordionist, had played *The Blue Danube* with his school group—but he was at a complete loss as to how to even begin.

It was then, Shony said, that he felt a powerful force take control of his hands. He said that he could actually perceive an angel guiding his fingers and the violin bow. To his astonishment, he began to hear beautiful music flowing out from the violin. It was without question Johann Strauss' waltz, *The Blue Danube*.

The guards began humming along with the melody, and the commandant was tapping the rhythm with his fingers on the table top. Shony knew that God had sent an angel to play masterfully a tune that he had never before even practiced.

When he finished, the commandant ordered Shony be given all the food that he wanted. Shony remembered that as hungry as he was, he began eating rather cautiously until the brutal guards with the iron rods left the dining room.

Later, Shony was transferred to the Natzweiler camp system in France, then to Dachau, where he was liberated by U.S. troops in April 1945. He did perform a Kreisler composition on Radio Munich before he emigrated to the United States and became a composer and a professional violinist.

"My life was saved so that I might live to become a father and a grandfather," Shony once said. "I owe everything to an angel who really knew how to play a violin."

An Angel Appeared to Anchor the Line in a Blinding Snowstorm

Douglas, who is now in his late forties, believes that he and twenty others owe their lives to an angel who mysteriously appeared when he was a fifteen-year-old guide caught in a sudden Rocky Mountain blizzard.

Douglas's father began taking him along on mountain hikes and climbs when he was barely three years old. By the time Douglas was thirteen, he had become a strong climber and nearly inexhaustible hiker.

In the summer of 1974, a friend of Douglas's father decided that he wanted to create a wilderness camp that would give big-city kids an opportunity to experience some real Rocky Mountain highs. To make it even more appealing for the kids, he wanted to hire a bunch of youthful counselors and guides.

True to form, Douglas said, his father generously volunteered Douglas's services for the season to help his friend launch the new enterprise.

Douglas remembered that he and two other teenage guides had taken a group of eighteen kids—aged nine to twelve, eleven boys and seven girls—on a mountain trail for an afternoon hike "We were really very high when we were suddenly caught in a violent blizzard," Douglas said. "This would have been frightening enough with experienced hikers, but with eighteen little greenhorns from the city, it was every mountain guide's worst nightmare."

Accepting the grim fact that at the age of fifteen he was the *senior* guide, Douglas realized that it was up to him to get everyone safely down the mountain trail to the main camp. They really had no choice other than to head back down. They had no tents, no blankets, no intention of camping out. This was a completely unseasonable, unexpected storm.

"The freak storm might have been all melted away in a couple of days," Douglas said, "but by that time we all could have been dead."

Douglas divided the main body of hikers into three groups of six, each one led by one of the teenage counselors. Dean was another fairly well experienced fifteen-year-old. Phil was seventeen, the oldest of the counselors, but he had never spent any time in the mountains and was as green as the greenest. Phil had been chosen as a counselor based on his talents as a folk singer and banjo player—to be a sing-along leader at the campfires.

Douglas tried his best to place the strongest of the children in two groups. He took the six weakest and least experienced of the kids with him, four girls and two boys.

Douglas will always be thankful that they had thought ahead to take some rope with them—enough so that each of the team leaders could tie their kids to them in connecting loops, like mountain climbers, so that they would be able to keep each group together.

The snow was coming down harder than ever, and the powerful wind was deadly on the breath at that altitude. Douglas knew they had to move out of the blizzard area as quickly as possible.

They were not many minutes into their retreat when Douglas began to regret his decision to take the weakest of the party with him. All of the children were crying in fear and confusion. The smallest boy kept stumbling and falling, and instead of helping him to his feet, the other kids had a tendency to keep walking and dragging him along—without notifying Douglas that one of their group was down.

As they were working their way around a jutting boulder in a narrow area of the path, two of the kids went toppling over the side. Without the rope binding the group together, they would have dropped thousands of feet to their certain death.

Douglas began to worry about the next narrow passageway. If three or four of the kids should fall off the path at the same time, he didn't know if he had the weight or the strength to keep the rest secure. They might all go plummeting over the edge. Douglas began praying as hard as he could for a nice warm cave or some other miracle.

Then he heard a voice shout, "Hey, guys. Steady now!"

Douglas was astonished to see very dimly in the whipping snow an anchorman at the other end of the rope—a husky, broad-shouldered kid who was bracing his feet solidly against a jut of rock. The rope grew taut as the stumbling children's weight tugged at it, but the anchorman's added strength helped to hold the group firmly on the narrow ledge. Douglas's own grip grew stronger, and he demanded that the kids stop screaming in panic and watch their step on the treacherous trail.

In the violently swirling snow there was no way that he could make out the face of the anchorman at the other end of the rope, Douglas said. "My only thought at the time was just getting the kids safely down the mountain. I figured that either Dean or Phil had recognized the foolishness of my bravado in taking all the weaker kids with me and had selected one of the stronger hikers from his group and sent him to add an eighth member to my cluster of stumbling, crying little kids. I just didn't recall any of our young greenhorns being that big and bulky."

Douglas told us that the grim truth was that his group of six children would probably never have made it down the mountain trail that night in the terrible storm if it had not been for the unknown anchorman.

He emphasized that he would always have to add the designation "unknown," because by the time they reached a plateau of safety where the adult sponsors of the camp were waiting for them in vans and station wagons, the eighth loop that had been tied around the waist of Douglas's mysterious anchorman was dragging empty. The welcome anchor of strength had become a roped ring of nothingness.

Douglas, the other two teen counselors, and the three adult sponsors counted noses. All eighteen greenhorn campers were present and accounted for, and there were no extra kids.

Both Phil and Dean, along with the kids within each of their groups, had noticed the eighth member of Douglas's team, and they all commented on his surefootedness and his apparent strength and bulk. Since all members of the other two groups were visibly present within their own rope loops, everyone wondered where the extra kid had come from. Another strange aspect of the mysterious anchorman was that no one could remember seeing him leave.

For more than thirty years, Douglas has expressed his sincere belief that the unknown anchorman who enabled him to get all the kids to safety was an angel. "Just before the angelic anchorman materialized," he said, "I was about to start crying louder than any of the frightened little greenhorns. I was just a fifteen-year-old kid who was doing his best to act responsibly. I know that that angel with muscles was the answer to my prayers that stormy and treacherous night on the mountain."

Getting in Touch with Your Guardian Angel the Gentle Way

We first met Tom T. Moore in the 1980s when, with his wife, he owned and operated an international wholesale tour company and, as an avocation, sponsored seminars and lectures in the paranormal. We recognized at that time that Tom, a graduate of Texas Christian University in Forth Worth, was a serious student of metaphysics.

A few years later Tom became active in the entertainment business and optioned film rights to Brad's metaphysical novel, *The Hypnotist*; he even entered a float dedicated to the project in the Cannes Film Festival. It was about that time that Tom developed a knowledge of communicating with his Guardian Angel and a method of requesting "Benevolent Outcomes" that could be used in both business affairs and in his personal life. He became president and CEO of his own international motion picture and television program distribution business in Dallas, and he has been co-executive producer of several films and television productions. Tom travels extensively to international film markets in Cannes, Milan, Budapest, and Los Angeles, and he also speaks at conferences and special events on how to request Benevolent Outcomes the "Gentle Way."

The following information comes from Tom T. Moore's book *The Gentle Way* and is used with his permission:

> Learning how to be in touch with your Guardian Angel is truly a simple process. Making it a part of your daily routine is the hardest part, as we are all creatures of habit. Adding something new to our daily lives, even though highly beneficial, takes some work.

> About ten years ago, I kept noticing that several of the spiritual books I was reading kept using the word "benevolent" to describe suggestions from the Angelic realm. Robert Shapiro, in his inspirational book *The Council of Creators* from the Explorer Race Series, wrote, "... seek out more benevolent experiences for yourself. Seek out more benevolent companions and experiences of benevolence for you and your companion or your family or your people."

> These suggestions seemed a little vague, but I was intrigued. Benevolent is not a commonly used word in everyday language, so it was quite noticeable to me. *The Webster's Dictionary* defines "benevolent" as "a kindly disposition to promote happiness and prosperity through good works, or by generosity in and pleasure of doing good works." I wasn't exactly sure how that related to what I was reading, but my curiosity was aroused.

> Then I read a suggestion in Robert Shapiro's book to request a Benevolent Outcome for a specific need. That sounded interesting, so I decided to try it. I realized that in order to see if my "experiment" worked, I would have to have some immediate feedback. Therefore, I began by requesting, out loud, a Benevolent Outcome for finding a parking place next to where I went

daily to pick up my mail. There is limited parking, not helped by having a busy veterinarian next door and a fast food restaurant next to the veterinarian.

It worked fantastically well! Someone would pull out of a parking space just seconds before I arrived. I also tried it out when we went to the theatre and when we would go out for dinner. It worked again and again, with the only exceptions being my reluctance to pass by a parking space a little farther away. Then, as we walked up to the door of the restaurant, I would see the vacant parking space waiting for me, had I chosen to continue to drive closer to the entrance.

I gradually expanded these requests to every phase of my life—business and personal—with the same success. Let's begin with some basics.

How Do Benevolent Outcomes Work?

A Request for a Benevolent Outcome is a request to your Guardian Angel for assistance.

A Request for a Benevolent Outcome has to be for exact intentions. You are asking for something specific.

It can only be used benevolently, even if it is accidentally (or otherwise) said in some way that isn't benevolent.

It will only work if the experience is benevolent for everyone, including those who cooperate consciously or on a subconscious level in bringing about your request.

A Benevolent Outcome must be a request for something you wish to happen, not something you don't wish to occur.

And the request has to be for *you*, although others with you may be benevolently affected too.

Again, a request for a Benevolent Outcome is not just words you say, it is a *request for assistance* from your Guardian Angel. There are times when you can even feel energy after your request. I think that it is a feedback of love from my Guardian Angel. Putting *emotion* and *feeling* into the request also helps. You are asking for a specific connection with a person or persons that encourages people to do something that they might otherwise do anyway; but your request asks them to do something at a specific time and that is not against their will or best interests.

There is no limit to the number of requests you can ask during your lifetime. You will not go "over quota." If you can, imagine enormous stacks of forms all around you, each one of them saying, "I request a Most Benevolent Outcome _____ ."

The rest is blank and ready for you to fill in your request. After you have written your request, you add, "Thank you!" I estimate that I have requested at least 10,000 to 15,000 Benevolent Outcomes over more than 10 years, and I still have that huge mound of forms that will never diminish in size.

8

Encountering Angels Unaware

Readers familiar with the Bible know that angels sometimes appear so human-like that they are mistaken for ordinary men and women. Hence the Apostle Paul's admonition in Hebrews 13:2 that we do not neglect to show hospitality to strangers, "for thereby some have entertained angels unawares."

His Father Was in Good Hands

When his grandfather passed away in 1997, Kevin was very sad that his father and his granddad had not seen eye to eye for several years. "They were just beginning to act once again like father and son when grandfather suffered a severe stroke," Kevin said. "We all knew that Grandfather wouldn't be coming home from the hospital, and Dad was taking it very hard. My grandmother, Dad's mother, had passed away nearly 27 years before, and now Dad was losing his other parent."

After Kevin's grandfather passed away, family members left the hospital in separate cars. They had reserved a section in the rear of a restaurant for the family to gather and remember their grandfather.

While on the way there, Kevin's father, who was driving alone in his car, ran out of gas on the freeway.

"A man pulled over and gave my dad a ride to a gas station," Kevin said. "During the whole time my dad was in the car with the Good Samaritan, he did not mention that his father had just passed away. When they returned to Dad's car, he thanked the man for the ride, got out, and started walking toward his car with the gas can.

"As he began walking, he heard the man who had just given him a ride say the following to him: 'Your father is with your mother and Suzanne (my cousin who passed away a couple years before) now. Your parents are very proud of you.'

"Shocked by what he had just heard, Dad turned around to say something to the man—but he was gone.

"Dad got into his car to drive to the impromptu memorial knowing that his father was happy where he was and was in good hands with his mother and cousin," Kevin said, concluding his account of his father having met an angel unaware. "My grandfather was a very special man whose memory will live on through my son, who was named after him."

An Angelic Nurse Told Him That He Couldn't Leave Just Yet

Rich and his fiancée were to be married on February 21, 1970. In preparation for their honeymoon, his Volkswagen camper was in the shop for a tune-up, which meant that he would have to ride his father's motorcycle to work.

"Motorcycles were always a part of my young life," Rich said, "so I was grateful when Dad offered the use of his that day. It was a brand new, top-of-the-line Honda, less than two months old. Whereas San Diego is a temperate climate year-round, winter mornings can be quite chilly. I dressed in layers that morning. In 1970, there were no helmet laws in California, but Ramona was a long ride. At the last minute, I grabbed my helmet thinking that, at the very least, it would keep my ears warm."

Work passed uneventfully. Rich's boss was aware that he was to be married the next day, and he teased him relentlessly the entire day. But, Rich said, his boss was a good sport when around 2:30 p.m., he said, "Rich, why are you still here? Don't you have something to get done?"

When Rich walked out of work he found that the afternoon had turned into one of those beautiful, warm, sunny days that native Californians like to gloat about to their snowbound friends and family in the East. He decided to forego the jacket and helmet for the ride home, and he secured them to the saddle.

He had gone only a few miles when he became aware that the jacket and helmet were going to need attention. He found a spot to pull off the highway and resecure the load.

"When I stepped off the bike," Rich recalled, "I had a chill run through me. Since the sun was so low in the sky, I knew that the canyons of Highway 67 would be cooling quickly. I opted to put on the jacket and helmet. Later, I would give much thought to that action. I was back on the road in a flash.

"In 1970, State Highway 67 was a nasty little winding, two-lane road between Lakeside and Ramona and had had more than its fair share of fatal accidents. I wasn't thinking of that. I was 20 years old and invulnerable and in love.

"As you pass the turnoff for Poway, heading southbound, the road makes a gentle rise, and then drops into a winding canyon grade. I noticed a car parked off the pavement a half mile to three-quarters of a mile ahead of me."

Rich did not see an occupant, so he assumed the vehicle was abandoned. It wasn't! Someone suddenly popped up from the seat, roared onto the highway, and proceeded to make a U-turn right in front of Rich.

"Anyone who has been in an accident will tell you that there is this feeling that envelopes you," Rich said. "Time, for all intents and purposes, is suspended. Everything is in slow motion. I knew instinctively at that moment that I was going to die."

When Rich regained consciousness—or thought he had come to—he was in the middle of a very dark place with no one around him.

"It was a swamp," Rich said, describing the strange environment. "It was very gothic, very spooky. Yet I wasn't feeling particularly frightened, because there was this sound, a sound that I liken to the sound of a large bell. It was a continuous sound, like what you hear after a bell has been struck, constant and unwavering, but far away.

"I was finally able to determine where the sound was coming from, and I started walking in that direction. I hadn't gotten very far before I realized that I was going to have to cross the swamp. It was very foul smelling but didn't appear too deep. I took one step, then another.

"The third step was into what I can only describe as quicksand, except much worse. I began to sink deeper and deeper. I was in past my mouth and nose when I cried out, 'God, please help me!'"

At that moment, Rich found himself in a hospital bed in the intensive care unit of El Cajon Hospital. There was a nurse at his bedside, gently stroking his arm, saying, "It's okay, Richard, you're loved. You can't leave just yet."

"I never will forget her," Rich said. "Her touch and her voice were so soft and soothing. I couldn't see her face because the light was behind her, but she just seemed to glow as she took my pulse."

Rich didn't reawaken for some time. When he did, he learned that his right leg had been shattered. The accident had severed all the arteries in his leg, and as he came to find out later, there was a fear of exsanguination (severe loss of blood). His collarbone was fractured, and he had suffered a severe concussion, which caused the doctors to place him into an induced coma for just under a week.

When Rich was able to talk about what had happened, he asked his doctor if he could send a note to the nurse on duty the night of his recovery—the nurse with the soothing touch and voice. The doctor smiled and asked Rich if he knew her name by any chance.

"I told him no," Rich recalled. "I was a little too doped up to know much of anything at that time. The doctor told me no problem and asked if I remembered what she looked like. I proceeded to describe her, with all of the details I could recall. She was slim, mid-twenties, blond hair, medium height.

"Just tell her thank you," Rich requested, "for the soothing touch and for what she said to me that night."

A day or two passed before Rich spoke to the doctor again. "I asked him if he had found out the identity of the nurse the night of my recovery," Rich said. "He got a very strange look on his face, then smiled and told me that on that particular night, there was no nurse fitting the description I had given him. Furthermore, had I regained consciousness in post-op ICU, there would have been a note on my chart. No note, no nurse."

Rich understands that a cynic could say that what he experienced was nothing more than drug-induced hallucinations. "But I will never believe that," Rich said. "I hope that by the grace of God, I will some-day be able to bow before my Lord and his angel to say, 'Thank you.'"

Their Angel Came Calling Unexpectedly on Christmas Eve

One Christmas Ruth and her husband Keith decided to stay at home instead of making the usual out-of-town trip to visit with family. It had seemed a good idea at the time. No long distance drives after dark. No worrying about running into ice storms or blizzards. No sleeping on couches in family recreation homes. No indigestion from meals prepared by an aunt who had been a heavy smoker and had nearly scorched her taste buds beyond regeneration and put too much pepper and spice in every dish because she herself couldn't tell hot sauce from strawberry jam.

However, at nightfall on Christmas Eve, they were alone and feeling quite lonely. They had just finished dinner and were trying to find some Christmas music on the radio or a classic holiday movie on television when the doorbell rang.

"When I answered it," Ruth said, "there was this beautiful lady standing in the lightly falling snow. She was asking directions to a Catholic institution where they were expecting her for the night."

Keith came into the hall, and the two of them invited the stranger in out of the cold. Ruth helped her remove her coat and boots and won-dered if she wouldn't like some hot chocolate.

Meanwhile, Keith made a phone call and got the information the lady needed to get her to her final destination.

"While we talked and shared some hot chocolate," Ruth said, "we felt we didn't want her to leave. She was so compassionate and loving.

We felt so blessed that she had stopped at our house. She told us she was a nun and had traveled many miles in bad weather to visit a friend. It seemed like a miracle that she had taken Sylvester Road instead of Sylvester Street and ended up at our place."

The nun expressed her feelings by thanking them for the kindness and the warm welcome that had been extended to her. "Her sincere, humble, and compassionate expressions convinced us that she was an angel sent from Heaven to cheer us up and bring special joy to our home," Ruth said. "She was a Christmas gift money couldn't buy!"

Ruth and Keith spoke often the next few days about the strange "accidental" misreading of street signs that had brought such a lovely and loving sweet lady to their home on a snowy Christmas Eve when they had felt so alone. In their opinion, they were definitely "touched by an angel."

She Met Two Angels Unaware: One in a Washroom, Another in a Parking Lot

M. Bryant, a licensed clinical social worker, told us that in the mid-1990s she was struggling to complete the requirements for state licensure for her clinical social work certification. Part of this training involved traveling to Seattle for consultation with a qualified clinical social worker who had a private psychotherapy practice.

"This happened once a week," she explained, "and involved getting up at about 4:30 a.m. to get ready to catch a ride with a friend who was in training/consultation with me. Then we'd drive the fifty-six miles to the ferry, leave the car, and walk aboard as foot passengers. Once in Seattle we would walk the many blocks to our supervisor's office. When the meeting was over we'd rush back to the ferry, cross Puget Sound, drive back to the peninsula, and usually immediately go back to work. It was exhausting but necessary, and we were usually fairly tired most of the time."

The day she had her angelic encounter was warm and sunny, almost hot. She and her friend had left their consultation session, dashed to the ferry, and barely made it on board before the ferry pulled away from the dock.

"I got a cup of coffee," she recalled, "took a few unhurried breaths, and tried to relax. I was tired, slightly sweaty, and frazzled, weary from having to rush around all the time and work so hard. Everything seemed hard right then.

"I decided to use the bathroom before the ferry docked and we had to begin our 90-minute drive home. While I was washing up in the bathroom there was a minor commotion behind me. A young girl, about eight or nine years old, was trying to help her younger sister wash up. In the process, she had gotten water on the younger girl's dress.

"The little one screeched, and the mother began scolding the older girl loudly and severely for getting the little one damp. My heart went out to the older girl. She'd been doing her best to help a fairly unruly little sister and was being publicly humiliated for her efforts.

"When I dried my hands and turned around, I made a point of catching her eye and I gave her a big 'I think you are a cool kid' smile.

"Suddenly," Bryant recalled, "her face was transformed. Her eyes suddenly blazed with the truest sky blue, her face began to glow, and she gave me a smile that almost knocked me over! It literally took my breath away.

"As I turned around and walked away I felt 15 years younger and 20 pounds lighter. I walked back to the rear of the ferry in a sort of daze and told my friend, 'I think I just saw an angel.'"

"She, of course, wanted to go find the little girl and see her. Somehow, I knew that wouldn't be the right thing to do, and I refused. I wasn't even positive that family was still on the ferry!"

M. Bryant admitted that she really didn't know what actually happened. "An angel suddenly peered out at me from behind that sweet and pretty little girl's face," she said. "It was a smile full of fierce love. It was *fierce*. That was the thing that stunned me. It wasn't a sweet smile; it was dazzling, brilliant, literally breathtaking, and it pierced me to the heart.

"The rest of my day and indeed many days after that were considerably lightened by that unexpected encounter," she said. "Since that day I have wondered what she saw when she looked at me. I hope that my angel was smiling fiercely back at her!"

M. Bryant told us another remarkable story of an encounter with a mysterious being who helped her to find a valuable earring that she didn't even know was missing:

A couple of years ago I decided to give my little granddaughter a treasure chest for a Christmas gift. I found an old-fashioned jewelry case and began haunting the Internet for vintage jewelry sales. On eBay I bid on several lots of estate-sale jewelry and had a wonderful time when it began to arrive. I would sort it out and wash and repair everything that was a suitable treasure for a four-year-old.

It was an interesting process. I found myself thinking a lot about the women who had owned this costume jewelry, wondering which things they had liked best and worn most, wondering about their lives in general. I kept thinking, "I wonder what the story is behind this piece?" There were dozens of "pearl" necklaces, pretty pendants, old pins with rhinestones and paste jewels in them, bracelets, and even rings.

The earrings were a problem. I didn't want to give her any pierced earrings for fear that she would start pestering her mother to let her get her ears pierced! So I sorted out all the pierced earrings. While I was doing this, I came across a very nice pair of badly tarnished, silver hoop earrings. They were several cuts above all of the other things I'd been handling, and I put them aside to look at later.

When I finally got back to them I discovered that they were sterling silver, hollow-bodied hoops, with an intricate and very secure catch. There was a nice, solid feel to them, and they looked special.

The treasure chest was a huge success for a Christmas gift. My granddaughter loved every piece of jewelry and has had enormous fun dressing up with appropriately matching "jewels." I loved the silver earrings and took to wearing them quite often.

Now we have to fast-forward to the following spring.

I came out of my office in the afternoon. I was the only therapist working that afternoon, and the only cars in the parking lot were mine and an older, small, domestic vehicle that was stopped directly behind my car. The other car's engine was running, and an older man was walking around the car looking for something on the ground.

I was tired and I wanted to go home, but I couldn't move my car because the other car was directly behind mine. I watched him for a moment. He was tall and had white hair. He was wearing a white, almost sheer shirt, the kind someone might wear on a hot day in a tropical climate or in the deep South. His search was exaggerated, almost a pantomime of a search.

He ignored my presence until I approached him. I asked, "What are you searching for? May I help you try to find it?"

He immediately straightened up and looked directly at me. "No," he said, "I'm not going to find it here," and pointed to the ground around his vehicle.

He abruptly straightened up, folded his long body back into the little car, did a U-turn in our parking lot, and drove away.

I was intrigued by now and thought, "Why would he be looking for something out here in the middle of the parking lot? That just doesn't make any sense."

But I walked around the area where his car had been parked, and scanned the ground.

Nothing.

Then, still scanning, I walked back to get into my car. Suddenly, I saw something reflecting the sun on the ground about six feet from the front door of my car.

I walked over and picked it up. *It was one of my earrings!*

It had evidently fallen out of my ear as I walked into the building in the morning, and had lain in the parking lot all day. It seemed untouched, even though it was a minor miracle that no one had driven over it.

Then I began to think about the entire strange encounter. If that man had just been searching for something in another part of the parking lot, I'd have given him a quick look, backed up, and driven away. But I couldn't drive away because he was parked directly behind me.

The clothes he was wearing were vintage southern, not the sort of clothing that people wear around here. And he'd sparked a small "treasure hunt" desire in me, which was why I was scanning the ground on my way back to my car. If that hadn't happened, I'm sure I'd never have found the missing earring.

I think that old gentleman was linked in some way to that earring, that he wanted it found and taken care of. I don't think he was an angel, but he was certainly, somehow, the spirit guardian of that earring.

Do Not Neglect Hospitality to Strangers

One "unimaginably hot and humid day," Darlene Phares was driving down a busy four-lane highway.

"I had just realized how thankful I was for the car's air conditioning when I saw a man walking along the side of the road," Darlene told us. "He was dirty and carried a filthy backpack over his shoulders. He must have weighed all of eighty pounds. My gut instinct immediately said, 'Pick him up,' but I drove another twelve miles arguing with myself about how dangerous picking up strangers can be."

Finally, Darlene said, her conscience got the best of her and she turned the car around and headed back toward where she had passed the man. "I told myself, 'If he is still walking, I will give him a ride to the other side of my hometown.'sure enough, I drove the twelve miles back down the road, and there he was, still walking."

Darlene pulled up behind him and lightly tapped on her horn.

"I startled him, without meaning to," she said. "He jumped off the side of the road. I put the car in park, opened my door, and got out. I asked him, 'Would you like a ride? I can take you about fifteen miles down the road.' At first he looked at me like I was half crazy! At that moment, I had to agree, I felt crazy for offering a complete stranger a ride. He seemed just as nervous as I was!"

The hitchhiker agreed to let Darlene drive him down the road. "As we drove," she recalled, "we talked. Our conversation centered around modern-day religion. I admitted that I was confused about what to really believe when it came to religion. He said to me, 'You must look into your own heart to know what is real; there are many forms of false religions and many false teachers. Beware of those things that will lead you astray.'"

He told Darlene that he had been walking for three days, sleeping at the side of the road and eating dried fruit. He would reach his destination in five more days if he walked fifteen miles a day. He commented that he was almost sixty years old.

Darlene offered him money for food, knowing he must be starving. He declined, saying what she was doing was more than enough.

"He thanked me for the ride seven times before I stopped and dropped him off where I told him I would," Darlene said. "He had tears in his eyes as he thanked me for the final time. He told me, 'You have no idea how much I appreciate you giving me a ride. That twenty-minute ride may not seem like much to you, but to me, it took one day off my travels. Please remember what I said. God bless you.'"

He got out of Darlene's car and started walking down the highway again.

"He turned back at me with a smile and he waved," Darlene said. "The incredible peace that surrounded this experience is something that I can never forget. I turned my car around and headed back into town.

"When I looked in my rearview mirror, the man had vanished."

A Hungry Beggar Granted a Miracle for an Unselfish Mother

Priscilla Garduno Wolf, an artist and *curandera* (healer) from New Mexico, shared with us the miraculous encounter experienced by her friend, Steve. As Steve related the account:

It was a very hot, dry summer. My father had deserted us. My mother Kathy tried her best to raise us kids. I was the oldest at age seven; Adam was five, and my baby brother Donald was only a few months old. Donald was born very ill. We kept him in a cardboard box by the wood stove and the door. I helped by babysitting my two brothers while Mom went to work cleaning homes. We were so poor that we never had enough to eat, and we never had any extra food to share with anybody.

One hot afternoon, we had our door open to keep the house cool while mother fixed something to eat on our old wood stove. Suddenly there stood a strange-looking man at our door. He looked so poor and dirty; we knew that he must be homeless. He asked my mother for a cold drink of water and food to eat.

Mom was so kind she could not deny anyone food. I knew we had nothing to spare, but Mom asked him in to share our meal. The man sat at the table and enjoyed the food, then he thanked my mom for being so kind.

He started out the door, then he looked down at my baby brother, Donald, and he asked what was wrong with the baby. Mom replied that Donald was born sick and that he was dying because she had no money for doctor care. The man bent down on his knees and blessed my brother and told my mother that Donald would be all right.

We all watched the strange man walk out the door and begin to walk down the dirt road—then he vanished before our eyes.

My baby brother got well within a few days and has never been sick again.

We knew that it was Jesus who came to our door appearing as a beggar and who ate with us and healed our baby brother.

Many readers will be familiar with those well-known verses from Matthew 25:31–40 when Jesus is speaking of the Final Judgment and how the Lord will bless those who have pleased him and welcome them to the kingdom created for them. Addressing those "sheep" he has separated from the "goats," the Lord will say, "When I was hungry, you gave me something to eat, and when I was thirsty, you gave me something to drink. When I was a stranger, you welcomed me, and when I was naked, you gave me clothes to wear. When I was sick, you took care of me, and when I was in jail, you visited me" (Contemporary English Version).

Those who have pleased the Lord are puzzled. When, they ask, did they do all those things for him?

And then the Lord utters the response that has inspired individuals of good will for centuries: "Whenever you did it for any of my people, no matter how unimportant they seemed, you did it for me."

Was it Jesus who visited the home of a young mother who, even though she had been deserted by her husband, valiantly worked to support her three sons and keep just enough food on their table for them to survive?

Or was it an angel who appeared as the ragged beggar, asking for food and receiving a guest's share of the family's meager dinner?

While no one can answer those questions with certainty, one marvelous thing the family does know for certain: Little Donald, just a few months old, born ill and barely hanging on to life, was healed by the mysterious beggar and never again suffered illness. Kathy responded to the plea of a hungry stranger, "no matter how unimportant" he seemed, and received a miracle in return for a meal.

9

Meeting Spirit Guardians during Near-Death Journeys

We've all heard of people who die or nearly die and come back with a sense of divine intervention. Fifty-seven years ago, Fred W. had a near-death experience. He remembers going through a tunnel and meeting someone surrounded by a bright light.

"It was the most momentous experience," he told us. "I've never forgotten it. I was never afraid of death after that. I do remember a figure who talked to me and who sent me back. And I clearly recall the wonderful sense of calm, peace, and acceptance that I felt in the presence of that being."

Returned to Earth

R.J.B. was in surgery for approximately five hours when his heart ceased to beat after having been resuscitated for the third time. "This time, though, it didn't start back up after a moment or two," he stated in his report to us:

> This was when my soul was separated from my physical body. An entity with a beard said that he was to be my guide. No words were needed to feel a warm, calm presence of peace eternal. I had left the physical plane of existence, but I was still aware of myself as an individual.
>
> The entity and I moved through what might resemble a time/space cylinder. It opened into what could be described as an electrically charged, highly lighted area with no containment. The light seemed to come from everywhere, and yet there was a focus ahead of me. I was ushered throughout this aspect of the experience by a voice that could only be described as "Absolute." Never having been one to disobey when a sense of superiority is present, I proceeded.... My questions were all answered although I was not aware of such at that time. Information was given to me that I would not be able to understand until time had passed. It was decided that I needed to return and complete the divine mission that had been given to me....
>
> Within a thought, I found myself back in the hospital room surrounded in a beam of irradiating light and goodness. My soul lay down within my physical body, and for the next seventy-two hours, I was in a coma.

Encountering Angels and Deceased Family Members during a Near-Death Experience

As Norma writhed in pain on the gurney headed toward the operating room, she seemed to be suddenly spinning around and around, and she heard a strange kind of crackling noise, as if stiff paper were being crunched up into a ball.

"Then I ... or my consciousness ... or my soul was bobbing around like a balloon on a string," she recalled. "That's the best comparison I can make. I was like a shining balloon attached to my physical body by a thin, silver string. I could clearly see my body below me, and the two interns were chattering about their plans for the evening. I thought how wonderful it was to be young and to be able to plan for the future. I assumed that I was either dead or in the process of dying. Which I guess I was."

From her new perspective, Norma could see her doctor walking hurriedly down the hall. Dr. Mandel took a last puff of a cigarette, then put it out in an ashtray filled with sand.

Within seconds, he stood beside Norma's body. He looked at her carefully, then became very angry. He swore at the two interns as if they were schoolboys. He shouted down the hallway and two nurses came running. Norma was quickly wheeled into the operating room.

"It seemed obvious that something had gone terribly wrong," Norma said, vividly recalling her near-death experience. "It was equally obvious that my soul had left my body or I wouldn't be up above everything looking down. My face was contorted in pain, and I was ashen, as if all the blood had left my body. I thought of leaving my husband Jack and my kids, and I began to cry."

As if from very far away, Norma heard Dr. Mandel shouting at the staff, but she didn't really want to observe what was going on in the operating room, so she thought of her bedroom at home, a place where she had always felt comfortable and secure—and suddenly she was there.

Then she heard bells tolling, as they do after funerals, and she thought that she must surely be dead.

"But suddenly a deep voice told me, 'Not yet!' And I felt myself being pulled upward and upward, like an arrow being shot into the sky," Norma said.

Next Norma was aware that she was no longer a kind of shining balloon but seemed once again to be a replica of her familiar physical self. Standing before her were a number of figures in bright, glowing robes. To Norma they seemed to glow with an inner radiance, and they seemed to her to look exactly like angels should look. One of them stepped forward and told her that she could stay with them, but she would have to go back.

"That's when I understood what the 'not yet'statement was all about," Norma explained. "I had assumed that I had died, but now I had received a second declaration that I was not going to stay wherever I was for very long."

At the same moment that she was admiring the vivid beauty of this bit of heavenly space with the angels, it occurred to Norma that she should be able to see her parents.

"In a twinkling, Mom and Dad were standing there beside me," Norma said, "and the three of us were weeping tears of joy at our reunion. I was surprised to see that neither of them looked as old as they had when they died. Dad had passed when he was seventy-six, and Mom had gone when she was nearly eighty; but both of them now appeared as I remembered them from my childhood."

Norma said that she talked with her parents on a bench in what appeared to be a lakeside park. She remembered seeing ducks swimming about, and a number of deer drinking at the lake's edge. After a time, Norma and her parents were joined by her maternal grandparents, Alf and Marta Jorgensen, and by her paternal grandparents, Sal and Benedette Marino.

"I had never met Dad's parents, since they were killed in a train accident before I was born," Norma said. "It was all so incredible. Like the best kind of family reunion."

As they spoke, Norma saw a small crowd of men and women gathering and encircling them. When she asked her mother who the other people were, she was told that those were relatives from many other previous generations of her father's and mother's families, but she would not have time to meet them before she had to leave.

"I remember feeling waves of love coming from my ancestors crowding around us," Norma said, "and it was as if I was somehow made up of bits and pieces of the soul energy of all of them. I had always kind of made fun of some cultures with their beliefs about their ancestors' ghosts hanging around, but maybe we really are the sum total of all those who have gone before us."

Norma and her parents walked along a lakeside path for what seemed like hours, then one of the angels in a white robe came for her and informed her that it was time for her to return.

"No sooner had he told me this than I was bobbing around in that shining balloon near the ceiling of a hospital room," Norma recalled. "I was shocked to hear a Catholic priest giving the last rites to my poor old body on the bed below. Jack was crying, and I had an impression of my younger sister Nancy outside in the hall with my children. A nurse had been standing at the left side of the bed with her fingers on my pulse, but all of a sudden, she walked out of the room."

Norma heard the same deep voice telling her that it was not yet her time—and then she heard that same crackling noise, like paper being wadded into a ball. "I had a weird feeling. I had been lighter than a feather and now I felt heavier than an elephant. I had a sensation of red, the color red, all around me. And then I began to realize that I was somehow back inside my physical body."

Norma remembered moaning with the pain of her illness and the just-completed surgery. When she opened her eyes, her husband and the priest were smiling. Norma's first words were to whisper that she had been to Heaven.

The priest chuckled and said that she had them all very worried that she might very well be knocking at Saint Peter's gate. Dr. Mandel said that he had given her only a matter of a few minutes to pass the crisis point or to die. A priest from the hospital chapel had been called to administer the last rites, because her chances to live had seemed almost nonexistent.

Norma firmly believes that her experience was genuine. "When I was alone with my sister," she said, "I told her that I saw Mom and Dad in Heaven—and I know that Nancy believed me."

There Is Always a Spirit Entity Who Helps in the Transition from Death to Life

The psychiatrist Dr. Elisabeth Kübler-Ross (1926–2004), who gained world fame for her work with death and the dying, said that the turning point in her work occurred in a Chicago hospital in 1969 when a deceased patient appeared before her in fully materialized form. Kübler-Ross had been feeling discouraged about her research with the dying because of the opposition that she had encountered among her colleagues. But the apparition of her former patient appeared before her to tell her not to abandon her work, and that life after death was a reality.

"Death is simply a shedding of the physical body, like the butterfly coming out of a cocoon," Dr. Kübler-Ross said. "It is a transition into a higher state of consciousness, where you continue to perceive, to understand, to laugh, to be able to grow—and the only thing you lose is something you don't need anymore, and that is your physical body."

What is more, as Dr. Kübler-Ross and other researchers have stressed, there is always some spirit entity there to help in the transition from life to death.

When Tom Purcell was twelve years old, he suffered a severe attack of bronchial asthma. Before his parents could summon their family doctor, the boy felt himself slipping into unconsciousness.

"All at once I felt peaceful and completely relaxed," Tom wrote in personal correspondence to us. "I remember clearly feeling that the real part of me, I guess you would say my soul, just seemed to float above that poor wheezing body on the bed. You know, I was concerned that the physical me couldn't breathe, but on the other hand, I had never experienced such a wonderful sense of freedom."

Although more than fifty years have passed since Tom's near-death experience, he remembers it as vividly as if it had occurred just last week: "I felt myself drifting, floating upward. I seemed to pass through the ceiling of my room, and I was soon looking down on our neighborhood.

"Then everything became rather surreal, and I felt as though I were drifting into another dimension of time and space. Ahead, I could see what looked like a tunnel through which I knew that I must pass. As I drew nearer to the opening, there seemed to be a force that began to tug and pull at me. That was the first time I felt anything at all like fear. I became concerned that it might not be a good thing to be pulled into the tunnel."

During those first moments of anxiety, Tom recalled that he was suddenly surrounded by a bright light. "It just seemed to appear, then wrap itself around me. I had the distinct feeling that it was some form of intelligence that had materialized to calm me or to protect me."

To Tom's recollection, the tunnel was a place of swirling darkness, and he was relieved when both he and the light emerged into a place of bright sunlight and green, rolling hills. "In the distance I could see a city that seemed to be made of crystal. The sunlight reflected off roofs and towers, and it seemed all in all like a magnificent place. I knew with all my heart that I wanted to enter the city. Even from that distance I could feel love, perfect love, emanating from its walls."

Tom began to take a few steps on a pathway that he knew would lead to the crystal city. "That's when the beautiful light that had enveloped me suddenly swirled into the form of a very commanding angel."

The heavenly being, attired in a brilliant white robe, appeared somewhat stern in its facial expression, yet Tom could feel its very presence projecting feelings of unconditional love. Although it did not have the familiar wings that angels bore in his Sunday school books, the angel still looked exactly the way he somehow knew that angels should.

"You're not ready to go there," the angel said in a voice that seemed to vibrate within Tom's soul-body.

"But I feel that I belong there," Tom protested. "I feel as though it is my true home."

The angel only smiled, then indicated that Tom should look into a crystal that it held in an outstretched hand.

"Within the crystal the angel held before me, I could see Dr. Mueller come puffing into my room back in the Earth dimension," Tom said. "The real me in my soul-body in Heaven thought, 'Oh, no, now he will make me breathe again, and I'll have to go back to that clumsy, awkward, imperfect, chubby body.'"

Tom watched as Dr. Mueller injected something into his arm. "The moment that he gave me a shot, I began to feel myself being pulled away from the angel and from the sight of the beautiful crystal city. The angel only smiled and nodded."

Tom remembered that at first he tried his best to resist being pulled back into that lump of clay that was so susceptible to disease and physical ailments. "Then the angel brought the crystal up to my eyes once again, and I saw Mom and Dad—and they were both crying. I didn't want to hurt them, so I stopped struggling and let myself be pulled back into my physical body."

He opened his eyes, took a deep breath, and was at once conscious of terrible pain in his chest and back.

"That was over fifty years ago," Tom reminded us, "and I have valued every day of my life here on this physical plane. I have a wonderful wife, three grown kids who are doing very well for themselves, and five grandkids who are my little Earth angels. But I knew from that day on that to die is to enter a free, spiritual state, and I have never feared death. It is only a doorway that will return us to our true home in Heaven."

The Near-Death Experience Is a Revelatory Experience

In his book *Life at Death: A Scientific Investigation of the Near-Death Experience*, Dr. Kenneth Ring, professor of psychology at the University of Connecticut, states that he considers the near-death experience (NDE) to be a teaching, revelatory experience: "They vouchsafe both to those who undergo them and to those who hear about them an intuitive sense of the transcendent aspect of creation. These experiences clearly imply that there is something more, something beyond the physical world of the senses, which, in the light of these experiences, now appears to be only the mundane segment of a greater spectrum of reality."

Dr. Ring's research has led him to isolate five elements that constitute what he has labeled the "core" of the near-death experience:

1. Peace and a sense of well-being
2. Separation from the body
3. Entering the darkness
4. Seeing the light
5. Entering the world of light

Dr. Ring concludes his book by admitting that he, personally, believes that humankind has a "conscious existence after our physical death and that the core experience does represent its beginning, a glimpse of things to come."

A Series of Near-Death Experiences Led Sherry Steiger to Visit the New Jerusalem

Sherry Steiger has often stated that there is absolutely no question in her mind that her childhood and adult near-death experiences and her contact with angel guardians had a profound effect on the choice of her life path as a minister, social reformer, teacher, and spiritual seeker.

Sherry supposes that it is very likely that she first left the physical plane on a visit to other dimensions when she was just a few months old and nearly died of pneumonia.

Her second excursion to the Other Side occurred when she had a severe bout of rheumatic fever at the age of six. She slipped in and out of her body many times during her long siege with the illness, and Sherry can still vividly recall the shapes, lights, and geometric patterns that she observed in another dimension of reality.

When she was eight years old and attending a summer camp in Upper Michigan, she was privileged to see a dramatic manifestation of the angel that she had felt around her ever since her struggle with rheumatic fever. Several other girls also witnessed the appearance of the heavenly figure.

The angel, who appeared to the children's eyes as a female entity, came down through the ceiling of the cabin in which Sherry was staying, and most of the startled girls went down on their knees and folded their hands in prayer. The angel emanated a brilliant bluish-white light and appeared to be the most loving, beautiful, and gentle woman imaginable.

Sherry and a few of the other girls heard the angelic being tell them how very special they each were and how very much God loved them. There were other messages, but memory has dimmed most of them. Sherry's eyes were brimming with tears, and she saw that many other of the girls were also weeping.

After the angel had vanished, Sherry sensed that on some level of her consciousness she had been given important insights into the sacredness, interconnectedness, and oneness of all of God's creation.

As CCV organizes and empowers Ohio Christians to speak out against this abortion initiative, we wanted to start by calling the Church to pray.

That's why we composed this prayer devotional. The six-week structure honors Ohio's Heartbeat Law, which prohibits abortion at the moment an unborn child's heartbeat can be detected—generally around the sixth week of pregnancy.

Our hope is that you, your family, your small group, and your church would join us in kicking off this campaign to protect the innocent by earnestly seeking the Lord in prayer.

A note on praying:
For years, I struggled to get into a consistent rhythm of daily prayer. But over time, the Holy Spirit revealed it was because I fundamentally misunderstood prayer as transactional—a spiritual ATM by which I made deposits and withdrawals—rather than a gift of communion with God.

Prayer is an invitational interaction with the Holy Spirit, allowing Him to transform and renew our hearts and minds through reflection, glorification, and engagement with Jesus Christ, and with His commandments, beauty, and sacrifice.

It's why I believe so deeply in praying Scripture, and why for each week in this book, we provided one short devotional per week, with Bible verses on the theme to guide our prayers each day. When you read the daily scripture, I encourage you to reflect not only on the promise or commandment in the passage, but primarily on what the passage teaches you about the heart of God, especially in the light that He choose to communicate this specific thought to you through the Bible.

Every morning when I pray, I find it helpful to structure my prayer time around the acronym ACTS. I start with Adoration, then Confession, then Thanksgiving, and Supplication (prayer requests). I encourage you to resist the temptation to jump straight into supplication, or even confession. Start with basking in the glory of God and adoring Him, and allowing this light to lead you into what you should be offering to the Lord in prayer.

My friends, let us not become discouraged by the perilous state of our culture. Instead, let's be encouraged that God has called you and me to Ohio *for such a time as this*. What's more let's trust the promise that although the mountain we have to climb to defeat this abortion amendment and save 30,000 lives every year is massive, *with God, all things are possible.*

Foreword

Alistair Begg, Senior Pastor, Parkside Church

Then Jesus told his disciples a parable to show them that they should always pray and not give up. — Luke 18:1 (NIV)

The widow in the parable who represents the poor, needy, and oppressed kept coming to the judge who neither respected God or man. Although he is reluctant to grant her justice, he eventually accedes to her request so that she won't come back. Persistence is her only asset, and she makes full use of it.

Jesus then makes his point. If an unjust judge finally grants the woman's request, how much more will God hear the prayers of his people. The comparison is between the reluctance of the unjust judge and the willing generosity of God our heavenly father. Instead of losing heart Jesus encourages us to pray persistently for justice. He closes the parable with a question: "When the Son of man returns, will he find faith on the earth?" The kind of faith that **asks** in the confidence that we will receive, **seeks** believing we will find, and **knocks** expecting the door will be opened.

Jesus then argues from the lesser to the greater. If your son asked for bread, you would not give him a stone. So, if you know how to give good gifts to your children, how much more will your Father who is in heaven, give good things to those who ask him.

When we pray, we place matters in God's hands, we express our dependence upon Him and we say: "Your kingdom come, your will be done on earth as it is in heaven." We can do more than pray, but only after we have prayed and not until! We have yet to see what God will do in response to the six weeks of prayer that are about to begin. It is imperative that we exhort and encourage each other so that we do not miss this opportunity.

In Shakespeare's Julius Caesar, Brutus says to Cassius:

When Sherry was accidentally given an overdose of ether during a tonsillectomy at the age of nine, she had the sensation of moving toward a wondrous light. When she recovered from that near-death experience, she had acquired a distinct knowledge that there were other dimensions of being that were to be taken seriously.

She felt like a stranger in a strange land after that experience. She would go off by herself to sit in the woods near her family's home in Minnesota and become completely enraptured by the patterns that she saw everywhere present in nature. She still had the bizarre dreams of the brightly colored geometric shapes zooming toward her, and she now began to notice fascinating geometric designs all around her. She also began to observe the incredible harmony that seemed inherent in the natural patterns and designs of nature.

During a shark attack that Sherry experienced when she was twenty-four, she saw those same sparks of light and colorful shapes zooming toward her. Sherry was pulled under the surface of the water three times by her monstrous adversary before *something* made the shark release her, and a sea park ranger managed to pull her to shore.

Sherry awakened in a first aid station, her legs covered with blood and scraped raw by the shark's rough skin. After the ranger pulled out the shark's tooth embedded in Sherry's left foot, he immediately issued a shark warning and cleared the beaches of all swimmers.

As medical personnel were tending to Sherry's injuries, the ranger theorized that the monster must have been toying with her before making Sherry its main dinner course. Later, it was suggested that a team of dolphins had arrived on the scene to distract the shark. In addition to the rescuing posse of dolphins, however, Sherry remembered the swirling lights that signaled the presence of her guardian angel.

When Sherry "froze" while serving a dinner party at age twenty-eight, she was rushed to a hospital where three cardiologists advised her that she must submit to immediate open-heart surgery or die within twenty-four hours.

Because she was more out of her body than in it, Sherry was able to see a much wider spectrum of reality and could somehow understand that the cardiologists' diagnosis, though well-intentioned, was not the true story. Sherry did accept their assessment that that she had a hole in her heart that had been precipitated by her childhood bout with rheumatic fever, but she knew that such dramatic surgery as they were prescribing was unnecessary. She thanked them for their concern and checked herself out of the hospital.

Later, when Sherry submitted to additional medical testing, she learned that her intuitive assessment had been correct. While the hole in her heart was present, it would have been unnecessary to have had her chest opened. Perhaps the sound had been somehow amplified by the doctors'stethoscopes, thereby causing the leak in her heart to seem larger than it really was.

Although it must seem as though Sherry was trying for a record in near-death experiences, a few years later she was stricken with a kidney infection that sent her temperature to 106 degrees, the near-fatal mark for an adult. Sherry lay in and out of a comatose state for ten days, her body packed in ice and hooked to all kinds of tubes.

Sherry now considers that those ten days in a coma may have been a time of deep teaching for her. Although she was in a terribly weakened physical condition when she left the hospital, she knew that her time on other planes of consciousness had shown her that all of the many disparate things that had occurred to her during her life on Earth did have meaning and purpose. She felt compelled to spend more time researching various spiritual paths and the scientific disciplines that might cast greater understanding on the techniques and applications of the ancient wisdoms.

Sherry began to practice meditation seriously, and it was during an astonishing five-hour meditative experience in 1985 that she was given the spiritual impetus to pull together all the scattered memories of her childhood near-death experiences to gain special meaning for the remaining years of her earthly walk.

Sherry remembers that her Real Self was met by a loving and caring angelic Light Being who escorted her through a beautiful, mystical adventure. Sherry was taken to a place that perhaps could best be described as a diamond or a crystal city where she beheld unearthly beauty, colors, and lights much different from those on Earth.

"Maybe I beheld the New Jerusalem," Sherry said. "Its beauty was beyond anything I've ever dreamed possible. It was like a crystal or diamond world, reflecting and refracting the purest, most brilliant colors. The light all around was effervescent, as if it were alive—as if it were alive and the very essence of *love*. This love was deeper and more complete than anything experienced here on Earth. I myself seemed to become a living crystal, and I became fused with the light. I became the Light."

This dramatic visionary experience became a life mission for Sherry, and she became more compelled than ever before to tell everyone that God's promise to humankind is, indeed, real. Life does continue after death.

"The most important thing in life that we can do is to be loving and to meet all experiences with love," she said.

Shortly after she received the powerful vision, Sherry was led to research what was eventually to become known as fractal geometry, a "new" mathematics. By 1988 she had assembled a powerful multimedia presentation utilizing slides and computer-derived images of fractals that evolved into remarkably effective healing seminars. In addition to testifying that the viewing of such images prompted tears to their eyes and healing energy in their physical bodies, numerous seminar participants said that the geometric shapes had also triggered memories of their own near-death experiences, which they had not been able to put into words until they had experienced Sherry's seminar. It was not until he viewed Sherry's presentation that Brad Steiger saw designs that closely approximated the geometric images that he had been shown during his own childhood near-death experience.

Somehow, Sherry's out-of-body viewing of the New Jerusalem—or whatever it truly was—filled her with a wonderful sense of oneness with All That Is that allowed her to visit the dimension of spirit from which her soul had come to Earth. Perhaps that is the true spiritual home for all of humanity, Sherry has said: "A place that we call 'Heaven,' a dimension of time and space where we truly shall be one with God ... one with love."

10

Angelic Love and Guidance Are Always Present

For many years, Lori Jean Flory has been sharing inspirational messages that she receives from the angels. She makes her home in a beautiful area of Colorado and spends as much time as possible in nature, meditating upon and communing with the angelic intelligences who first contacted her when she was three years old. The author of The Wisdom Teachings of Archangel Michael *(1997) and the loving, compassionate teacher of hundreds of men and women who come to her for guidance, Lori never fails to share an inspirational message to warm the heart and soul of those who may have felt frozen in their spiritual development due to the icy indifference of a harsh and often cruel world.*

Modest and self-effacing, Lori emphasizes that she is no more special to the angels than anyone else, but she admits that she began to feel a bit different from others when she was three years old. "I can't recall ever being around anyone else who had the same kind of experiences that I did—nor was there anyone to explain to me what was happening to me," she said. "I don't recall that I shared a lot of my experiences with others as I was growing through childhood and my teenage years. I have been told by Spirit that the reason for this was that I might have been talked out of my angelic contact by skeptics and by others who might try to convince me that I was dreaming or imagining things. I have always been very sensitive and intuitive in that way." Daephrenocles, Lori's principal angelic guide, has told her that little spirits used to hover around her when she was three, but she said that she doesn't remember seeing them.

"I do recall that when it would be time to go to bed at night, I would have experiences that were otherworldly," Lori said. "First there came the sound of a beautiful angelic bell, and then I would hear a frequency that would begin to rise in pitch. I would not be able to move my physical body, for that pitch would create an out-of-body experience and I would travel to another dimension. Sometimes this would happen more than once in a night. I never really understood these experiences as a child, and during the day, I was just a regular kid, running around and playing and doing things that kids do."

Daephrenocles has told Lori that she agreed to be of service to God before her present lifetime. "I came into this life to be a teacher of the Light," she said. "It was meant to be a part of my pathway for soul growth to radiate to others the truth that we are love and that we are here to experience love and to live love through our feelings, words, actions, and thoughts.

"I agreed to strive to fulfill a mission that would have me be on the Earth, but not of it," Lori continued. "I am to seek to integrate Heaven and Earth into one through the knowing that we are divine entities having a human experience, rather than being human entities seeking a spiritual experience. The truth is that everything we do is spiritual—even washing the supper dishes—if we do it with all attitude of love and gratitude."

As she has evolved spiritually, Lori has learned that the sacred exists in each person and that love is a mission in this life for us all. "Each day we can imbue the special and the divine into our lives," she said. "It doesn't have to be some big, grandiose thing. Sometimes the greatest and most profound moments and truths truly come in the simple, small experiences that are of and from the heart. It is the special moments of the heart that we take with us in life."

Lori told us that she had many out-of-body experiences that went on through her childhood, teenage, and young-adult years. Lori went on to tell us that she had seen the "tunnel" described by so many near-death experiencers, as well as the Light, but none of these experiences brought her near death.

"I have heard the rushing wind in the tunnel, and I have emerged on the Other Side," she said. "I have heard a loud, booming voice shout, *'Go Back!'* just before I crossed the threshold.

"Since childhood on, what usually sparked these experiences were the Masters focusing a beam of light on the 'third-eye' region of my forehead," Lori said. "I have always been able to hear, feel, and sense it; but since I have never had any control over the light, I just learned to flow with it. But in none of those instances was I ever near death. I was always fine and healthy.

"Once before I was returned to my body, I remember looking through a white arbor and seeing grass, gardens, and flowers every-where. There were lots and lots of roses. On the Other Side, roses emit musical harmonies."

It was just as Lori was about to walk through the arbor that she was swept back to her physical body in a matter of seconds.

On most occasions the laser-like bursts of light from the heavenly beings would strike her third-eye region when she was lying down, rest-ing. "Within my third eye I would see light and letters and words of light," she recalled. "I would also hear celestial sounds. This all seemed to be a gradual process that the angels employed to open things up within me—which is probably why they started attuning me when I was only three. I never really understood what was happening to me all those years, and I did not think this procedure was that much fun. When I was a little older, the Masters apologized to me, saying that they had not intended to upset me, but it was necessary for me to undergo such a series of attunements if we were to work to together when I was an adult."

Saved While Stuck on a Cliff

It was in the summer of 1978, between her junior and senior years of college at California Lutheran College in Thousand Oaks, California, that Lori formally learned that her special angel guide was named Daephrenocles. That was also the summer, while she was working at Yellowstone National Park, that an angelic presence saved her life and helped her to develop new facets of herself.

Lori and a friend had been hiking in the so-called Grand Canyon area of Yellowstone when she suddenly found herself in a precarious position on a cliff that was more than 200 feet straight down. She knew that if she made one wrong move, she would fall to her death.

She knew that her angels were there with ready hands to help steady her, but there really was not much for her to hold onto in the way of rocks or bushes. All she could do was to lean forward and use her hands and feet like a spider's clutching onto a wall.

In retrospect, Lori said that it seems as though that afternoon God and the angels were giving her a choice: "Are you going to do any more reckless, crazy things that you know you should not be doing—or are you going to concentrate more upon spiritual growth?"

"It really did seem as though I was standing at a crossroads in my life," Lori said, "because in so many ways I was feeling unhappy and insecure while at the same time receiving emotional, mental, and spiritual strength from the angels."

After what seemed an eternity of her taking little "ant footsteps," Lori did reach the top of the canyon, where pine trees, grass, and much firmer footing awaited her. She also rose high enough from her precarious perch that her friend was able to reach her and pull her up to solid ground.

Lori felt weak, faint, and relieved. "I knew that I would never do such a thing again. I knew that I would definitely concentrate more on my spiritual growth. I knew that there had been an invisible presence all around me that had kept me from falling. I would be grateful to God and the angels forever."

In 1988 Lori was told that the reason for her early childhood experiences was to raise her consciousness or spiritual vibration one step at a time, so that when she was older, spirits would be able to come through her and so that she might assist, help, and uplift others.

"I never saw the angels as physical beings when I was a child," Lori said, "but I did hear and feel them around me. For some reason it was a long time before I had the courage to open my eyes and see what was there. I know now that we all have many helpers of love around us who are constantly guiding and helping us."

Now in her mid-forties, Lori conducts special counseling sessions for those seeking information about the heavenly realms. The following information about achieving angelic contact was received from Lori's principal angel guide, Daephrenocles:

As you awaken to the grandeur within you, we angels shall empower you. When you have awakened fully to our presence, we are also fully empowered to assist you in your growth. Truly, you are clothed in the skin and bone of physicality, but we have come to tell you that you are so much more than this. You are light; you are divine; you, too, are Beings of Light.

Forever do we watch over you. Never are you alone: We are one. An angel's love is the reflection of your heart. An angel's love creates the perfect space to see your true self within the heart.

Truly do each of you have your own unique music of the soul that is audible to us of the Light who love you. Truly, we are mirrors of you, here to awaken you gently to who you really are: You are beings of light, pure love, wisdom, and truth. We have come to remind you of your divinity, of the beauty that you are. The more you love, grow, share, care, and help others, the brighter your auric beacon becomes—and the more noticeable you become to us who love you.

Allow the healing vibrations of angelic music to enfold and encompass you. Allow your wondrous selves to be lifted and filled through the heart. We are here to love you and to help you. Blessed Ones, we are partners of light.

You are each an instrument of God's light. You are in partnership with the light. Many paths lead to the light of God—none better or lesser than another.

We have a relationship of working with you, as partners in God's Light, to assist you in seeing the incredible soul beauty of your own to have compassion, to help one another as we are helping you. There is a celebration of joy within the angelic kingdoms every time an expression of love radiates from the heart of one of you. We ask you to value one another, to love one another, to respect and to have faith in one another. Reach for the Light, beloved ones. We are right here, standing ready to lift you up.

As Lori has matured, her mystical experiences began to broaden in scope, and she developed such gifts of the spirit as clairvoyance and clairaudience. However, she is always quick to protest that she does not accomplish any great things by herself: "It's not me, but the Light flowing through me. I work in partnership with the Light."

Lori has often mentioned to us how the angels can find inspirational lessons in what one would consider the most common objects. Below are two teaching messages from Archangel Michael prompted in one instance by observing a leaf floating in a forest pond and in the other by watching a trumpeter swan in flight:

Float Gently as a Leaf

Like the tiny still leaf, gently, silently floating deeply upon the verdant forest pond, let your heart be the clear reflection of our love for you. Let our love reflect clearly upon the emotional waters of your heart. Let your emotions be as tranquil, as peaceful as the tiny leaf, fragile and vulnerable, that silently floats gently upon the waters of life. Allow yourself to be still and to be centered within, like this beautiful leaf. Truly the most profound truths are simple and are to be found in nature reflecting the light of the soul.

Let it be known to each heart that the sacred stillness within is the I AM THAT I AM IN ALL THAT I AM ... peace be still, dear heart. For within the heart are the doorways of light to the heaven realms—to the inner world of each one where divinity and infinite light express and reside. It is the sparkling rainbow bridge between the heavenly realms and the doorways, the hallways of the essential temple of light existing within.

We come to show you how wondrous you are. We come to show you that there is a place of peace, serenity, tranquility, and solace that exists within. There is a place of rest from life's traumas within. There is a place to be soothed and healed within.

Simply allow your emotions within to be like the little leaf, floating peacefully upon the pond of the waters of your soul. Beloved ones, we shall always shower the light of God upon you like an iridescent waterfall of sparkles. Love deeply. Love often. Love well.

You are loved greatly.
Archangel Michael

Wonder of a Trumpeter Swan in Flight

Flowing elegantly through the currents of air, moving on the wingtips of love and light, is the white trumpeter swan. Such a being when airborne is the pure definition of grace, poise, and flow. Beloved one, know you that when such a one is in flight, every feather, every nuance and element of its being is involved in the process. Each aspect of its essence works together as a single creation of God's beauty. From the tip of its beak to the end of its feathered tail, from its webbed toes to its keen eyes, it soars naturally and instinctively.

Beloved One, I now wish you to envision the beauty of this sky being in your mind's eye and to feel the sensation of watching a swan in flight. For a moment, I ask you to think of nothing else. Allow your mind to be encompassed in the sheer, awesome beauty of this magnificent being.

Now ask yourself if you can live as one who is natural and sure of self. Ask if you can live as one who naturally without question accepts self and the God Light within. Allow your intuitive knowing to flourish as God's voice within your own being. Be centered, not whipped back and forth by the winds of others' words and opinions that may not be your truth. Stand in God's truth—the gift within your own heart.

As the elegant swan rises in flight from the clear waters of the lake, allow the pure love and the pure light of your soul essence to rise above material concerns. Be confident of God's light within you. Know that you are always guided and never alone. Let the sweetness of your soul express its grace through the look in your eyes, the glow in your heart, the compassionate touch of your hand on that of another. Remember well that there is always someone who faces challenges far more difficult than your own.

Observe again the swan. See how it appears to take much delight in the activities of its flight. It would seem to have many moments of peace and calm as it glides surely along the waters of the lake. Comfortably, without inner struggle, it follows the plan of God within its own instincts. Allow yourself to be in many ways like unto the wondrous and elegant swan. Revel sometimes in the wonder and the creativity of the light within you. Other times, permit yourself simply to listen to the voice within, then just know, just be. Know that all there is around you is part of God's plan.

Yes, Beloved One, strife does exist upon the Earth, but such conflicts are not caused by God's Light. Calm yourself. Quiet yourself. Center yourself—and you shall find yourself in a different space from the chaos around you. You always have a choice in how to react to life's challenges. And remember, you are never alone. The Angelic Host is always with you.

Archangel Michael

11

Shamanic and Totem Guides

We first met Priscilla Garduno Wolf, a Native American artist and storyteller, at a gathering of tribes in Oklahoma City in the 1970s for which Brad Steiger was the keynote speaker. We have kept in touch with "Little Butterfly," her Jicarilla Apache name, ever since. Priscilla is also a curandera, a Medicine woman, of great ability.

Priscilla said that the Native Americans are coming out in the open more and more as the Medicine people from the different tribes meet. They believe their legends of the Wakan Tanka spirits and know that these spirits watch over them. She explained that the Lakota words *Wakan Tanka* mean the Great Mystery, thus Wakan Tanka spirits would be equivalent to angels or benevolent beings.

"When I moved to Adelino, New Mexico," Priscilla told us, "many strange things took place in my life. I am very close to my friends, the

Lakota Medicine man Pete Spotted Horse and the Cherokee Medicine man and chief Paul White Eagle. We share the power of Medicine people of being able to go to the past or the future. We see clearly the connection of humans and animals, and know that we are one. Wakan Tanka spirits can visit you and let you see beyond."

Priscilla described a peaceful day when she and some family members picnicked beside the Rio Grande. Later, when they took a walk along the river bank, Wakan Tanka spirits allowed them to see back to the beginning of God's creation:

Suddenly, in front of us was wild grass as tall as we were, maybe even taller. When we moved the grass to make an opening for us, we were suddenly back in time, like a flash! We walked on, amazed at what we saw. All the land was free from bridges, homes, and outsiders. What a lovely sight! The grass was pure green in color. The water was pure white and blue, untouched by the human race. Birds were singing in the trees.

We walked for five miles. I felt no pain. I was complete, just as the day that I was born. I looked beautiful, younger, my long black hair was clear to my waist. Yet we had the same clothes on as we did at the picnic.

We came upon a flat opening where the land seemed to form a pure white platform. I saw the eastern sky open, and a golden curtain moved aside to allow two Indian men to appear and walk toward us. They were beautiful like the gods of water, and they were singing, praising the Great Spirit. They stood upon the white platform, and from the east came hundreds of people, surrounded by a golden glow, singing and praising the Great Spirit as they came nearer the two men. On these two men were signs of lightning, like thunder rods, painted in black. They touched the people as they reached up to them to be blessed.

All the while, I kept hearing voices singing and the sounds of drums, *Wakan Tanka! Wakan Tanka!* One of the men on the platform pointed to the south and spoke: "Whites have entered; times will change."

I reached out and touched one of the Wakan Tanka healers, whose body was glowing like the sun. We left that place with spiritual understanding that the Great Spirit was with us and our people. We all felt wonderful and healed as we returned to present time.

Defining Shamanism

The ability to communicate with the unseen world probably began soon after humans first conceived the idea that some part of them survived physical death and existed in some other place in spirit form. Among early tribes of humans, those individuals who demonstrated their ability to visit the place of the dead were known as shamans. Originally, anthropologists applied the term to the spirit doctors and exorcists of the Tungus, an indigenous people of Siberia, but eventually the title was applied as well to the Medicine men and women of the various North American tribes who also serve as mediums, healers, and visionaries for their people.

The Latvian anthropologist Ivar Lissner (1909–1967), who spent a great deal of time among Native people, defines a shaman as one "who knows how to deal with spirits and influence them.... The shaman loses outward consciousness and becomes inspired or enraptured.... [The shaman] sees dreamlike apparitions, hears voices, and receives visions of truth."

A crucial element in shamanism is the ability to rise above the constrictions and restraints of linear time. In his text for *American Indian Ceremonial Dances* (1972), John Collier comments upon the shaman's and the traditional Native peoples' possession of a time sense that is different from Western society's present understanding of the passages of minutes, hours, and days. Once all people possessed such freedom, Collier says, but the mechanized world took it away from us. If we could exist, as the Native people in their whole lives affirmed, "in a dimension of time, a reality of time—not linear, not clock-measured, clock-controlled, and clock-ended," Collier suggests that we should gladly enter it, for we would expand our consciousness. "In solitary, mystical experience many of ourselves do enter another time dimension," he continues, but the "frown of clockwork time" demands that we return to chronological time.

Achieving a deep trance state appears to be the most common way that shamans regularly abandon linear time restrictions in order to gain entrance to that other dimension of time. By singing their special songs received in vision quests or dreams, shamans put themselves into trances that permit them to travel with their spirit helpers to the land of the grandparents, a place free of "clockwork time," where they gain the knowledge to time travel, to heal, and to relay messages of wisdom from the spirit people.

Spirit Helpers

When spirit mediums speak of their control or guide, they are referring to the entity who assists them in establishing contact with deceased humans on the Other Side. The spirit guides of mediums usually claim to have lived as humans on Earth before the time of their death and their graduation to higher realms of being.

In many shamanic traditions, the spirit helper serves as an ambassador from the world of spirits to the world of humans and often manifests in animal form to act as a kind of chaperone during visits to other dimensions of reality. In most Native American shamanic traditions, the spirit guide or spirit helper is usually received during the vision quest. Before initiates embark upon this ordeal, tribal elders and shamans tutor them for many weeks on what to expect and what is expected of them.

Speaking as a *curandera*, Priscilla Garduno Wolf advised us to take at least five minutes every day to be at one with our spirit guide and the Great Spirit. "Always thank your guiding spirit for all you do," she said. "Without it, we are nothing. I always give my spirit a gift for allowing me to be part of it. The spirit guide is what makes us more powerful. Around my home are gifts that belong to my spirit."

The Totem Animal

Among the shamanic teachings of the traditional Native Americans, the totem animal represents the physical form of one's spirit helper, the guide who will lead the shaman into the spirit world and return him or her safely to the physical world. Contrary to the misinterpretations of early missionaries, the Native people did not worship these animal representations of their guides as gods.

The ethnologist Ivar Lissner states in his 1961 book, *Man, God, and Magic*, that his seventeen years of research among shamans demonstrated to him quite clearly that totemism is not religion. Lissner ponders the mystery of why those anonymous Franco-Cantabrian cave artists of more than 20,000 years ago never left us with any clearly defined self-portraits that would depict the actual physical appearance of our ancestors. Aside from a few mother-goddess statuettes, we are left with a rather strange collection of ghostly creatures and a great variety of two-legged beings with the heads of animals and birds. Why, so many anthropologists have wondered, did these cave painters, despite their remarkable artistic gifts, never pass on a representation of their own features? Why did they confine themselves to portraying beings that were half-human, half-animal?

Lissner proposes that it is possible that the Stone Age artists really were portraying themselves, but in something more than in human shape. Perhaps they were depicting themselves "in the guise of intermediary beings who were stronger than common men and able to penetrate more deeply into the mysteries of fate, that unfathomable interrelationship between animals, men, and gods." Lissner suggests that what the ancient cave painters may have been telling us is that the "road to supernatural powers is easier to follow in animal shape and that spirits can only be reached with an animal's assistance." The ancient artists may have been portraying themselves after all, but shamanistically, in animal guise. The spirit guides, appearing as totemic animals, guide the shamans to the mysterious, transcendent reality that leads beyond the material world and leads them into another dimension of time and space wherein dwell the inhabitants of the spirit world. It is through such a portal that shamans must pass to gain their contact with the benevolent beings, the grandfathers and grandmothers, who reside there. With their spirit guide at their side in the form of a totem animal, they can communicate with the spirits and derive wisdom and knowledge that will serve their tribe.

The Story of Cruz and Angel

Priscilla Garduno Wolf loves to share a story passed on to her by her grandmother, Matilde Fernandez Trujillo.

In a small northern town in New Mexico in the year 1915, there lived a young Indian man by the hillside whose name was Cruz. Cruz was a quiet, lonely man who lived in a small cabin just big enough for him.

Cruz had to carry his water from the small creek below, and one day a white dog appeared from out of nowhere and went up to Cruz in a friendly manner. Cruz named the dog Angel because it had appeared like the wind and followed him everywhere, just like a guardian angel.

One time Cruz suffered from a bad fall, causing a sore. Angel sat quietly as Cruz washed it and tried to put cactus juice on it. A few minutes later, Angel went up to Cruz, licked his sore, and healed him.

Angel and Cruz became very attached, as best friends; to Cruz it seemed as if Angel was looking over him all the time.

One day a bad rainstorm overcame Cruz and his Angel dog while they were by the creek. Cruz fell into the storm-swollen creek while trying to get some water, and his faithful dog tried to save him. They both drowned during the storm.

Cloud Angels saw what had happened to the two friends, and they came down to Earth to see that Cruz and his faithful dog were buried beneath some big rocks so their spirits would ascend.

Cruz and Angel did not realize they were dead, and they began to walk home. Soon, they were puzzled when they came to a fork in the road where it split into three paths, marked 1, 2, and 3.

Cruz and Angel took the path on the right, marked 1. At the end of the road was a gate guarded by a tall man dressed in black. "You can't enter here with that dog!" the gruff man told Cruz. "Leave him out here, and I will walk you in."

Cruz answered that he could do no such thing. He said firmly that he and his dog would not separate.

With that, they walked away back to the beginning of the fork in the road and began walking the center path marked 2. At the end of the path there was another gate with a guard, but this time the man was dressed in purple. Once again Cruz was told he could not enter with his dog. He would have to send Angel away if he wished to pass through the gate.

Again Cruz said no, and he and Angel went back to the beginning to path 3. They were so sad, for they seemed lost and just wanted to go home. But as soon as they started walking path 3, they were surrounded with beautiful flowers and tall green trees. Up ahead, though, was another gate, and Cruz wondered if once again they would be denied passage. The man at gate 3 had hair white as snow and wore a white robe. The gate glowed in gold, and the white-haired man's voice sounded like music.

Angel wagged his tail and was so happy, but Cruz held on to him. "Come enter my gate," the guard bade him.

"I cannot do that," Cruz replied. "I will not leave my dog behind."

"Oh, you do not have to leave him," the white-robed man said. "Bring him in with you. You will see other owners with their pets in my garden beyond. Animals are free to roam here."

As Cruz and Angel entered the garden, they both knew that they had finally reached their true home. Here, they would exist happily ever after.

Priscilla said that her whenever her grandmother told the story, she would whisper softly that there were spiritual lessons to learn: that God, the Great Spirit, loves all creatures, and that Angel had been Cruz's guardian angel on Earth and now was a real angel dog in Heaven.

The Vision Quest

The personal revelatory experience and the contact with the spirit world received during the vision quest is a fundamental guiding force in the shaman's power or Medicine. Those who would be traditional shamans set out alone in the wilderness to fast, to exhaust the physical body, to pray, to establish their own contact with the dimension of spirit, and to receive their individual Medicine power. The dogma of tribal rituals and the religious expressions of others become secondary to the guidance that one receives from his or her own personal visions.

"The seeker goes forth solitary," writes Hartley Burr Alexander (1873–1939) in *The World's Rim: Great Mysteries of the North American Indians*, "carrying his pipe and with an offering of tobacco. There in the wilderness alone, he chants his song and utters his prayers while he waits, fasting, such revelation as the Powers may grant."

In the Native American tribal traditions, the power granted by the vision quest comes from a vast and impersonal repository of spiritual energy, and those who partake of the quest receive their personal guardian spirit and a great vision that will grant them insight into the spiritual dimensions beyond physical reality. Far from a being a goal achieved, the vision quest marks the beginning of the traditional shaman's lifelong search for knowledge and wisdom.

Alexander saw the continued quest for wisdom of body and mind—the search for the single essential force at the core of every thought and deed—as the perpetually accumulating elements in Medicine power. The reason the term *Medicine* became applied to this life-career function is simply because those attaining stature as men and women who had acquired this special kind of wisdom were often also great healers. The true meaning of *Medicine* extends beyond healing to the arts of clairvoyance, precognition, and the control of weather elements. Perhaps most of all, the power received in the vision quest enables the shaman to obtain personal contact with the invisible world of spirits and to pierce the sensory world of illusion that veils the Great Mystery.

Discovering Your Own Totem Spirit Guide

Silver Cloud, one of Brad Steiger's early mentors, had undertaken the traditional vision quest when he was a young man living with the Winnebago tribe. "One thing that we were taught is that we must never call upon our guides until we had exhausted every bit of physical energy and mental resource possible," he said. "Then, after we had employed every last ounce of our own reserve, we might call upon our guide and it would appear."

When the Steigers were conducting Medicine seminars, Brad fashioned the following visualization to simulate a vision quest of the mind to discover the totem animal and spirit guide. In this exercise, the subjects would first be placed in a state of relaxation and visualize themselves as individuals on a traditional vision quest.

Those who may wish to go mentally on this vision quest to discover their totem spirit should first employ a relaxation technique. One may have a trusted friend or family member conduct the relaxation process, or one may prerecord the process and the following exercise in his or her own voice. Soft, floating music, such as a selection of Native American flute music, would be ideal to help one relax and to prompt appropriate mental images.

Once a state of relaxation has been achieved, the following exercise should be read:

See yourself now on a vision quest to discover the identity of your totem animal or spirit guide. Know and understand that you have relaxed the physical self. Know and understand that your body is relaxed so that your spirit can soar to the Great Mystery.

Feel now your body becoming very tired ... very heavy. See yourself lying down on a blanket in a clearing in a forest to relax ... relax ... relax.

Slowly you become aware of a presence. Someone has approached you and has come to stand next to you. You feel no fear. You feel only peace and love.

As you look up from your blanket, you see two spirits who have come from the spirit world of the grandparents to view you on your quest. You see that they are majestic in appearance. They smile at you ... then disappear.

Your inner knowing tells you that they came to you to show you that in many ways, on many levels, you have great a partnership with the world of spirits. The grandparents have given you a sign of the reality of your oneness with all spiritual beings.

You have but a moment to ponder the wonder of the spirit visitation when you become aware of a globe of bluish white light moving toward you. You are not afraid, for you sense a great spiritual presence approaching you.

As the light swirls and becomes solid, you behold before you a man or a woman in spirit whom you regard as a saint, a great Medicine Chief, a master, an illumined one. This figure, so beloved to you, gestures to your left side. As you turn, you are astonished to behold a marvelous link-up with other holy figures from all times, all places, all cultures. You see that these great spiritual beings form a chain of Spirit from prehistory to the present and into the future.

The sacred one before you smiles benevolently, then bends over and gently touches your eyes, your ears, and your mouth. You know that this holy touching symbolizes that you must share your revelations with others.

As the holy one begins to fade from your perception, you now perceive a brilliant white light so bright that you must cover your eyes. You feel no fear, only love emanating from the bright light. Your inner knowing makes you aware that within this powerful light is your spirit helper, whose identity will soon be made known to you in physical form.

Now, in a great rush of color and light, you are made aware that you are being elevated in spirit. You know that your spirit helper has taken you to a higher vibrational level. You have moved to a dimension where nonlinear, cyclical time flows around you. The energy of the Great Mystery touches you, and you are made aware that you are becoming one with the great pattern of all life.

You see before you now an animal, any animal that enters into your consciousness. Become one with its essence. Become one with this level of awareness. Be that animal. Be that level of energy expression.

See before you now a bird, any bird that enters into your consciousness. Become one with its essence. Become one with its level of awareness. Be that bird. Be that level of energy expression.

See before you now a creature of the waters, any creature of the waters that enters your consciousness. Become one with its essence. Become one with its level of awareness. Be that creature of the waters. Be that level of energy expression.

See before you now a creeper or a crawler, any creeper or crawler that enters your consciousness. Become one with its essence. Become one with its level of awareness. Be that creeper or crawler. Be that level of energy expression.

See before you now an insect, any insect that enters your consciousness. Become one with its essence. Become one with its level of awareness. Be that insect. Be that level of energy expression.

See before you now a plant, any plant that enters your consciousness. Become one with its essence. Become one with its level of awareness. Be that plant. Be that level of energy expression.

Know that you are now one with the unity of all plant and animal essence.

Know now that you are one with all things that walk on two legs or four, with all things that fly, with all things that crawl, with all things that sustain themselves in the waters, with all things that grow in the soil.

And now your spirit helper will show you the image of your animal totem.

At the count of three, you will focus upon that creature. You will see its beauty. You will become one with its life essence. At the count of three, you will know that this animal is now your totem, the symbol that will often come to you in dreams and represent your spirit helper on another level of reality.

One ... the image is beginning to appear before you.

Two ... you are beginning to see clearly the image of your animal totem, your spirit helper.

Three ... you see clearly the image of your animal totem!

At this eternal second in the energy of the Eternal Now, at this vibrational level of oneness with all living things, at this frequency of awareness of unity with the cosmos, your animal totem is permitting you to receive a great teaching vision of something about which you need to know for your good and your gaining. Receive this great vision now! *[Allow approximately two minutes to pass before speaking again.]*

You will return to full consciousness at the count of five.

You will be filled with positive memories of your vision quest. You are now fully aware of the identity of your animal totem, your spirit helper. You will awaken feeling better and healthier than ever before in your life, and you will feel a great sense of unity with all living things.

One ... coming awake. Two ... more and more awake. Three ... feeling very good in mind, body, and spirit. Four ... coming awake. *Five* ... wide awake and feeling wonderful.

12

Sacred Places Where Miracles Happen

Contact with benevolent beings often occurs on sacred ground. These ancient sites, both marked and unmarked, are scattered across the globe. Sacred places may also be highly personal places where we pray and meditate and where our communication with higher beings seems to be facilitated.

A Father Finds Hope

The artist, storyteller, and healer Priscilla Garduno Wolf recalled a story that her cousin Jose told her about a miracle that had blessed his father, Felipe, when he left to seek work in Casa Grande, Arizona.

It was a very hard time for the poor Mexican Indian family, and while his father was away from home in search of work, Jose was left in charge of the family. At age ten, all he could do was work the streets, asking tourists to buy the rosaries and other items that his mother had made.

Felipe had left with a small bundle of food and water and the only horse the family owned. He encountered great obstacles in his journey, eating only dry, hard bread and drinking water to survive. After he arrived in Casa Grande, he stayed with a family that he knew while he sought work. Felipe found nothing but disappointment, so he decided to make the two-day return trip to his family.

He was hungry, wet from the rain, tired, and cold. He rested beneath a big bush and prayed to God to provide him with an answer on how he might provide for his family. He put his need and trust in God's hands.

Early the next morning, Felipe continued on his journey home. As he approached Tierra Blanca, he caught a glimpse of a fire and a camp. Felipe knew his prayers would be answered, for he had entered sacred ground, a place where miracles happen. Felipe knew there were no coincidences. Everything in life happens according to a plan. His faith had opened the door for a miracle. All things were possible through divine intervention.

As Felipe came closer to the camp, he could see three Apache men enjoying the warmth of the fire and eating. The sight made him very happy. He would ask them for food and warm up, then be on his way.

The men welcomed him and fed him and told him not to worry because God, the Great Mystery, would provide for him. As Felipe mounted his horse to leave, he turned around to thank them for the food, hospitality, and words of inspiration. As Felipe watched, the three men vanished before his eyes. The fire, the encampment, the men— everything disappeared.

Jose said that his father came home a changed man. Felipe told his family of his ordeal trying to find work away from home and of his encounter with the three Apache men, who were apparitions of higher spiritual beings. These three spirits had assured him that the Great Spirit would provide for him and his family.

Soon, as the three spirits had foretold, Felipe was able to find work close to home, and he was able to provide very well for his family.

This is a true story, Priscilla Garduno Wolf said, and it helps her family members always to remember that faith can remove all obstacles and to give thanks to God, the Great Spirit.

Miracles Are the Great Spirit Speaking Directly to Us

Our friend Wolfman Dan, who follows the traditional ways and who is guided by his spirit totem, Stardancer, a wolf, defines such miracles as the Great Spirit speaking directly to us. He tells the following story:

Miracles happen because some have a path yet to walk. It is not the Great Spirit that wishes for people to burn to death, for example. Death is a fact of life. Perhaps those who perish have already learned the lessons that they wished to learn in this existence, and it was merely their time.

I look at the miraculous as intervention by the Great Spirit. Mishaps, I take as lessons learned ("that which does not kill us makes us stronger"). Not only that, but from some of the stranger, more harmless mishaps, I can take comfort in knowing that the Great Spirit—and probably a few other spirits— gained a good chuckle. Problems are only as harmful as one makes them.

For the past fifteen years, ever since Stardancer came to me, I see every day as a blessing, come good or bad. I've had many strange things happen, and thinking about them is what keeps me both sharp and grateful for the time I have. Some may see this as just a matter of a choice, but I know better. I am learning the lessons that the Great Spirit has intended for me. I do not fear death. I know where I'm going and I know my duty once I reach the next plane. I feel sorry for the skeptics and cynics of the world, who seem to thrive on the fact that all they have is this solitary existence and that they will only disappear when this life is over. How secluded must one be not to live in a world of magic, miracles, and mystery.

May you be blessed by the Great Spirit, and forever may he shine light on your path.

An Afterlife Communication at a Sacred Site

Shortly before Brad and Sherry Steiger left on a tour of the sacred sites of Peru in 1988, Sherry received a strong intuitive impression that her son, Erik, who had died in an automobile accident on the Sunday before Christmas when he was nine years old, would give her a sign while they were traveling.

Several days later, when the Steigers were high in the Andes approaching a sacred site by bus, a beautiful white horse appeared completely out of nowhere. At first, the magnificent animal kept pace with the bus, running next to the window where the Steigers were seated. Then, in a great burst of speed, it crossed in front of the bus ... and disappeared.

There were no farms, ranches, or villages near. They were high in the mountains. There were nothing but craggy rocks alongside the narrow road. This incredible white horse came directly from the spirit world as a sign sent by a loving son to assure his mother that death is but a change of worlds.

Why a white horse?

Because Sherry is of Chippewa, as well as Swedish, heritage—and because she has spent a great deal of time studying with Native American shamans—she was aware that for many tribes a vision of a white horse represents the spirit of Death coming to accompany the soul to the land of the grandparents. On the morning of his death, Erik had awakened Sherry to show her a puzzle that he had assembled that pictured a single white horse grazing in a beautiful green meadow. He solemnly informed her that the puzzle must not be dissembled and put away. It was a special present for her.

On that Sunday morning, as Sherry rushed to get the children ready for church and steadied herself for travel over icy roads and blizzard conditions, she did not have the time to ponder the significance of Erik's gift of a white horse. Since his earliest childhood, Erik had been enthralled with many of the myths and legends of the Native tribes, and he always wore the beaded bracelets and medallions of his mother.

Sherry did have an ominous feeling that stormy day as she set out in an unfamiliar, rather dilapidated vehicle with a passenger-side door that would not stay closed. That uncomfortable foreboding was horribly realized when the vehicle flipped over on the icy roads and Erik was pinned under it. Erik was buried with his cherished star necklace, placed on his chest by his mother and his sister, Melissa.

Angels Rose out of a Sacred Lake into the Night Sky

An afterlife communication with Sherry's son was not the only miracle that the Steigers experienced on that expedition to Peru's sacred sites.

As longtime researchers into UFO phenomena, they would often ask villagers if they had seen any "flying saucers" or "mysterious lights in the sky."

In almost every instance, once the Steigers had made themselves as clearly understood as possible with their rudimentary Spanish, the villagers would smile, nod, and correct their visitors politely by explaining that they must be speaking about "angels." Glowing angels, the Steigers were told again and again, were frequently seen in the skies and in the waters of the region.

One night, not far from the sacred Incan city of Ollantaytambo in Peru, the Steigers'shaman guide said that he would take them to a sacred lake where every night one could see such angels entering and leaving the water. The only condition to his offer was that the Steigers and their friends maintain the secrecy of the lake's location.

It was on an extremely dark night that the Incan shaman took them to the sacred lake where the Steigers and their companions witnessed numerous illuminated beings or UFOs or angels emerge from the lake's surface, soar through the night sky in a peculiar zig-zag flying pattern, and then—at least some of them—descend and submerge under the water.

In spite of the chill in the night air, there were barefooted villagers walking about in the darkness, carrying grain and water to their families in jars atop their heads. To those who could speak Spanish, the Steigers asked them their thoughts about the mysterious lights. Some answered that the lights were spirits of the grandfathers. Others called them the Old Ones. But most of them declared that the lights seen leaving and entering the lake were angels.

Among the group accompanying the Steigers, opinions were equally varied: Space Brothers. Extraterrestrials with an underwater base. Some strange, unknown natural phenomenon. Survivors of an ancient race. Or angels.

Sherry was inspired to attempt an experiment. She began projecting thought-messages to the glowing lights to zig to the left, zag to the right, spiral upward, dive into the lake, and so forth. Incredibly, as everyone witnessed, the "angels" complied with her requests.

As impressive as this demonstration was, it raised many new questions about the true identity of the glowing lights and answered none of the old ones.

Remarkable Multidimensional Phenomena at Sacred Sites

Ever since the early 1970s when numerous metaphysical groups began conducting pilgrimages to ancient sacred sites around the world, many individuals have returned claiming dramatic sightings of UFOs, Light Beings, or other mysterious entities hovering above the sacred areas.

The Steigers themselves have witnessed remarkable manifestations of multidimensional activity—most often reported as UFOs—at Petra, the ancient Nabatean city in Jordan; Machu Picchu, the Incan metropolis located high in the Andes in Peru; the Great Pyramid of Giza and the Great Sphinx in Egypt; the mystical city of Luxor in Egypt; Masada, the hilltop fortress at the edge of the Judean Desert in southern Israel; the remains of the Essene community at Qumran in the West Bank; the transformational vortex areas of Sedona, Arizona; the powerful Kahuna shrines of Hawaii; the Temple of the Sun in Cuzco, Peru; Mount Nebo in Jordan, the legendary burial place of Moses; the ancient Incan healing springs at Tambo Machay, Peru; the gigantic, sprawling mystery lines in Peru's Nazca Desert; the sacred Peruvian city of Ollantaytambo; tribal Medicine power places in Santa Fe, New Mexico, and the Four Corners area of the Southwest; and numerous Navajo, Hopi, and pre-Navajo sites in Arizona.

In addition to having observed UFO or angelic materializations at these sacred sites, a number of spiritual pilgrims also claimed a personal mystical encounter with otherworldly intelligences. To many of these experiencers, the contact that they received during an encounter with a multidimensional intelligence at these holy places served as an initiation into higher awareness. Interaction with an intelligence that had previously existed far beyond their normal world of ordinary expectations served as an impetus to awaken their consciousness to consider previously undreamed-of facets of the universe.

A sacred site remains energized and charged regardless of what present-day edifice may rest atop it. Throughout Europe, many churches are constructed over previous so-called pagan temples. Some researchers believe the original pagan sites of worship were built on natural energy lines, or "ley lines." In the Americas, if one were to investigate the history of the site where a church or synagogue now stands, one would more than likely discover that it rests on a former Native American power place or Medicine area.

Since the most ancient of times, tribal elders, priests, and religious orders have worked to develop traditions of spirituality to provide inspiration for life's challenges. Rituals and rites were designed to reveal certain truths, explain various mysteries, and present a process by which initiation into a higher awareness might be achieved. Spiritually, the significance of initiation lies in the death of the egoistic, physical self and its rebirth in the divine, transcendental order.

In some sacred traditions, such special knowledge and power were kept secret and remained exclusive to the initiated. Other great teachers focused their energies on arousing the sleeping spiritual senses of their students, thereby bringing about enlightenment through a personal mystical experience. These wise masters were aware that the individual mystical experience was the catalyst that awakened the initiate to the Inner Voice that speaks of a sense of Oneness with All That Is and the wisdom that the Great Mystery dwells within each soul.

Many great spiritual teachers have declared that initiation may be bestowed upon the sincere seeker by benevolent beings that exist on higher planes of being.

Discover Your Own Sacred Place

Perhaps some readers are now feeling somewhat estranged. They are unable to travel to faraway sacred sites and receive miracles and initiations. Fortunately, one need not put self or spirit on the sacred ground of others, because we all have within us our memory of our very own sacred place.

Certain scholars who specialize in such subjects as anthropology, mythology, and religion have theorized that all of our various ritual observances have their genesis in a faraway beginning time, a sacred event to which a particular culture can trace its origin. A familiar illustration for those in the Judeo-Christian-Islamic tradition would be the story of Adam and Eve and the Tree of Knowledge. For at least three thousand years, the creation of humanity, species consciousness, and the world has been traced to that symbolic event.

So it is that each of us has our own personal myth of "the beginning" of a special kind of consciousness regarding the external, material world around us. Each of us has a memory of a special time to which we might return in our own individual sacred moment and our unique ritualized measurement of reality.

Brad Steiger can remember being a small boy as young as two or three and crawling into the midst of a clump of lilac bushes, where he sought refuge from the demands of physical reality. From this magical spot, he was able to perceive the world from his own special vantage point.

Brad can remember that whenever it seemed as though the confusions and the frustrations of the outside reality—the one that he shared consensually with his parents and others—became too much for his budding psyche to comprehend, he could retreat into his sacred space in the lilac bushes and take some time to process just exactly how best to deal with the present stressful challenges.

Even now, as an adult in his seventies, whenever he feels that the consensual reality that he shares with family, friends, and colleagues becomes a bit too much for him to handle, he returns in his memory to his special, magical place—his own mythical moment of the advent of his consciousness as an individual spiritual entity in a very strange material world.

When he needs a sturdy fortress and a temporary respite from the stresses and pressures of external reality, he mentally returns to his sacred place in the lilac bushes. He need only withdraw from the place of stress or conflict and find some place where he can be quiet and alone for a few minutes. Then, after taking three or four comfortably deep breaths, he follows a procedure that anyone can accomplish:

Remember the magical place with all of your senses.

With the memory of your sight, recall every detail of your mystical spot's appearance.

With the memory of your sense of smell, remember any odors that are associated with your secret spot.

With the memory of your sense of hearing, remember any particular sounds that you heard when you retreated to your special place.

With the memory of your sense of taste, remember if there were any tastes connected with this place.

With all the memory of all your senses, allow yourself to recall how calm and peaceful you felt in your own secret sacred site. Remember how loved you felt and how you became one with All That Is. Remember the sights and sounds and smells that may have manifested together with the knowledge that beside you at all times was a benevolent being who would always be there to love you and to watch over you.

After you have sat or lain quietly for a few more moments, you know that it is from this eternally safe and secure psychological vantage point that you are able to regroup your energies, recharge your psyche, resume your mission on the planet with renewed strength, and return to deal with the stresses and conflicts that prompted you to retreat for a few moments to your own sacred place.

In *Healing States* (1987) by Alberto Villoldo and Stanley Krippner, the shaman Don Eduardo speaks of the true meaning of initiation:

Initiation represents a readiness to assume responsibility for the planet and for serving humanity.

Initiation helps one to forge a link between oneself and an ancient lineage of knowledge.

Initiation is not graduation. It is only the beginning of the great work that lies ahead of the initiate.

Initiation is basically a salute to the spirit of a person whose consciousness has been awakened.

As Don Eduardo emphasizes, initiations are taking place all the time: "Initiations can occur on the way to the supermarket or on top of the Himalayas. And the most powerful initiations ... are bestowed from the hands of the masters who work directly from the 'overworld.' These initiations may occur in our dreams or during meditation or may take us by surprise ... when we least expect them. But in the final analysis we make the choice to be initiated ourselves."

Take a few minutes now to identify your own personal sacred place and moment. Each of you has a similar magical, mythical place—perhaps it was in your bedroom closet or under the dining-room table or beneath a bush in the backyard—a sacred spot to which you retreated as a child and felt secure and protected from the fears and awful awareness of a reality external to you and to your inner spark of divinity.

Once you have reviewed all the sensory details of your sacred place, then you are ready to pull in the power of your internal myth and use it to help summon the teachings from benevolent beings you most need to assist you in a successful accomplishment of your mission on Earth.

13

Grandmother Is My Guardian Angel

Over the past fifty years of our collective research, we have spoken to many men and women who have told us that their guardian angel is a deceased loved one who manifests from the Other Side. As we have stated earlier in this book, theologians from the Jewish, Christian, and Islamic religions will state firmly that angels are an ethereal species created apart from humankind. According to these religious scholars, the angels were fashioned by the Supreme Creator long before humans were shaped out of the clay of Earth.

Although we have been consistent over the years in echoing the conventional theological dictates concerning the identity of angels, in this book we are presenting a much wider spectrum of just who the "real angels" might be and examining as complete a range of definitions of these benevolent beings or guiding spirits as we possibly can. In other words, we very much recognize that we cannot be dogmatic in our view of who among the unseen world might be suited to the requirements of a guardian angel.

We humans also are multidimensional beings in that we have a soul temporarily inhabiting a physical body. Throughout our lives we often define our physical world in terms of our dreams, visions, inspirations, feelings, and emotions—all important determinants that are invisible to others. Many of us have had out-of-body or near-death experiences in which our soul, our Essential Self, has left the physical body to soar free of the mundane limits of time and space. How much more is the soul, the Real Self, free to move through otherworldly dimensions when it leaves the body in the final projection of death? And who is to declare with full assurance that our loved ones cannot serve at least for a time as our guardians and guides?

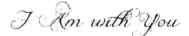

I Am with You

We had begun to reconsider our strict position on guardian angels a few years ago when we shared the grief of Mardai Harricharan's death. Mardai was the wife of our dear friend John, the award-winning author of *When You Can Walk on Water, Take the Boat* and *Morning Has Been All Night Coming*, and they had been married for twenty years. We knew that even with his solid belief in the afterlife and in the continuation of the soul after death, John would be struck with the question of how he and their two children would continue in life without Mardai.

In the days that followed, John told us there were times when he looked around him and perceived life as a meaningless mess. But there were other times when a quiet voice would whisper in his heart that life was not as it appeared to be. Life was much more than a short span on Earth. A lifetime was but a blink in eternity.

One day as John pulled up at a red traffic light behind another car and was waiting for the light to change, he silently said, "Mardai, if you are around, please let me know. I would feel much better." The light changed, and as the car in front of him pulled away, John saw on the license plate *MEH 711*. MEH were Mardai's initials, and 711, July 11th, was the date she died.

A calmness and joy welled up within him, and John heard a voice in his mind say, *"I am with you."*

John told us that from that experience many others followed. "They seemed to come at times when I most needed reassurance about life and its direction."

After a while it became commonplace for John to see Mardai's initials on billboards and license plates, and he would look at a clock for no apparent reason only to find that the time would be 7:11. He became so used to seeing such signs that as time went on, he ignored many of them for fear of becoming too dependent on them. Still, he found a strange, beautiful comfort in such reminders.

Sometimes John would be thinking of Mardai, and at that very moment a song that she loved would play on the radio. It was as if she were saying to him, "I just want you to know that I love you and that I am with you whenever you think of me."

It is now John's belief that our loved ones continue their lives in an area just beyond our physical senses. "I feel that they reach out to help, to guide, to comfort us in a most loving way," he said. "There are signs of their presence all around us if we but look more closely and listen more attentively."

Furthermore, John explained, he believes that the bonds that exist between those who love deeply are stronger than death itself. Perhaps, he commented, love is the greatest reality in the universe.

Although he no longer sees Mardai's physical form nor hears her lovely musical voice, John knows that she exists, and he believes that she is closer than he thinks. "Sometimes I meet her in my dreams, and at other times I feel as if she speaks to me in the quietness between my thoughts," he said.

John's father died a few years before Mardai, and he continues to feel his presence as well. "Those whom we love will always be with us," he said. "Sometimes on a beautiful, cloudless, starry night, I sit on my porch and look into the woods behind my house," John told us. "I hear the voices of my loved ones in my heart and in the very whispering of the wind through the leaves. I look up into the sky and see the second star on the belt of Orion the Hunter, and I can see Mardai smiling at me."

As John looks and listens in the quietness of his soul, he hears Mardai say:

> I have always loved you, and I have known you from eternity.
> When you are sad, I feel your sorrow, and when you are happy, I

rejoice with you. You must finish the work that you came to Earth to do. Time will lighten the heaviness in your heart, and then I will be able to communicate with you more clearly.

I watch over you and our children, and I know how difficult it can get at times. But you are not alone. There are others here who also watch and help. Our work on Earth was finished, so we had to go on. We are all brilliantly alive.

I visit you sometimes in your dreams. The veil that separates your reality from mine is very thin indeed. In your quiet moments, you sometimes pierce that veil and obtain a glimpse of our reality. It is gloriously exciting where we are, and one day we shall all meet again. You have much to do before you join us, but know that we will be with you every step of the way.

My dearest John, I will love you through the Halls of Forever. When you are ready to come here, I will be the first one waiting to greet you. Live life joyously and fully.

John has continued to live life as gloriously as he can, fulfilling his mission as a spiritual advisor to hundreds of men and women. His son and daughter are happy, and John finds joy and comfort in the simple things around him.

"I know that our loved ones are always with us," John said. "I know that love prevails over everything—even over death. Listen to your heart, and you will hear the sounds of eternity. You will feel the ties that bind you in an everlasting love."

His Grandmother Is His Guardian Angel

James Mohr of Texas told us that he knows that his grandmother is his guardian angel and that he learned that indisputable fact when he was driving a rented truck, moving from Omaha to Dallas in 1997.

"My wife was following with the kids in our van about a day or so behind," he said. "I had gone on ahead to meet her two brothers at our new home, and the plan was that we could get the furniture unloaded before she and the kids arrived to complete the move."

Mohr was getting low on gas and was very sleepy when he saw a small gas station and diner up ahead. He planned to pull over, fill up with gas, and get some coffee and a sandwich when he got a whiff of something familiar and very out of place. He was clearly and distinctly smelling his grandmother's lavender-scented powder. He had smelled it on her since he was a little kid, and he would know it anywhere—even though his grandmother had been dead for more than ten years. The recollection of the familiar scent brought him a clear materialization of Grandmother Mohr.

"As solidly as I see you now," Mohr said, "I saw Gram sitting opposite me in the cab of the truck. 'Jimmy,'she said, 'you just keep on driving to the next gas station. You don't want to go in that place up ahead. Stay clear of it, my little man. Something very bad is about to happen there very, very soon.'" Mohr said that he didn't have to think twice about the admonition from the spirit of his grandmother. She smiled at him, said she would always love him and watch over him until he walked in Heaven beside her, then she disappeared.

"I didn't intellectualize that I had been driving too long and was hallucinating," Mohr said. "I knew it had been Gram. First there was the smell of that lavender powder of hers, and then she called me 'little man.' Even after I got to be over six feet and way over 220 pounds, she still always called me little man. I put the pedal to the metal and kept driving right on by the gas station and diner where Gram said something bad was about to happen."

Late the next afternoon, just before he arrived in Dallas, he was having lunch in a restaurant outside the city when he saw a segment on the local television newscast that showed the very traveler's oasis at which he would have stopped the night before. The gas station had been robbed, and one attendant had been brutally murdered and another seriously wounded in the thieves' cruel efforts to leave no witnesses.

"The time of the robbery and assault on the attendants checked with the exact time that I would have pulled into the gas station and diner," Mohr said. "If Gram's ghost had not appeared and told me not to stop but to keep on going, I would have been another victim of the robbery. I couldn't ask for a better guardian angel than Gram. We were very close when she was on Earth, and I guess we're even closer now that she's in Heaven."

Generations of Guardians

As the Steiger Questionnaire of Mystical, Paranormal, and UFO Experiences provides a great many such accounts of deceased friends and relatives serving as guardian angels for their loved ones on Earth, Brad began to reassess one of his earliest childhood memories, the nocturnal visits of a somewhat stern-visaged couple who frequently walked into his bedroom at night and stood for several minutes at his bedside, looking down at him. Brad remembers that at first he would hide his head under the covers for a few minutes, then peep out to see if they were still there. They always were.

Brad soon came to understand that they meant him no harm, and even though he never once caught them in a smile, he had the distinct feeling that they liked him. The man had a full beard and wore a black suit, white shirt, and dark tie. The woman wore her hair in a rather severe bun, and she was attired in an old-fashioned dress with a lace collar. Years later, while paging through an old family album, Brad saw pictures of his great-great-grandparents Ole and Marit, who had immigrated to Iowa from Norway in 1881, and he recognized them as the nocturnal visitors of his childhood.

Because of this early visitation around the age of three, coupled with a chance close encounter with a multidimensional being when he was five and a near-death experience at the age of eleven, Brad has been aware of the presence of unseen entities for many years. On numerous occasions throughout his life experiences a voice from some invisible entity has shouted at him to "step back" or to "stay away" or to "get out of here fast" and saved him from serious injury, if not death. Why could those warning voices not have issued from the solicitous spirit of a loved one, as well as from a guardian angel?

She Met Her Spirit Guide in a Heavenly Garden

Diane Ching of Arizona said that she met her spirit guide, her great-uncle Chang Yun, on the Other Side when she nearly died during the crash of a small airplane in which she was the passenger.

"My friend Aaron had just received his pilot's license, and he wanted to show off to me," Diane said. "I had a bad feeling, a premonition, that I should not go with him that afternoon, but I wanted to show my confidence in his abilities. Next time, I will listen to my inner voice."

Diane underwent a classic near-death experience. She saw herself moving down a dark tunnel toward a speck of light that grew larger as she drew nearer. She was aware of an entity, a kind of spirit guide, near to her as she moved closer to the light. And then suddenly, she was standing on a small footbridge that stretched over a fish pond in a beautiful garden.

Gradually she became aware of people moving around her. They all seemed very friendly, and they were smiling and welcoming her. Diane said that they were people of all ethnic groups—white, black, yellow, red, brown—every hue of humanity—and they all seemed delighted to see her.

Just as Diane was growing accustomed to the concept of her death, a tall Chinese gentleman stepped forward and told her that her stay would be very brief.

"He was very imposing, but in a gentle way," she remembered. "He had a beard, the kind that traditional Asian wise men wear. He came closer to me and held out his arms so that I might embrace him. In a soft, yet commanding voice, he informed me that he would always be near me and watch over me. Then he asked me to look more closely at the lovely goldfish swimming."

One very large fish caught Diane's attention, and as she watched its supple and graceful movements, it began to swim around and around in circles. The next thing she knew, she was waking up in a hospital.

Diane was in for a hospital stay of nearly two weeks and a long period of convalescence in her parents' home. She was not married at that time and was only two months out of college.

"I had not yet found a steady job," she said, "and my parents were kind enough to extend their love and care to me as they had when I was a child."

One day, to pass the hours, Diane's mother brought down a number of old family scrapbooks. As the two paged through the photographs depicting the pictorial history of their family's acculturation into American society, Diane felt a little shiver of recognition when she saw a photograph of the distinguished gentleman who had embraced her in the lovely garden on the Other Side. In the picture, he stood with two little boys, one of whom Diane recognized as her father. The other, her mother identified as one of her father's childhood friends.

Then Diane asked about the adult standing with the boys. Mother told her that was her grandfather's brother, her great-uncle Chang Yun.

"He was a very wise and good man, known widely for many acts of kindness," her mother said. "He died very young when he was trying to rescue a small girl who was drowning. He was only about thirty years old. I barely knew him. I was only six or seven when he died."

Diane told her mother of her near-death experience and her visit to the gardens of paradise where she had met Chang Yun. "He embraced me, Mother, and said that he would always watch over me."

Diane said that her mother got tears in her eyes and told her with great emotion that she could not have a better guiding spirit to look after her.

A Dream of Grandfather Looking after Her Son in Iraq

Sometimes a person can learn that a dear one on the Other Side is still looking after family members by experiencing a vivid dream of such interaction. On April 26, 2006, Mary Crofts included this account when she submitted the Steiger Questionnaire:

> In 2003 my youngest son, Eric, was in Iraq with the U.S. Army. I prayed to God and asked my spirit guides and my grandparents to be with my son and give him guidance. I had not heard from him in several weeks. My grandfather visited me in a dream and told me that he was with Eric and would watch over him. I felt relieved, knowing Eric had family with him. The visit was so real, but there were few I could talk to that would understand because of their strict religious beliefs.

When we asked Mary for additional details, she kindly responded with the following:

> The dream was so real! Granddad sat down for a visit, but at the time I didn't remember anything he said. The next morning, as with most dreams, I had forgotten it entirely. Then my

husband said something, probably about Eric, that vividly brought the dream back—and I *knew* my grandfather was with Eric and that grandfather had assured me that my son was all right. It was very emotional. I was filled with joy knowing that Eric had a special spirit guide with him. My granddaddy still had the same personality as before he passed over.

As I said earlier, I had the dream in early May 2003. I hadn't heard from Eric in almost six weeks. Other families in our support group had received emails and phone calls from their soldiers, but we had heard nothing from our son. His Civil Affairs unit was embedded in the Third Infantry Division, and no one here knew where he was. I prayed constantly to God and my spirit guide. Then I began talking to the spirits of my grandfather and grandmother, asking them to be with Eric and watch over him.

My grandfather and grandmother were special people. I feel they are still with me, especially when I visit their home place. Strangely enough, as I write this, today would have been Grandfather's 106th birthday! My brother is constructing a Web site in memory of Grandmother's art [http://marytrogdon.atspace. com/]. There is a picture of my grandfather on the site, as well. They were deeply in love with each other.

And it would certainly appear from Mary's account that they are still deeply in love with their family members who remain on Earth.

A Deceased Sweetheart Became Her Guardian Angel

Doreen told us that she and Kevin had known each other for several years and had become good friends long before they had begun to think of each other as potential sweethearts or marriage partners. Their sudden awareness of each other as lovers had one day seemed a most natural thing, and they could not help chiding themselves after having worked in the same insurance company for nearly three years.

Kevin, who had a mystical side to his nature, as Doreen soon learned, would philosophize that a Force-Greater-Than-They had for some reason seen fit to keep them apart, yet together, for so long. Kevin even theorized that he may have been her brother in a past-life incarnation.

When Doreen suggested that this was a "weird" notion, Kevin only shrugged and said that it could have been. He only knew from the moment that he had first seen her that he had felt very protective toward her. It was as if he wanted to be her bodyguard.

When Kevin proposed marriage after five months of serious dating, Doreen did not hesitate to give an overwhelmingly positive answer. Kevin was twenty-eight; she was twenty-five. They were old enough to know what they were doing, and young enough to enjoy doing it. They had not fallen in love—they had grown in love. They had been friends before they had become lovers.

Two months before the wedding, Kevin was killed instantly in an automobile accident.

Doreen has little memory of the first few weeks after Kevin's death. "I was left to try to put back together the scattered pieces of what seemed to be an irrevocably shattered life," she said. "It was well over a year before I began dating again. I know that I was too hard on the men who asked me out, because, in my mind, no one could ever begin to compare to Kevin. No one could ever satisfy me on as many levels as Kevin had. There were men with whom I didn't mind being friends, but I was not ready to consider any of them as my life partner."

Two years after Kevin's fatal accident, Doreen began to go somewhat steadily with Charles. After three months, he asked her to marry him.

"I was unable to give him an answer at the time," Doreen said, "and I asked for a few days to consider his proposal. I had tender feelings for Charles, but I also felt that I was not ready to marry him just then."

Doreen explained her feelings to Charles, but the man continued to court her for nearly a year. Finally Doreen agreed to marry her persistent suitor. Charles did not have the depth of feeling that Kevin had revealed, but he was attractive, had impeccable manners, and, on the purely materialistic side of things, drove a Mercedes and always seemed to have plenty of money.

One night, less than a week before the wedding, Doreen lay tossing and turning in bed, unable to sleep. Her mind was full of thoughts of Kevin, rather than Charles. Her entire being seemed to be suffused with a strange uneasiness.

"How I wished that it were somehow possible for Kevin to be there to discuss the whole business with me," Doreen said. "I knew that he would be able to give me good advice, just as he had so many times in the past."

She began to cry, and she became aware of Kevin's voice calling her name. She sat bolt upright in bed, struck with the sudden realization that she was not imagining the sound of his voice. She was actually hearing Kevin calling to her.

Doreen looked in the direction from which the voice emanated, and she was startled to see Kevin standing solid as life next to her dresser. So many images began to flood her brain that she feared that she would succumb to the shock of seeing Kevin standing there and faint dead away. Then she became strangely calm and pacified at the sound of his voice.

Kevin told her that her marriage to Charles was a serious mistake. "You must not marry him," the spirit warned her. "He is not what he appears to be."

Doreen was so moved, so impressed by the apparition of her dead fiancé that she feigned illness and told Charles that they must postpone their marriage in order to give her time to recuperate.

Less than a week later, Charles was arrested on charges of illegally possessing marijuana and such hard drugs as heroin and cocaine. During his hearing, conclusive evidence was produced to prove that while Charles himself was not a chemical substance abuser, he was a "pusher," a recognized dealer in the illegal drug network. Under examination by the prosecution, it was also revealed that Charles was already married and had a wife in an asylum in another state. Tragically, she had become a drug addict under the ministrations of Charles, and she suffered severe brain damage when he had once injected her with some "bad stuff."

Two years later, just a few days before she turned thirty, Joel asked Doreen to marry him.

"I felt almost certain that an apparition of Kevin, my dear friend and guardian angel, would once again appear to let me know if my choice was a wise one," Doreen said. "Three nights before my August wedding to Joel, Kevin appeared in my room. He looked just as solid as he had when he had materialized two years before to warn me about

Charles. I was not shocked this time, and I waited eagerly for some sign, some signal from him. This time Kevin only smiled at me, waved a hand, and disappeared. I knew that dear Kevin had given my marriage to Joel his blessing and that he had waved his hand in farewell."

14

Light Beings from Etheric Vehicles

Whenever angels appear, they are described as strong, swift, splendid, subtle as the wind, elastic as the light. No distance wearies them, and no barriers hinder them. An angel entered the fiery furnace to keep Shadrach, Meshach, and Abednego cool, and another entered the lion's den with Daniel and closed fast the jaws of the beasts. These beings are proclaimed to be so much more than human—and yet, there is always something very familiar about them that expresses itself to the deeper levels of the human psyche.

Angels or Aliens?

Ed, a postal employee from Arkansas, will always remember the night when he was six or seven years old and was awakened in time to look out the bedroom window and see a whirling, bright, silver UFO disappearing in the night sky.

"I believed that the entities that began appearing to me after the UFO sightings were angels," he said.

One night, to prove their corporeal, as well as ethereal, existence, he asked them to turn on a desk lamp in his room—a lamp with a particularly stiff switch. The light came on.

"When I got a little older, I began to receive mental messages that I was not of this earth," Ed said. "I was told that I had come here to perform a special mission.

"These messages came to me in dreams and in reverie states, and they were delivered by silvery and bright beings. They seemed quite tall to me, and they wore whitish or dark blue tunics. Some seemed like patriarchal males with longish hair. The females seemed to have a kind of 'Virgin Mary' feeling to them."

A Warning Voice Saved Her Life from a Sniper in Jordan

Anna, an administrative assistant from Brooklyn, told of the time in 1970 that she was riding in an open jeep in Jordan. She was in the backseat on the left, and a nurse was on her right.

"We were going down a highway when a loud voice shouted at me in English: 'Move!'" Anna recalled. She was so frightened by the booming voice that she immediately jumped to her left. "At that instant a shot rang out, and the nurse was shot. I would have been killed had the bullet hit me instead."

Anna asked the driver if he had yelled at her to move.

"Of course not," he said. "I didn't even see the sniper!"

Anna then recognized the warning voice as the one who had spoken to her from what she believed to have been a space ship that had touched down on her grandparents' farm in Georgia when she was only five years old.

"I remembered that I had wanted to go with them then," Anna said. "But one of them said, 'We'll come get you when you are grown.'"

He Always Listens to the Angel Who Called Him "Son"

Michael of Seattle was five years old, alone in the wooded area near the family home, when he heard someone call him by his first name.

He turned around to see a tall, slender, silver-haired, pale-skinned man with light blue eyes. At his waist was a belt buckle shaped like a "glittery pyramid."

The strange man opened his arms to the boy, and inside his head Michael heard the being say, "I am pleased with you, my son."

Michael recalled that such a salutation puzzled him. The man was not his father. "Who are you?" he asked the stranger.

The silver-haired entity smiled and told him that in the course of time Michael would come to know him. And then Michael heard inside his head the words that would puzzle him for many years: "I am all you are, have been, and will become."

At that moment, Michael remembered that he was distracted by the voice of his father, his true Earth father, calling to him.

When he looked back to the stranger, he was astonished to see him fading from sight. "Don't forget me," the entity said. "Always remember me."

Today, at age forty-two, Michael stated firmly that he never has forgotten the being. From that remarkable day forward, the pale-skinned, silver-haired entity has come to him in his dreams or sometimes by voice only.

"Sometimes, he tells me things that are about to happen to myself, family, or friends," Michael said. "It always pays to listen to my angel."

Angels, Light Beings, Space Brothers and Sisters

When seen on Earth, angels have always appeared youthful, physically attractive, and commanding. They are, in fact, described the same way that contemporary UFO contactees describe their "space brothers and sisters." The place of origin for these benevolent beings has been identified as Heaven, hell, other worlds, other galaxies, or other dimensions. But as the eighteenth-century philosopher Voltaire once observed, "It is not known precisely where angels dwell—whether in the air, the void, or the planets. It has not been God's pleasure that we should be informed of their abode."

Although angels are considered to originate from a spiritual realm and a higher plane of existence than humans, it is often implied in the Bible that angels also may, at least for a time, manifest corporeal bodies to accomplish an earthly assignment. When in a physical guise, angels often have been mistaken for ordinary humans. However, many who have provoked a confrontation with the ethereal beings have felt the physical effects of their majesty. One touch of an angel's hand crippled Jacob after the two had engaged in a lengthy and prolonged wrestling match. The single stroke of an angel's staff consumed Gideon's offering. Zacharias was deafened by an angel's spoken word. Daniel's men fell quaking at the sound of an angel's voice.

While true angels steadfastly refuse to be worshipped by humans, they never turn down hospitality, and there are several accounts in the Bible and the books of the Apocrypha of angels breaking bread with their human hosts. By the same token, they fed prophets in the wilderness and undertook the great task of distributing manna, "angel's food, the bread of the mighty," to the wandering Children of Israel.

In relation to God, the Supreme Being, angels stand as courtiers to a king. They themselves are not gods but are created beings, as subject to God's will as are humans.

Is Jesus Returning in a Spaceship Piloted by Angels?

Noel, a musician from California, said that he has endeavored as a child, teenager, and adult to live as Christ would have him live. He testified that as a child he loved God first, Christ second, the Holy Spirit third, and his parents fourth—with those members of humankind who had been "saved" following after them. In spite of what seems to be a typical expression of evangelical Christianity, Noel also stated that from the time he was eight years old he has believed in the reality of UFOs, other intelligences in the cosmos, and the strong possibility that Christ will return in a space vehicle.

Eight-year-old Noel was riding with his parents near a Nike missile base when they sighted six UFOs. From that point forward, his family agreed that Earth was being visited by beings from another planet.

Visits to Giant Rock in Landers, California, a mecca for UFO enthusiasts, during the mid-1950s and 1960s introduced him to George Van Tassel and that colorful UFO contactee's belief in the benevolent Space Brothers. According to Van Tassel, he had traveled with the Brothers in their beamships, and he commented that although the benign visitors from outer space looked just like us, they were really more on the level of angels. Furthermore, a number of the Brothers had been living among humankind for quite some time.

Over the years, Noel, now in his early sixties, has had numerous dreams in which he envisions himself aboard the beamships with the space beings. And he maintains his belief that the Space Brothers and Space Sisters are warm and friendly, "angels in starships."

Do Guardian Angels and Spirit Guides Fly UFOs?

Is it possible that entities from UFOs are serving as guardian angels or spiritual guides for certain men and women of Earth? Or are we casting heavenly angelic guardians as alien beings because our advanced technology and our contemporary culture find extraterrestrial surveillance crews easier to accept than messengers sent from God?

Are the UFOnauts cosmic forerunners of Christ's return, or are they benevolent extraterrestrial missionaries intent upon disseminating spiritual teachings to the wayward sons and daughters of errant Earth? Are they, as some evangelists have warned from their televised pulpits, demonic servants of the Antichrist come to assist in the harvesting of condemned souls? And, of course, we must not forget one of the staples of science fiction: the *War of the Worlds* theme that fears that the UFOs sighted in our skies signal the arrival of malevolent entities from another galaxy who have come to reap the spoils of a soon-to-be-conquered planet.

If, however, we lower our expectations of visitors from other planets having arrived to colonize, convert, or conquer us, we must recognize that throughout the course of human history there have always been accounts of mysterious supernatural entities seen riding in fiery chariots, moving within mysterious globes of light, driving strange aerial vehicles, or appearing suddenly in blinding flashes of light. These beings—humanlike in appearance, yet somehow different—always seemed supernatural compared to the struggling and evolving species of *Homo sapiens*. These "Others" have been called Angels, Devas, Star People, Light Beings, and, on occasion, demons and devils, as well as gods and overlords. Whatever name was applied, the various activities ascribed to these entities have remained constant through the ages and consistent from culture to culture. If we are able to lower our expectations that every glowing sphere in the sky must come from "outer space," then we may consider the unidentified illuminated objects as "etheric" vehicles, rather than spaceships, and the beings who travel within them, benevolent or otherwise, of multidimensional rather than extraterrestrial origin.

In an analysis of the works of fifty writers of antiquity, the author and scholar W. Raymond Drake found references to such celestial phenomena as airborne lights, shields, fiery globes, strange ships, and warrior-like "men" with the ability to fly. In addition, he discovered mentions of two or more "moons," two or more "suns," new "stars," falling lights, unknown voices, "gods" descending to Earth, and "men" ascending to the sky.

Drake strongly believed that the old gods of Egypt, Greece, Rome, Scandinavia, and Mexico were not simply manifestations of lightning and thunderbolts. "By some strange twist of the human mind," Drake once mused wryly, "we worship prodigies in old Palestine as manifestations of the Lord, yet scoff at identical phenomena occurring at the same time only a few hundred miles away."

A UFO Became Her Agent of Transformation

Sherri of Brooklyn, New York, experienced her initial contact with multidimensional beings when she was eighteen. She was lying in bed one night in that borderline state of consciousness when two entities in dark, hooded robes floated through her closed bedroom door. Sherri was totally terrified, not only because they had broken into her bedroom in the middle of the night, but because they seemed so aggressive.

The two hooded beings pulled at her blanket and asked, "Are you ready?"

Sherri screamed at them, and they disappeared.

Her next experience with the beings occurred in her mid-twenties. She felt something gently touch her shoulder. Her husband was sound asleep, so Sherri knew it wasn't him. She clicked on the bed lamp, turned, and saw the "visitors" once again. As before, they disappeared when Sherri screamed at them, but just before they vanished, she was able to catch a fleeting glimpse of a large, pyramid-shaped light hovering over the bed.

Sherri's "ultimate contact" occurred a week later. At 4 a.m. she was awakened by a "visitor" calling her name in a soft voice. As she got out of bed, she saw a large, glowing object at her window.

"To my surprise," Sherri said, "I saw two figures peering out at me from inside the object. It was so well-illuminated that I actually saw the interior of the craft, and there were other beings inside, moving quickly back and forth."

Sherri opened the apartment window to get a better look at the figures and their glowing vehicle, but the craft suddenly appeared to transform itself into a flame. She remembers attempting to shout at them to get away from the apartment building before it caught fire, but then she heard a voice inside her head say, "Don't be afraid. Look at us. Stay at the window until we leave. Look ... look ..."

Ten years after the second multidimensional visitation, Sherri's assessment of the experience remains firm that it was a mystical one. She believes that night she began to undergo a spiritual transformation. "I became more compassionate toward people," she said. "I became cosmically oriented toward the evolution of humankind. I think about God. I often ponder the purpose for my existence. Sometimes I feel as though I am on the outside looking in at this planet. The UFO and the visitors altered my state of consciousness."

Snatched from the Path of a Truck

In nearly all accounts of angels, the beings seem to be paraphysical in nature; that is, they are both material and nonmaterial. Although they apparently originate in some invisible and nonphysical realm or dimension or vibrational level, they manifest as solidly in our reality as the humans whose lives they seek to affect.

When Bobby of Asheville, North Carolina, was five years old, he ignored his mother's warning and ran out into the street after his toy race car.

Too late, he saw the semi truck bearing down on him. "I'm now thirty-seven years old," he said, "and I can still remember just freezing, not knowing what to do. When I was able to move, I stumbled over my own feet and fell directly into the path of the truck."

Bobby remembers that it was as if time suddenly slowed, maybe even stopped for a few seconds. A husky man with straw-colored hair materialized from nowhere and pulled him away from the huge tires just in time. He rolled Bobby to the side of the street, right up against the curb, then reached down and rubbed his head affectionately.

"It's not your time yet, Bobby," he told me.

Then everything went back to normal time—cars were honking, tires were skidding, brakes were screeching—and Bobby's mother was screaming, picking up her son, and crying about a miracle.

In 1982, Bobby had a sighting of a UFO while he was vacationing in Wisconsin. "I thought right away of the angel who had saved my life when I was a little kid," he said. "I got the same kind of feeling when I saw that UFO as I did when I saw that big blond angel."

Are the Increasing Manifestations of Light Beings a Sign of the "End Times"?

In both the Old and the New Testaments angels are divided into two vast hosts: one, obedient to God and active in good ministries for humankind; the other, intent on annoying and harming humans and bringing about the enslavement of their souls. The angels may appear benevolent, like friendly travelers one might encounter on a lonely road. On other occasions, deceitful etheric beings have been accused of abduction, kidnapping, sexual assault, and even murder.

As we have noted in previous chapters of this book, in the teachings of Islam there are three distinct species of intelligent beings in the universe. There are first the angels (*malak* in Arabic), a high order of beings created of Light; second *al-jinn*, ethereal, perhaps even multidimensional entities; and then human beings, fashioned of the stuff of Earth and born into physical bodies.

The Qur'an suggests that while a certain number of *jinn* act benevolently toward humans and may even serve as guardians and guides, the great majority of the ethereal entities are dedicated to performing devilish acts against humankind. Normally invisible to the human eye, they are capable of materializing in our three-dimensional world; while they are in the physical plane, they are notorious for kidnapping human children and seducing adults into acts of sexual intercourse.

Such a division of etheric entities may remind the metaphysically minded of the famous psychic Edgar Cayce's concept of the primal warfare on Atlantis between the benevolent Children of the Law of One and the evil Sons of Belial. *Belial*, by the way, happens to be Hebrew for "person of baseness" and is often used to designate the prince of the dark angels, Satan.

The observation that the presence of Light Beings among us seems to be increasing has caused many individuals to conclude that we are drawing near to what some refer to as the End Times and the event that some religionists foresee as Armageddon, the final great battle between Good and Evil. The large number of angels or aliens witnessed by vast numbers of people in recent years is seen by some contemporary students of scripture as a certain sign that the supernatural warriors of the Apocalypse are arriving for that great final conflict.

Historians have observed that angels, demons, and other spiritual beings are always popular characters in apocalyptic writings. Skeptics dismiss current reports of angels and aliens as merely the externalized projections of fearful men and women who fantasize the images of benevolent beings in order to assuage the terror of existence in our contemporary world of chaos and conflict. Theologians and other spiritually minded people disagree and declare that the benevolent beings are increasing their manifestations because they have been placed in charge of the cosmic order of the universe and because times of crisis, such as those currently shaking the planet, summon them into the fray.

"I Am That I Am— Past, Present, and Future"

Pat, a schoolteacher from Ohio, recalled the summer day when she was eleven and saw two strange, glowing objects hovering above the lake near their home.

"That night something awakened me," she said, "and I saw a shining, silver humanoid being standing at the foot of my bed. I remember at first feeling the sensation of undistilled terror, but that soon changed to awe and wonder as I watched the being disappear."

Pat did not see the entity again until that Thanksgiving when she accompanied her father to take her grandmother home after her holiday visit with the family. "Dad and I wound up on a dark, winding road," she recalled. "It was icy and slick because of a sleet storm. Dad asked me to roll down the window and to watch to make certain that we didn't slide off the road and down the steep banks."

Pat remembers feeling very frightened, and it was obvious that her father was nervous and concerned for their safety. There was a very real possibility that they could slip over the edge of the highway, crash, and freeze to death.

"It was cold, and my face was numb and stinging as I looked into the darkness from the open car window," Pat said. "Suddenly I saw directly behind us and just above us a brilliant white light with a bluish center. I did not hear a voice, but I was unmistakably getting a message from the light—or from something. And I knew somehow that the message was something connected with myself.

"I survived that frightening, freezing night with the deep certainty that the white light had told me, '*I am*.'"

Pat said that it was not until many years later that she learned the significance of the *I am* concept in theology, as exemplified in the experience of Moses when the voice from the burning bush identified itself as *I am that I am*. But from that childhood Thanksgiving evening onward, Pat has been keenly aware that the message that came to her from the brilliant white light with the bluish center was the assurance that there was within and outside the very essence of her being an aspect that exists in the now, in the past, and for all time.

15

An Ancient Order of Spirit Teachers and Healers

Who are these mysterious hooded entities who visit humans to teach and to heal? Are they angels in a less familiar guise? Could they be a special group of "monastic angels" who relay messages of spiritual growth? Or are they members of an ancient order of beings from another dimension of time and space, another world, another universe?

A Child Meets His Angel

As a child, Jonathan suffered from severe allergic reactions to almost everything. He remembers his mother once sighing in frustration that it seemed as though Jonathan was allergic to planet Earth.

In the account he provided to the Steiger Questionnaire of Mystical, Paranormal, and UFO Experiences, Jonathan said that his sole form of solace came from an angel who always appeared to him as a cowled figure, much like that of a monk. Jonathan remembers the benevolent being's voice as gentle and soothing, filled with wisdom and love. The hooded angel's name was Jedidiah.

Jonathan said that he first met his angel when he was about five years old. "I started to fall down the stairway," he said, "and someone reached out and pulled me back to a sitting position on the landing. I looked up to see this bearded man bending over me and smiling at me."

Jonathan's twelve-year-old sister, Sarah, who was supposed to be babysitting him, saw him totter at the top of the steps, start to topple, then appear to fly backward up to the landing. Jonathan clearly recalled his sister's declaration when she ran up the stairs to check on him: "You must have a guardian angel!"

When he turned sixteen, Jonathan was startled one night to see a strange manifestation of a greenish, glowing ball of light that appeared in his bedroom shortly after he had finished saying his prayers.

"The glowing object just seemed to shoot around my room at great speed, yet never hitting a wall, any of the furniture, or the ceiling," Jonathan said. "And then suddenly it seemed as though my spiritual essence was out of my body and racing along beside the glowing ball! This remains one of the most exhilarating experiences that I have ever had—zipping around the room like an accelerated ping-pong ball that never had to touch anything in order to bounce. And then my spiritual essence and the glowing ball seemed to soar up through the ceiling and upward into the dark night sky. We seemed to dance among the stars. The feeling was absolutely ecstatic!"

After that liberating experience, Jonathan found that all of his debilitating allergies had left him. It was as if he had left his cocoon of illness and pain and emerged as a butterfly, free of blights and blemishes.

"I still had the occasional sinus headache, but all in all, I felt wonderful," he said. "I knew that it was Jedidiah, my guardian angel, who had assumed the form of the mysterious glowing ball to set my physical body free of all those restrictive illnesses and allergies."

When Jonathan contacted the Steigers, he was a twenty-eight-year-old high school sociology teacher and guidance counselor, who was popular and well liked by his students. "Jedidiah will sometimes enter my consciousness and speak through me to the students," he admitted. "Of course, neither they nor my superiors on the staff know that on occasion I channel an angel during some of my guidance sessions. Jedidiah has a knack for saying what people *need* to hear, rather than what they *want* to hear, so while some of the students might be stung by his initial comments, the truth of his counsel always rings true. And best of all, it always seems to help them."

Who Are They?

Brad Steiger's encounters with a hooded spirit teacher began with the image of an illuminated greenish-colored ball of light that transformed into the figure of the cowled being. At the time of the first visitation, Brad was thirty-six years old and was already the author of more than thirty books on the unknown and an experienced paranormal investigator who had witnessed a great variety of spirit, ghost, and UFO phenomena. And yet upon the hooded being's initial two visits, Brad was instantly rendered entranced so that he could receive a vast amount of information in a brief period of time. On a subsequent visitation ten years later, Brad was given more information, and upon the next encounter, Brad was given a dramatic healing.

Brad came to call his spirit teacher Elijah; Jonathan received the name of Jedidiah for his cowled benefactor. In spite of numerous positive encounters with these mysterious beings, too many people prejudge the manifestation of hooded entities as messengers of evil or negativity. Here follow the accounts of individuals who benefited greatly from an interaction with the cowled beings.

Healed by Hooded Beings

The Experiences of Douglas, a High School Teacher

Many reports and articles have come and gone about the frightening aspects of the hooded being phenomenon. I totally agree this experience can be very scary; however, my experiences with them have been beneficial to the extreme. My mother and I have been recipients of healings of catastrophic medical problems by the hooded ones.

My healing comes first in chronological order. To give some background to the report, I lived in those days in Salem, Oregon, in the northern middle part of Oregon's Willamette Valley. It was the summer of 1971, and I was a thirteen-year-old boy. During that summer the Willamette Valley was subjected to a major strep epidemic of a form that was very difficult to treat, even with the antibiotics of the day. I simply was not getting better, and I knew from the conversations in hushed tones by my doctors that I might die.

One night as I lay in the hospital bed something happened that shocked me and changed my life forever. Coming into my room was this "nurse" with a monk-like hooded cloak. I interpreted her as a "she," although in truth I do not know for certain the gender of the being. She was a bit on the chubby side and stood around five feet, five inches in height. Her face was nothing but eyes and a V-shaped ridge for a nose, with only an indication of a mouth. Her skin looked like more like plastic sheeting than skin. When she communicated, it was mind-to-mind, I never saw her mouth open.

She communicated to me that she had a solution to my problem. From out of her overly long sleeve emerged her hand holding a metallic rod, which was very knobby and looked like brushed aluminum. When she pressed the end of the rod against my hip, instead of injection pain, I felt instead a sensation like an ice cube pressed against the skin. By about 11 a.m. the next day, my fever broke for the first time, and I started getting better!

The Healing of Douglas's Mother

My mother had been having a series of strokes that left this physically vital woman totally drained. One night a series of events occurred that gave us a second experience with the hooded ones.

I was my mother's medical caregiver in those days. I had gotten her to bed and had gone to watch television and to unwind from the day's work. Around 12:45 a.m., about a half hour after my mother had gone to bed, her bedroom-access hall light came on. I went to check on my mother, found her quiet and asleep, so I returned to my TV program. About ten minutes later the light came on again, so I went to check things out. But I got only to the end of our dining-room table when some unseen force caused me to sit down and just look down the hallway. Through the guest bedroom door came three hooded entities who crossed the hall and entered my mother's bedroom. They never opened any door, and they moved in a floating, not a walking, motion. They came back and forth from the guest bedroom, as if it was some sort of staging area, and they carried their equipment in containers colored a flat-finish gray about the size of large facial tissue boxes.

To describe the Beings, they wore hooded monks' outfits, which looked very much like the garb worn by the old Spanish monks. A feature about them that struck me at the time was that they were very thin compared to their height, which was around six feet tall. They were almost pencil-like in their thinness. Their faces were solid black. I could make out some curved dimensions to their faces, but there were no features at all. Their heads were like eggs sitting on point and painted solid black with a felt pen.

They kept on with their work for what seemed like more than two hours. The next day my mother was totally better, almost as if she had never had those strokes. Mother stayed that way for around six and a half years, until a major stroke forced her into a nursing home.

I have no idea whether my mother witnessed any of the activity done for her benefit by the hooded beings. I never talked about the experience with my mother. Interestingly, there were physical traces as evidence of Mother's healing. There was caked blood left on her pillow case, which required discarding; and in the guest bedroom from which the hooded beings had come and gone, there was an ozone smell like that of a burned-out electric motor. All I really know is that I have a debt to the hooded ones that I don't know how to pay!

Douglas Finds Another Case
of Intervention by the Hooded Beings

A couple of years ago on a rainy night I went into the library of Oregon State University. I set up a one-night-only chatroom on Yahoo to check if I could get any reports of hooded beings.

I received one major intervention case of a woman in her mid-thirties who was a teen runaway from an abusive home. She made some bad decisions that led her to become the live-in girlfriend of a high-level biker gang leader in northern Arizona. This guy was abusive as well. She decided to leave the biker and change her life around, but the biker wanted nothing of her leaving.

The hooded entities showed up and thrashed the biker. She refused to provide any contact info, including where she was living at the time.

An Account of a Miracle Healing from Lee Moorhead,
Well-known Psychic-sensitive and Medium

I am going to share something that happened to me just after my twentieth birthday.

I had been trained originally to be a high diver, and I was practicing one of my dives when I misunderstood my coach. I thought he was giving me the signal to dive from a thirty-foot board, but the signal was actually for the man who was on the fifteen-foot board. So when I dived off, I looked below and there I saw my fellow diver just below me. We would have crashed and maybe been killed, so I threw my body out of position and ended up away from him, but on my back and unconscious.

I woke up in a hospital and kept drifting in and out of consciousness. They sent me home with my mother, who was a registered nurse, and she continued to care for me. It seems I had mangled one of my kidneys, which has not worked since.

But the part of the story I want to get to is that the first day home, my mom had to leave the house to get my prescription filled, and I was sleeping. Suddenly I awoke, and standing there next to my bed was a hooded being that I felt was male. He was standing there next to me, not saying a word, but I knew that he was reading out of a book, which I have always thought was a Bible. I opened my eyes to look at him, but I kept drifting in and out. The hooded being remained there, reading from this book. I was in a paralyzed state and could not speak, cry out, or move, but I did not fear him. Then he turned and went away.

Overnight my fever broke, and in a few days I was up and on my feet again. The doctor had told my mother that I should never have children, because I would only have the use of one kidney.

I paid no attention, and I had my family just a few years later. I felt that I was healed by the hooded being, and until this day I have told only a very few people about the experience. Now I am sharing it with you.

Using the Image of a Spirit Teacher as a Teaching or Problem-solving Device

The Steigers have employed this visualization technique very successfully in their seminars. Use the same relaxation technique that is given in Chapter 3, beginning on page 25, to place yourself in a state of receptivity for the following problem-solving device. Read the step-by-step process of complete body relaxation so you are as fully prepared as possible to meet the image of your spirit teacher. Although the masculine pronoun is used in this exercise, you may of course use the feminine pronoun if you wish to do so.

After a state of complete relaxation is achieved, have someone read the following text to you. You may also prerecord the instructions in your own voice. Soft, gently flowing music may intensify the experience. Be certain that the music contains no lyrics and that you have allowed at least an hour in which you will be undisturbed to be able to undergo the relaxation technique, the visualization, and time afterward to sit quietly in reflection.

See yourself walking up a narrow mountain trail in the light of a full moon. The trail is easy to see in the moonlight, and you have no fear of falling.

You are approaching an ashram, a place of spiritual retreat, wherein resides a very ancient and wise spirit teacher from a sacred order that is thousands of years old.

Take a moment now to experience fully your emotions as you walk up the mountain trail to meet the spirit teacher.

Feel deeply. Savor your expectations. The spirit teacher whom you are seeking is said to be able to answer any questions sincerely put to him. You are pleased that you have received an invitation from this ancient teacher to visit his ashram in this dimension of time and space and to ask him any question that troubles you.

Now you turn off the mountain trail and begin to walk up the path that leads to the front gate of the ashram. Be aware of your inner thoughts and feelings.

As you enter the gate, you are able to see the dancing flames of a great open fire burning in the center of a courtyard. You are able to see a hooded being dressed in robes sitting near the fire. You know that it is the ancient and wise spirit teacher.

Become totally aware of the spirit teacher. See his clothes, his body form. Look beneath the hood and see his face, his eyes, his mouth, the way he holds and moves his hands.

He gestures to you that you should be seated, and he hands you a cup of his favorite tea.

Raise the cup to your lips. Taste the tea in your mouth. It is a very special tea, exceedingly flavorful, yet mild, gentle to your palate.

The spirit teacher nods to you, indicating that you may now ask a question that is important to you—one that is troubling you.

As you ask your question, notice how the spirit teacher responds to your words. See how carefully he listens. See how thoughtfully he considers your question.

Observe the spirit teacher closely. He may answer your question with a facial expression alone.

He may choose to answer your question with a gesture of the hands or a shrug of the shoulders.

Or he may answer your question at some length with carefully selected words.

He may show you something. Some object or symbol may appear in his hands.

However he responds, he will answer your question. At the count of three, you will receive that answer. One ... two ... three. He is answering you *now*!

[Pause here for about two minutes to allow the impressions to come.]

What kind of reply did he give you? What answer did you receive?

How do you feel about his answer? Are you pleased or displeased?

How do you feel toward the spirit teacher? The spirit teacher tells you that it is now time to return to your dimension of time and space. Before you leave, he reaches into his robe and brings forth a leather pouch. He tells you that he has a very special gift to present to you. He wishes you to take the object with you.

He opens the leather bag and removes your gift. Look at it. See what it is.

Tell the spirit teacher how you feel about him and his gift. Say good-bye, for now you must leave.

As you walk down the path to the mountain trail, open your hands and look at your gift once again in the moonlight. Turn it over in your hands. Feel it. Discover all you can about the gift.

What deep significance does this gift have for you?

Understand that you have the ability to use this gift wisely and to its most positive effects to help you solve any problem that may confront you.

Now begin walking down the mountain trail, carrying your gift and the spirit teacher's answer to your problem with you.

And now, with the thoughts of the spirit teacher firmly in your memory, with the true meaning of his gift and his answer firmly impressed in your awareness, begin your return to full consciousness.

At the count of five, you will be fully awake and filled with the wonderful feelings of love, wisdom, and knowledge from your spirit guide and guardian.

One, coming awake. *Two*, coming more and more awake, filled with love. *Three*, coming more and more awake, filled with unconditional love from your spirit guide and guardian. *Four*, coming awake, opening and closing your hands. *Five*, wide awake, opening your eyes—and feeling wonderful.

The Mission of the Hooded Spirit Teachers

Although their original duties may have been assigned to them even before the Earth was fashioned, it seems that the hooded spirit teachers maintain as a considerable portion of their mission the task of guiding us toward ever-expanding spiritual awareness. As well as having been assigned to be present on occasion to give us humans a helping hand, it seems that it is also an integral part of their terrestrial assignment to lead us to a clearer understanding of our true role in the universal scheme of things.

Furthermore, it seems to be very clear to many humans who have interacted with the hooded beings that while these entities cast themselves in the roles of our tutors, they truly favor teaching us by example and inspiration.

It is in this crucial area of noninterference that the good spirits and angelic beings differ markedly from the entities who emanate from the Dark Side. The less benign beings have no compunction about interfering with humankind's spiritual evolution. On the contrary, they appear to delight in their attempts to thwart our spiritual destiny.

Throughout human history the benevolent beings have shown by their examples that the impossible can be accomplished, that the rules of our physics are made to be broken, and that the physical laws of this planet were created to serve, rather than subvert, the human spirit.

16

There Is a Timeless Garden of Love within Each of Us

Julian West is a young philosopher, poet, musician, and mystic whose insights have grown steadily in awareness and spiritual strength. Julian participates in Brad Steiger's group called the League of Seekers, and when the discussion turned to the hooded beings and their true identity, he wrote the following account of a series of inspirational encounters with such a mysterious teacher:

Prior to my initial encounter with a hooded entity in November of 2003, I had on several occasions over the previous two years dreamt of a feminine presence that I began to associate with the Jungian "anima" archetype. I was at the time struggling as a freelance writer, and I was having a difficult time finding the proper direction. Without going into detail, each of these dreams was somehow indicative of my adopting a style of writing that was more aphoristic and mystical.

In the weeks leading up to the incident I wrote in a journal entry: "I believe that conscious life recognizes the obligation—or rather the *joy*—in assisting life to be more conscious ..."

Then, on November 27, 2003, I awoke with a sharp pain in the left side of my head and neck that never abated. On the 28th it became even worse, and at work I found that I could no longer keep my eyesight focused, and from time to time a searing brightness would come over my eyes that almost seemed to temporarily blind me. No form of pain relief seemed to work. I got very cold in temperature, almost as if I was feverish, and began to experience spasms running through my whole body. I also experienced a very warm dripping sensation coursing through the middle of my head and neck.

Strange sensations of ballooning and numbness overcame me in the middle of the day. I was ready to check myself into the emergency room when all of a sudden it came to a shuddering halt. The pain completely stopped. It did not fade or taper off; it simply stopped. I was stunned.

The following morning, November 29, at approximately 5 a.m., I was awakened by a hooded or cowled figure (the height and size perhaps of a ten-year-old child) standing at the side of my bed. This figure I perceived as feminine even though I could not see any defining features, but only a hooded silhouette. There was a dim, ruddy glow behind her, which served to outline her silhouette and give the cowl she was wearing the appearance, at least, of being ruddy in color.

She took my right hand in hers. This was what fully alerted me to her presence, and I was immediately wide awake. I opened my eyes. She seemed to caress my hand, as if to say, this is real, this is actual, tangible; or perhaps, "I am real, I am actually here, I am touching you."

She spoke to me. I realized I had my earplugs in (I am a light sleeper, and after the previous day's pain, I wanted to ensure a full night's sleep), and I reached up with my left hand (she was still holding my right) to pull them out. I recall feeling quite warm and mildly sluggish, and I was having a difficult time coordinating my left hand in removing the earplugs. She let me know that removing them was not necessary—and I quickly realized that her words were telepathic!

She comforted me about the pain I had just been through and informed me that there was more to come. I got the sense from her words that it had been some kind of purgative or transformative physiological process that had caused the pain. She informed me of some sort of great task or undertaking that I would be embarking upon and indicated that some sort of realization I would soon be coming to, or some kind of experience I would soon be having, would be shattering. She told me that she would always be with me, as she always has, as my guardian and guide. I was, indeed, beginning to realize that "she" was somehow familiar to me.

Then all was dizziness and darkness. There was a bright light, and I seemed to fall back into slumber. I awoke again about fifteen minutes later, knowing that it had all been real and tangible.

Being well acquainted with various religious and philosophical traditions, I was immediately reminded of one of Joseph Smith's admonitions, given in the scripture the Mormon Church calls Doctrine and Covenants. (For the record, I was not raised in the Church of Jesus Christ of Latter-day Saints, but in the late 1990s I studied its scriptures and history in depth and still remain fascinated by the character and the paranormal experiences of their founding prophet.) The section I had in mind is section 129, which reads, in part:

"When a messenger comes saying he has a message from God, offer him your hand and request him to shake hands with you. If he be an angel he will do so, and you will feel his hand. If it be the devil as an angel of light, when you ask him to shake hands he will offer his hand, and you will not feel anything; you may therefore detect him ... whereby you may know whether any administration is from God."

I began to get the sense that this feminine personage, this hooded entity who claimed to be my "guardian" and "guide," knew very well that I was familiar with this passage and that I would use it as a gauge to measure not only the veracity of the encounter, but also her true identity and intentions. I began to identify her as something much like an angel.

Over the next few months my writing began to change shape. I began to formulate a different perspective, one I began to call "writing from within the Garden," from an *unfallen* state of being. In January of 2004 I wrote:

"There is a Garden in each of us, where we exist unfallen: where the illusion of the Fall holds no sway. Where Time has never begun, and where Life and Death are understood in all their wonder and perfection. Where Man and Woman are perfectly equal, and the relations they hold with one another are coequal to their relations with God. Where God is fully manifest in all our tasks and undertakings, and where God is always present and near and alive. Where we lack nothing, and where all desires and passions are simply the sacred urge of the Divine to explore the Creation in all its richness and fullness."

During this time I once again began to have dreams in which the same anima figure was present. I also found an aphorism by the Hindu mystic Sri Aurobindo that both comforted and inspired me: "They proved to me by convincing reasons that God does not exist, and I believed them. Afterwards I saw God, for He came and embraced me. And now which am I to believe, the reasonings of others, or my own experience?"

Then, on the morning of May 2nd, 2004, the hooded figure, my guardian and guide, returned. Having awoken from dreaming, but not yet fully awake (if I'm not mistaken, this is referred to as the *hypnagogic state*), I found myself kneeling down before her in a small, dimly lit room. I was kneeling not out of reverence, but in order to place myself at a similar height as hers. In her hands she held a small book, the cover and spine of which I never saw. On the right-hand page a single sentence was written. I blinked a few times and tried to focus on the words. The sentence read:

Within this lesser earth, a greater Earth has been planted.

As I read it with my eyes, I heard her voice reading it aloud in my head. As soon as I had read (and heard) the last word, that sentence quickly faded from the page, and another emerged into view. I read that one, and it was in turn replaced by another. I began having a difficult time reading the words, and the whole scene faded from view.

I opened my eyes, my heart racing, and grabbed pen and paper and scribbled that phrase down. Beneath it, I wrote: "Thus when the greater Earth bursts the shell of the lesser earth, it will seem cataclysmic. As a bud out of its seed. What is more surprising is that this phrase is definitely not nonsense!"

This type of occurrence repeated itself quite often beginning with the May 2nd visitation and continuing through August of 2004. I began to encounter her frequently just before awakening in the morning. In each of these encounters I would find my gaze transfixed upon an unnamed book held open by her. A single sentence or short paragraph appeared on the page. As my eyes examined the words, I heard her voice reading them aloud (or perhaps only telepathically in my mind's ear?). Her voice was calm and gentle, yet emphatic.

As soon as one recitation was completed, those particular words would disappear, only to be replaced by another sentence or paragraph. The pages were never turned, nor did I ever see the front or back cover of the book, or its spine. Several recitations would occur before I struggled to awake, that I might commit to writing whatever I was fortunate enough to remember. Later I began to have the same experience even in the middle of the day, or in the evening; it seems to occur in something like a hypnagogic state. Only my first encounter was physical and tangible.

As time went on, I became more adept at retaining the words shown to me, and I continued to record what I could remember in a bedside notebook I kept specifically for that purpose. Sometimes I would only see the words and would not hear her voice; other times I would only hear her voice and see nothing at all. On occasion it would happen in mid-afternoon if I had chanced to doze off for a bit. The hypnagogic space between sleep and wakefulness seemed to be the key to this phenomenon.

Occasionally what I recalled upon waking was only a fragment; a portion of those I tried to amend the best that I could, while others I left aside in their fragmented state, unfinished. I now have a few hundred pages of these fragmentary statements.

I currently have collected hundreds of these brief aphorisms or koans. I have just during the past two months decided to incorporate some of these fragmentary statements into the text of a metaphysical dialogue I've been working on. A portion of this dialogue can be found at http://upwinger.blogspot.com/2005/10/faith-of-future-dialogue.html.

I saw her again on the morning of November 5th, 2005. The very same morning I received an e-mail from Brad Steiger about the hooded entity phenomenon, and I very excitedly wrote to share the basics of what I have tried to recount here.

In this last instance, my guide presented to me a book very different from the one she had previously been "dictating" to me. This one was written in the "I AM" Voice of God. The book was probably only 100 pages in length. There was a preface of approximately seven pages, which covered the definition of the Great I AM in relation to both canonized and noncanonical texts, both affirming and criticizing the orthodox and heterodox views. Then she showed me the first chapter, the first paragraph of which I was allowed to read in detail. Upon awakening, I tried to reconstruct it:

I AM. Humankind is My incarnation on Earth, the representative of My Eternity in the present Here and Now.

Godly is your birthright, and Divine your proper estate, but this is never to be taken for granted. In all things done under the Sun, each Man, Woman, and Child must be inspired to explore the Infinity of his or her own inner Being, and the natural bliss of conscious embodiment must be guaranteed to one and all, and enjoyed to the utmost and highest.

In Mankind I AM the husbandman of Gardens both near and far; in Womankind I AM the midwife of both the newly born and the newly departed.

Although I do not recall her explicitly saying so, I got the impression that I was to bring this text to birth in our waking reality. It is a task I look forward to with great hope.

One incident I have remembered in connection with the above account is a dream a very close friend of mine had about five years ago. In the dream he was in a vast library where I was holding certain books open for him to read, very excitedly pointing out certain passages. The contents were indeed revelatory to him also. He tried to remember what he had read upon awakening, but never could. For days it haunted him, and he tried to recall what he saw written there. But he never did.

If the collected wisdom of many worlds could be compiled and arranged in a vast library, then I would regard the hooded feminine presence in my life as its master librarian. Perhaps she is currently engaged in the task of having a condensed version of this wisdom disseminated among us. Whatever the reason behind it all, I, for one, feel grateful and humbled by the tasks I feel she has entrusted to me.

17

Angels Do So Want to Help

Clarisa Bernhardt says that angels are all around us and want to help us. On several occasions, the angels have specifically said to her, "We do so want to help, but people must ask."

It is her earnest belief that all people can achieve their own personal communication with benevolent beings. The attractive, soft-spoken seeress, who currently resides in Winnipeg, Manitoba, maintains that every person should be able to receive guidance and understanding of a personal solution from his or her contact with angelic beings.

"I have been blessed with so many angelic communications since I was a child," she said. "My mother told me that even as a young girl of two and three years old, I always spoke of seeing angels. Growing up in the Bible Belt of Oklahoma, as I did, it was not easy for everyone to understand a little girl who said she saw and spoke to angels."

Clarisa has always been thankful—and sometimes amazed—for the many gifts of vision that have been bestowed upon her, but she firmly believes that all people are in communication with the higher realms much more than they realize.

"If you do not 'see' the angels with your physical eyes, you can be more easily aware of them by feeling their presence with the essence of your heart," Clarisa said. "Many people speak now of doing 'random acts of kindness' and remaining anonymous. This wonderful gesture is certainly mirrored in the angelic realm."

Guidelines for Angelic Communications

Clarisa told of an occasion when she was given the privilege of asking some questions of an angel who appeared to her. Clarisa knew that she and the angel had established telepathic communication, and Clarisa was trying to organize her questions so she might present them properly and respectfully.

"My thought field momentarily went blank," Clarisa said, "and while I was regaining my focus, I wondered to myself what the beautiful angel's name might be. I did not intend my unspoken curiosity to be a question, but I heard her say to me as she smiled, 'A name isn't necessary. It is work and effort that counts.'"

Clarisa also believes that it is important to acknowledge that an event that includes angelic communication additionally gives one the bonus of being able to turn earthly attentions inward to reflect on the higher radiance that may not always be easily visible to one's earthly vision.

Throughout the years, many people have told Clarisa that they have benefited from using the guidelines for angelic communication that she shares with them in her private counseling. We are pleased that she has consented to share a number of valuable lessons for this book.

On one special morning, Clarisa listened eagerly to the communication from the angels as they spoke to her from the sacred space that allows visions of another "somewhere" to manifest on the "inner viewing screen" of the human mind:

Perhaps it could also be described as a sort of "Star Trek" kind of communication that appears on a screen from "inner space," which sometimes occurs just as you are returning from a night's sleep—but not yet quite awake. I was back in the Earth realm with earth eyes still closed; and yet, I easily observed their peaceful manner, seeing them as they appeared so majestically. It was once again confirmed to me that angels *do have wings*!

In all my other visions, after a message is delivered, the angels usually go rather quickly. This time, however, they remained. This activated my curiosity, which was quickly resolved. One of the angels stepped forward and continued speaking to me telepathically, and powerful projections echoed through the ears of my mind in these exact words: "We are so surprised that more people don't ask us for help!"

Clarisa said that this angel was dressed in a white robe that matched the brilliant snow-whiteness of its wings. He stepped back to join the other two angels, and this time they instantly vanished.

Ever since that special moment, Clarisa has tried to share this message with others, saying:

> I want everyone to know that it is important to focus on the angelic realm and to be excited about these divine beings caring so much to want to help us here in the Earth realm. In moments of further meditation on this special visit from our winged friends, it became crystal clear to me that by our communicating with the angels and asking for their help in important issues and concerns in our lives, we are helping the angels to fulfill their mission of being of service.

> We can tell the angels our problems as we visualize them our own mind's eye, but we should keep our requests realistic, and we must always thank them for any help that they can bring to us or to others for whom we ask help. And of course we should never ask for anything that would cause pain to the heart of another.

Clarisa never fails to declare how very blessed she has been to have received angelic communications over the years, and she has often promised how delighted people will be when they learn to ask the angels for their blessings to be showered upon them. "You will be so thankful for the interesting solutions that will come about and for the lovely bonus of being in a better space with new opportunities to let your own light shine brighter," she said.

Clarisa reminds people to be prayerful and thoughtful in their requests of the angels: "Remember to use care in what you ask for—because you just might get it."

Sometimes peoples' life paths can be very stressful and painful, and Clarisa has herself found it so important to receive that bit of extra hope so magnificently brought about by angelic communication. "We can be lifted to new possibilities that are exceptional and that will manifest through angelic assistance," she said, "and sometimes angelic intervention can help the extraordinary to become possible."

The Angels Sing

In April 2004, Clarisa had become so overwhelmed by the pain and sorrows of others that she found herself in a vortex of despair. She meditated and prayed and asked for angelic help.

"The next morning as I was awakening," she said, "I heard a song that was just beautiful and filled with vibrant energy being sung by voices I somehow seemed to recognize. The song was so powerful, so lovely. I quickly ran to my computer to write down the lyrics, but to my dismay, the song's words just seemed to fade away."

Later in the day, Clarisa was thrilled to once again hear the beautiful angelic song, and this time it transformed itself from song into one of the most incredible visions that she has ever experienced. "It certainly is in my 'top-ten list' of visions," she said, "and the vision and the song seemed to be under the direction of the Angel Raphael, who actually appeared to me. Raphael is known for his healing abilities, among other blessings, so I was able to write the words of the song down quite easily—and this time I remembered the music that accompanied the lyrics."

Later, when she performed the song for David Williams, a friend of hers who is a singer, he made certain that Clarisa got the angel song produced professionally.

"While it was being recorded in the studio," Clarisa said, "David experienced angelic communications about the song even as he was singing it—as did others who were in the studio, including the sound engineers. And what was impressive to me was that these were people I had never met before, and they were aware that something most unusual was occurring—and it was to them seemingly angelic. It was impressive."

Many people who have heard the song feel that it has great healing qualities, and there are plans to release the recording so that many others may benefit from Raphael's gift to Clarisa and to all those who feel heavy of heart and under stress from the trials and tribulations of life on Earth.

"Interestingly," Clarisa observed, "this period seemed to be a time of visions arriving rather quickly, for within a month of the song given to me by Raphael, another message of encouragement was given to me by an angel to share. Hopefully it will be helpful to the readers of this book."

"Look to the Light"

The following is an "Angelic encouragement"™ given to Clarisa Bernhardt on May 14, 2004, at 6 p.m. by a shining angelic presence. This work is happily acknowledged and hopefully shared to offer encouragement to each of you as you travel on life's sometimes mysterious path.

Sometimes you cry for the things that could have been and almost became ...

And yet you must move on ...

For the call of eternity does not still with the night,

Its gentle urging comes deep from within

    and

You move forward once again ... not daring to look back or

To become imprisoned once more by the emotion

That locks the door to the heart.

So go forward and hold your head up high ...

    and

Look up as you listen to the call of your soul as it guides you through the night.

For certain there will be a turn and a twist in the road ...

Just keep your eyes on the light ...

    for

The dawn will return and with your soul as a guide ...

You will reach the end of the night.

18

Benevolent Healing Visitors

Many have had occasion to pray for the sick, asking for angelic assistance, when medical healing has reached its limits.

Waiting Room Angel

Gloria accompanied her friend to the hospital for emotional support when Jayne's three-year-old son underwent brain surgery for a mysterious growth that the doctors suspected might be a brain tumor. During the boy's surgery the two mothers were joined by their pastor, who prayed that God would send an angel to protect the child during his ordeal.

Gloria said that at the moment that the pastor prayed for an angel, she saw a broad-shouldered being manifest between them. The glorious entity wore a long, flowing robe that touched the floor. She said nothing about the angel's appearance because, as she said later, she was completely dumbfounded by the manifestation.

As Gloria sat awestruck by the magnificent angel, who stood not more than two feet from them, a nurse came into the waiting room with the wonderful news that the growth in Jayne's son brain wasn't cancerous and would pose no serious problems or after-effects in his life.

Gloria kept the appearance of the angel to herself for more than nine years before she finally made up her mind to reveal the experience to Jayne. She was amazed when Jayne admitted that she, too, had seen the angel and felt its blessing as it held its arms outstretched over them in their time of need.

Healing by a Beautiful Angel-Song

When Paula was thirteen she fell desperately ill with a rare blood disease, and after a long period of convalescence she was placed in a hospital. Her parents were very devout, and as she slipped in and out of consciousness, Paula heard her mother talking about taking her to Lourdes or to a healing shrine in the United States. That's when Paula knew her condition must be very serious.

Late one evening, after her parents had gone to the hospital cafeteria to get something to eat, Paula overheard a doctor and a nurse freely discussing her prognosis just outside the door of her room. The doctor had made the same assumption as her parents, that she was sleeping, but Paula could clearly hear him telling the nurse that it was doubtful that Paula would survive the night. He was confiding in the nurse that he was summoning the courage to tell her parents and admitting that the part of his profession that he hated was the task of informing hopeful parents that all hope for their child had passed. The nurse sympathized with the doctor and said she would call a priest to administer last rites.

Paula told us that she then began to pray with every ounce of what little strength of will and purpose she had left. She asked God to heal her, and in her thirteen-year-old state of innocence and belief, she fully expected to receive a miracle.

Paula clearly remembered feeling as if her hospital bed were tilting crazily. Then it was as if the entire room was spinning.

"I seemed to leave my bed and float up toward the ceiling," she said, "but I could see that *I* was really still on the bed. My consciousness, though—my spirit—was up on the ceiling looking down on the physical me."

At her birthday celebrations when Paula was very little, her father would often take a balloon, blow it up and tie the end, then rub it against his sweater or shirt to build up static electricity. Once he had performed this little ritual, he would stick the balloon up on the ceiling or on the wall way up high where none of the children could reach it. That was how Paula felt then, like a balloon stuck on the ceiling of the hospital room.

Paula was confused, then frightened: Had she died? If the doctor was right, then she had died without even getting to say good-bye to her mom and dad. That made her feel very sad. If she had died and this was God's idea of the miracle for which she had been praying, then the Almighty's concept of the miraculous certainly did not coincide with her own.

Paula felt herself moving through the ceiling. "It actually kind of tickled as I felt myself sort of oozing upward through the construction materials of the ceiling," Paula remembered. "And then, whoosh! I was somewhere way out in space."

At first there seemed to be nothing but darkness all around her. It was much better floating above her body in the hospital room, and she wanted to go back. Then Paula heard someone calling her name. "I recognized the voice as that of my Grandma, who had died about four years before. I couldn't see her, so I called out for her to come and get me."

A slim shaft of light pierced the darkness, and it seemed as though far, far away, Paula could see an image of her grandmother. She seemed to be beckoning her, and Paula could hear her urging her to move toward the little speck of light.

Paula remembered that at this point in the experience she was convinced that she had died. "I was saddened because of leaving my parents and my friends, but I had always really liked Grandma. She had always held me on her lap when we came to visit, and she would make special chocolate chip cookies with marshmallows for me. So I thought that if I would be with Grandma, then death wouldn't be so bad."

As soon as the slightest thought of acceptance of her transition came to her, Paula found that she began to fly toward the light with much greater speed. She could see a small cottage with a beautiful flower garden. Grandma had always loved flowers. And she could smell chocolate chip and marshmallow cookies.

Paula's flight was suddenly blocked by three tall figures in lavender robes. She clearly recalled that one had a beard, so he was definitely male. "I think the others were female," she said, "but they could have been androgynous beings. None of them really looked like my thirteen-year-old concepts of angels. They looked to me more like people from the time of Jesus and the disciples."

The bearded entity told Paula that she could not join her grandmother on the Other Side. "I was upset by this announcement," Paula said. "I thought he meant that I was going to be taken to some other place, that I would be separated from Grandma, that I wasn't good enough to be with her."

The being explained that what he meant was that it was not yet Paula's time to stay in Heaven. He said that she must return to her body.

Paul told him that was impossible. She had heard the doctor telling a nurse that she was dying. Besides, she had been so terribly ill that she really didn't want to go to that diseased little body of hers.

The bearded angelic figure informed Paula that she would not be returning to the same body. They would heal it before she left their sacred dimension.

"As strange as it seems," Paula told us, "it was at that point that all three of the angels opened their mouths and began to sing this most incredibly beautiful song. My entire spiritual essence began to vibrate and to glow. I remember somehow feeling at one with the angel-song and, well, everything—the angels, God, the universe. The next thing I knew, I was opening my eyes in an oxygen tent. Mom and Dad were standing there with tears in their eyes, and the doctor seemed really surprised."

Paula heard the nurse telling her parents that it was a miracle. The doctor shook his head and said in a tone of amazement, "I feared we might lose her, but thank God, she's come back!"

Paula knows for certain that "something happened" to bring about a miraculous cure of a blood disease that her doctors had decreed was incurable.

"And that is about as technical and scientific as the doctors were able to be: 'Something happened, and the disease disappeared,'" Paula summarized the official diagnosis with a slight satirical touch.

For the next four or five years, Paula was regularly examined by doctors to be certain that her disease was truly "in remission."

"By the time that I was nineteen, they finally pronounced me officially cured," Paula said, now a healthy thirty-year-old mother of two. "It may have taken the doctors six years to accept the miracle, but I accepted it the instant God gave the angels permission to heal me and I became one with that incredibly beautiful angel-song."

When a Healer Needs Healing, the Angels Are There to Help

Priscilla Garduno Wolf, the well-known Native American artist, storyteller, and *curandera* whom we affectionately call Sister Wolf or, by her Apache name, Little Butterfly, told us of a time when her life looked very grim and dark—until a healing angel arrived.

It was 1979. They say that God doesn't give you more then you can handle. Well, I had seriously begun to question if that was really true. My husband had deserted me and my five-month-old son, Erik, after he found out I had cancer. My marriage had been rocky for about a year, and the mental abuse had grown pretty bad. How do you explain to your children why their father left? The hardest questions are the ones left unanswered. Life has many roads and many pathways to good or bad—it's what you do after the hardships that counts.

I kept telling myself that God removes all the bad if you have faith, but then I lost my home and my teenage daughter began having problems. It was hard to support a family and keep it together. Everything happens for a reason. We learn from our mistakes. They are stepping stones.

However, when you learn that you have cancer and are facing many hardships, it does make you wonder where God is. Things got worse and worse. Why had God forsaken me? I had to live to know my baby and see him grow.

One day as I was lying in bed in great pain, I could hear my baby crying for me. Then I realized that the day nurse had not come. My baby was crying and wet. He kept calling out, *Mama! Mama!* I felt so helpless. I couldn't move, yet my son needed me.

He crawled to my bedroom door with his empty bottle in his hand—and then he stood up, like someone was lifting him. There was a bright flash, and a heavenly light surrounded my son. I could see the spirit of a man, and I knew he was my son's spiritual guide.

The spirit began to walk away from me, and my son started to move his hand, calling me to follow. "Get up," the spirit guide said. "There's nothing wrong with you!"

I forced myself to get up and walk slowly toward my son. As I struggled in the hallway, it seemed like a million miles to the kitchen. You never think you can become so helpless until it happens to you. I fixed my son's bottle, then I dragged myself to the sofa, grabbed the diaper bag, and changed him. He was so happy; he kept kissing me. I dragged myself back to the kitchen, pulled myself up to the kitchen sink, and drank water like I was a dried-up river full of dirt. I felt the water inside me—and then I felt a touch of life within me. Within a week, I was healed by that angel who had visited me.

Now I am a *curandera*, a healer with God's gift. The Great Spirit has been there for me. I have been sick and recovered. I have raised my son to adulthood, and now he has children of his own.

I believe that I suffered hardships and heartaches so that I can better understand all the terrible things that people can go through. I know how people feel when they fear that God has forsaken them. My granddaughter Jessica says God gets tired, too, and sometimes he goes on vacation. That is why he grants some of us the gift of healing—to take over some of the work while he is away.

My only wish in life is to help others. Before I die, I want to have made a difference and left something behind to help the poor.

I keep a journal of my life. This story was the hardest one I have written. It still breaks my heart. But my son came with a wonderful angel to watch over him, cure me of cancer, and help the family to survive.

I had spinal surgery on November 5th, 2004, at St. Joseph Hospital in Albuquerque, New Mexico. On November 8th I was taken to Lovelace Sandia rehabilitation center.

A week after the surgery I was having a difficult time attempting to walk, and I was in great pain. One night my friend Marina Sanzuez Vaca called me from her home in Texas. She was attending a prayer healing for me at her church.

That night happened to be one of my very worst for pain. I finally fell asleep. Then, in a dream-within-a-dream state, I saw a bright light appear on the left side of my bed. Within the light, I saw a man in a white robe. I could see his feet and hands, but not his face, as it was covered with light. His hair was long and brown. I kept staring, because he was sitting on a cloud or something not visible to me.

I noticed that in his right hand he held a beautiful, bright blue seashell, and the blue color shone through the small holes of the shell. With his left hand he dipped into the seashell and withdrew gold-like pearls that broke into golden flakes in the air. Next, he sprinkled the gold flakes on me. He started at my head and face and moved down to my feet. The flakes seemed to drift slowly downward and enter my body. Then the spirit in the white robe vanished.

Later that night, I was able to turn my body on my own. The next morning, I told the doctor and a few nurses about my vision. Later that day, I got up on my own. Three days later, I was walking without support.

I feel Jesus had sent an angel with a seashell full of prayers that were said for me, and that all those prayers were turned into gold.

As an interesting footnote, my Apache grandmother used fool's gold dust to heal. She said it helped keep the body pure.

Four Angels Manifested to Correct a Mistake and Restore a Dead Teenage Girl to Life

The following dramatic account occurred in the 1930s and has been told and retold to generations of young people as an inspirational promise of the good that can come of staying right with God and the angels.

At the age seventeen Sarah Gunderson was a bright girl with a promising future ahead of her. Her years of singing with the church choir had prompted interest from the director of respected university choir, and in the fall Sarah would be going off to college with a music scholarship.

Then came the day in early July 1934 that Sarah fell ill. Her father, Dr. Thor Gunderson, was a prominent physician in the region of Eau Claire, Wisconsin, and he rushed to his country home as soon as the message reached him regarding Sarah's illness.

Dr. Gunderson desperately rendered what medical treatment he could, then admitted to his wife in a helpless whisper that there was nothing more that could be done for their daughter. Sorrowfully, the older children were summoned home, and the family gathered around the stricken girl's bed to await the imminent arrival of the Angel of Death.

Sarah was in a coma-like sleep for many hours. Suddenly she roused herself and startled her parents by sitting bolt upright. "Mommy, Daddy," she exclaimed, "I just saw my own funeral. I was with my guardian angels, and I looked down from Heaven to watch my own funeral at Good Shepherd Church."

Dr. and Mrs. Gunderson hastily called the other children, and when the entire family had joined Sarah in her sickroom, the teenager told them of her vision.

"I had just died," she told them, "and you were all sitting around my bed, like now, crying. Only I was outside of my body with my angels and feeling very much at peace. I felt so sad that I was unable to talk to you or to find a way to let you know that I was all right. I tried and tried, but none of you were able to hear or see me.

"Then everything got kind of fuzzy, and when it became clear, we were in Good Shepherd Church. All of our friends and relatives were there, even Aunt Mary from South Dakota. Pastor Jacobsen had a nice sermon and said lovely things about me. The choir sang 'Beautiful Savior,' one of my favorite hymns, and then the congregation sang 'This Is My Father's World.' I watched everything from Heaven with my angels."

It was heartbreaking for the Gunderson family to hear their beautiful Sarah describe a preview of her own funeral, but there was a strange kind of luminosity about her face that eased the sadness of the narrative. It seemed as though Sarah had accepted the fact that she was going to die and that her vision sought to accustom her family to the sad event as gently as possible.

As soon as Sarah had completed the account of her visionary experience, she confessed to some weakness, but she still wished to sit upright in bed and to visit with her older siblings, whom she had not seen for many months. For the rest of the afternoon she appeared to suffer no debilitating pains. Other than an unnatural pallor and an admitted weakness, there seemed to be no indication that she was dying.

In the early evening Sarah experienced violent muscle spasms, and her face grew taut with pain. Her skin blanched, and her larynx ceased to function. Their transient hopes dashed, the Gunderson family reluctantly gave up all hope of Sarah's recovery. At last, she lay still and closed her eyes. She emitted a deep sigh, then moved no more. Dr. Gunderson solemnly checked his daughter's pulse and nodded in mute answer to the rest of the family's unspoken question. Benumbed with grief, no one stirred.

Then the miracle occurred.

A deep, masculine voice issued forth from the girl and proceeded to give the Gundersons instructions on how to revive Sarah. "Take both of her arms and rub them as hard as you can," ordered the rather gruff voice.

Sarah, just pronounced dead by a practicing and accomplished physician, had opened her mouth—and it was clear to everyone that the voice was issuing forth from her lips.

"Hurry!" the voice demanded. "It was not her time. She is not to stay here with us. Take both of her arms at once and rub them as hard as you can!"

Startled into compliance, the Gunderson family members found themselves obeying the command of the invisible task master. As if in a collective trance, they began to massage Sarah's limbs.

And then a different voice, decidedly more pleasant, almost musical in tone, began to speak words of encouragement: "Good. That's good. But you should be holding her upright as you massage her arms."

Increasingly confused and baffled, Dr. Gunderson gently raised the body of his daughter. Mrs. Gunderson hastily moved a supportive arm around Sarah's back.

The gruff voice was back. "If I could have her legs moved so she could be set up on the footboard, I think she might be all right."

Dr. Gunderson attempted to effect the unusual request, but he did not move quickly enough for the unseen advisers. The entire family watched in awe as an invisible force lifted both of Sarah's legs and placed them on the footboard.

Now a *third* voice spoke up to contradict the previous order. "Really, now, don't you think the body should be allowed to rest on its back again? Please, let's move it back to the previous position."

Once again the unseen power present in the room acted without hesitation and without the assistance of any member of the Gunderson family. Simultaneously, the angelic force nudged the doctor out of the way and gently lowered Sarah's body to its original position on the bed.

The bewildered Gunderson family stared at Sarah's body, by this time completely uncertain what would follow. No one dared moved for fear of not being at the ready for any new commands issued from the unseen trio of angels or spirits in the room.

Nothing happened for nearly fifteen minutes.

Then a *fourth* voice began to speak to them in a soft and gentle voice: "I know this has all seemed very strange to you, but a mistake had been made, and we were sent to correct it. You see, Sarah is not to stay here with us. It is not yet her time. Things got a little mixed up, and we had to correct matters. Sarah will be fine, and she will soon be awakened and placed back among you."

Remarkably, the unseen angel with the soft and gentle voice continued to converse with the Gunderson family for nearly three hours. The benevolent being described many aspects of the heavenly kingdom and advised them to maintain a prayer vigil around Sarah's body until she regained consciousness.

At last the invisible entity bade then farewell, and all was silent in the room.

Dr. Gunderson checked Sarah's pulse and found it beating feebly. Everyone could see that she was breathing in slow, measured breaths. With tears of joy replacing those of sorrow, they were comforted and elated to know that the angelic healing visitors from the unseen world had spoken truthfully when they said Sarah would return to them. The Gundersons decided that their mysterious guests had truly been angels.

The family gathered around Sarah's bed and obeyed the soft-spoken angel's final command that they maintain a prayer vigil until she returned to consciousness.

It was nearly dawn before Sarah awakened from the trancelike state that had held her for so many hours. Although she underwent a lengthy period of convalescence, Sarah truly had returned to her family from the dead. The astonishing ministrations of the unseen angels had restored her heaven-bound soul to her earthly body, where it remained for seventy more years of an active ministry as a performer of religious music.

Angels Sent Her a Strange, but Very Effective, Prayer Partner

Rachel said that her oldest son, Rodney, who is now in his mid-thirties, had an angel keeping an eye on him with he was eighteen and had returned from his high school senior trip.

Rodney had come home really sick, Rachel said. At the beginning, the doctors thought he had a kidney infection, but an accurate diagnosis was not at all forthcoming.

"A few days passed, and he was to the point that he had to sit up to breathe," Rachel said. "We could hear the fluid gurgle when he took a breath. The doctors were not sure what was wrong with him outside of kidney failure. They did not know what to do. I was really scared. I prayed to God if it was his time to die, please give me the strength to get through it."

A few minutes after she had completed her earnest prayer, there was a knock on Rodney's hospital door. Rachel went to the door, thinking it was a family member. "It was not," she said. "I did not know the young lady standing there. She was dressed in an old T-shirt and worn jeans. She asked if she could come in and pray for my son."

Rachel was puzzled. Rodney could not be seen from the door by the stranger. Who was she? And how did she know Rodney?

The young woman explained that she had been trying to clean her house for a Bible study at her house later that night, but God kept putting Rodney's hospital room number everywhere she looked. She said it came to a point when she could see nothing but the room number.

"We went over to Rodney and kneeled down at his bedside to pray," Rachel said. "We were holding hands while we were praying, but I felt other hands on my shoulder. I reached up to touch whoever was there—and there was no one! I could not say anything but, 'Thank you, Lord.'"

When they finished praying, the young lady stood up and told Rachel that Rodney would be fine, but she needed to take him to Birmingham as soon as possible. Rachel assured her unknown prayer partner that she would move Rodney to Birmingham.

"At Birmingham, the head urologist told me that Rod's oxygen assimilation was so low that it was remarkable that he had not been comatose for several days," Rachel said. "I told him that I knew that, but I also knew that Rodney was going to be fine. The doctor noted that Rodney's blood pressure had been 220/180 for several days. The doctor told me that, speaking frankly, he could not promise me that my son would live another thirty minutes. I told him I understood what he was saying, but Rodney would be fine."

In twenty-four hours, Rodney once again had a normal blood pressure.

"The doctors had no explanation for Rodney's sudden illness, and they certainly had none for his miraculous recovery," Rachel said. "But I knew without a doubt that the Lord and his Guardian Angel had taken care of Rodney. I also told Rodney that God had a job for him someday."

Rachel is happy to conclude her account by stating that today Rodney is active in God's work. He is a wonderful father and husband, and his family attends church regularly. He tries very hard to live a Christian life and to help his fellow man in whatever way he can.

"I have a lot to be thankful for to the Lord," Rachel said. "I only share this testimony when I feel led by God to do so. May someone be blessed by our blessed experience with the Lord and with my son's Guardian Angel."

19

Angelic Yentas Who Bring People Together

Sometimes angelic assistance becomes necessary to permit two people to find each other and fall in love. From the angelic perspective, what brings greater joy or is more important in this world than the generation of love?

When David Met Tina

Dave, who lives today in a medium-sized city in Missouri, told us that an angel first manifested in his presence when he was a child of five. Dave was playing in the woods near the family home in Idaho. At first he couldn't tell if the angel was male or female, but the voice he heard inside his head seemed to be more feminine.

"The voice was soft and gentle, kind of like hearing sweet music being played on a harp," he said. "I will never forget the image of the beautiful entity. She said she would always be with me, guiding me, looking after me. She told me not to be afraid of her, because she loved me."

The angel contacted Dave several times throughout his childhood. The second time, he didn't see her, but he definitely heard her voice warning him not to enter a cave. He wondered why he couldn't go in; he had seen some older boys crawl into the cave a few weeks before.

"Then I got a mental image of a rattlesnake," Dave said, "and I pulled out right away. A few days later, a hunter told my father that he had shot the granddaddy of all rattlesnakes near that same cave."

A couple of times after that, Dave thought that he might have caught a glimpse of his guardian angel, but as the years went by, he had to be contented with only the sound of her sweet, musical voice speaking to him inside his head.

Dave always wondered what he had done to deserve such a wonderful guardian angel. His family was not particularly religious. They went to church on most of the religious holidays, but not too much more.

Dave went steady with a girl during his senior year in high school, who became quite upset when they went to different colleges. They wrote for a time and carried on a long-distance romance for most of the first semester, but his feelings for her cooled. During the Christmas break, he told her that he thought they should start seeing other people.

Dave said that he had expected some tears, but she said a lot of cruel, personal things that really hurt his feelings. When he left her place, he felt confused and wondered if he had done the right thing. But then he heard his angel's voice clear as could be inside his head: *Don't despair. She is not the one with whom you should spend your life.*

It was Dave's turn to get really serious toward the end of his junior year in college when he bought an engagement ring for a stunning, dark-haired girl from Montana. He remembers her as vivacious, lovely, and filled with seemingly inexhaustible energy.

When he went home with her during one vacation break to meet her parents, he saw that her daddy owned a very large spread of ranchland. She didn't seem to be in any hurry to settle down, but Dave had decided that he didn't want to take any chances of her getting away from him. He made up his mind that he was going to pop the question one night after a lavish dinner at an expensive restaurant. He had even memorized of few lines of some romantic poetry to help him create the most dramatic effect when he brought out the diamond engagement ring.

However, Dave's angel whispered to him right after he ordered dessert and just before he brought out the engagement ring: *This would be a terrible mistake that you would always regret. She is not the one who will make a suitable life partner for you.*

With those words of warning inside his head, Dave told us, what had started out to be the night of nights became simply a marvelous dinner at a fine restaurant.

About a week later, the girl Dave had thought would be his life partner broke their date to go to the movies, pleading a bad head cold and a touch of the flu. But later that evening Dave and his roommate saw her dancing with one of the big men on campus, the son of wealthy parents, who belonged to the hottest fraternity.

"That's when my buddy leveled with me," Dave said, "and told me that he had heard through the rumor mill that the girl whom I had almost asked to marry me had been two-timing me for months. He had not wanted to hurt my feelings until he had some definite proof that she was messing around behind my back. Seeing her slow dancing with Mr. Silverspoon had pretty much provided such proof."

Dave said that he surprised his roommate when he said that he wanted to stop by the chapel before he went back to their room. Dave's roommate left him alone, thinking that he must be really broken up.

"Well, of course, I was hurt and upset," Dave told us. "But what I really wanted to do was to thank my guardian angel for saving me from making a very bad mistake."

Dave continued to date—much more cautiously—always looking forward to the day when the sweet, melodic voice of his angel would give him the go-ahead for a permanent relationship. It didn't happen for him until he was in his mid-thirties and becoming quite successful as a real estate salesman. He told us:

Tina, a very attractive young widow of twenty-eight with two small children—a boy and a girl—stopped by my office to discuss the various issues involved in listing her house with my agency. She lived in an exclusive part of the city, she explained, and because her husband had been killed in an automobile accident the year before, she did not feel that she could afford to keep up the mortgage payments on such a large house. Unfortunately, her husband had been woefully underinsured, and now she bravely accepted her responsibility to make the necessary adjustments in lifestyle in order to protect the future welfare of her children.

Dave nearly fell off his desk chair when his angel spoke up loud and clear inside his head: *This is the one: She is the one for you. She is the one we have selected as your helpmate on your lifepath. We have been waiting for her.*

That night, after work, Dave sat quietly in the darkness of his apartment and asked his angel aloud if she had truly meant what she had said about the young widow. The answering voice seemed to issue from all around him: *She truly is the one for you. She is the one for whom we have waited.*

Dave didn't mean to sound insensitive or unappreciative, but, he reminded his angel, the lady had two children. Not that there was anything wrong with that, but Dave said that he would feel somewhat awkward beginning a marriage with two kids already there. He felt he would need some time to get adjusted to married life before he could deal with children.

His angel answered: *It is part of your destiny to be a father. You need such life experiences for the gaining of your Soul.*

Dave protested that he was not saying that he did not wish to have children, but that he felt he would need some time to prepare mentally and emotionally for fatherhood.

Dave puzzled over the next response from his angel, but after saying the enigmatic words, she would speak no more that night: *You do not have the proper seed to father children of your own. The only children who will grace your home will be those given to you by another.*

The next morning he had an appointment with Tina at her home for the purpose of writing up a complete listing of the qualities and advantages that her residence might offer a prospective buyer. Dave arrived that morning at ten o'clock, and by three he hadn't even thought of his one o'clock luncheon date or of leaving the house. Before he realized what was happening, he heard himself asking Tina out for dinner that night—and what was even more incredible, he heard her accepting.

When Dave finally left her home at four that afternoon to drive back to his office, his angel was chirping happily: *It is as it has been foretold. She is the one for whom we have waited. She is the one for whom we have saved you!*

Dave stated that his angelically inspired courtship with Tina went so smoothly that it was as if some heavenly screenwriter were daily turning out the pages of a cosmic script that the two mortals were following to the letter.

They loved the same music, the same movies, the same foods, the same everything, it seemed. Dave had never felt so natural, so at ease with a woman.

"The very notion of seeing a lady with two rug rats would normally have terrified me," Dave admitted, "but her kids, Tammy and Rodney, were great. They were respectful and well-behaved, and they genuinely seemed to like me."

But the kind of biblical sounding angel talk about his "seed" not being "proper" troubled him greatly. He asked a friend of his who had once studied for the priesthood to consider, hypothetically, what an angel might mean if she or he referred to a person's seed. Once Dave had convinced his friend that he was not drinking and that he was really serious and really wanted to know, his friend told him that throughout the Bible a man's "seed" referred to his semen, his ability to propagate the species, to reproduce.

Dave thanked his friend, then hung up the telephone more troubled than before. Ever since Dave was five years old, his angel had always seemed to know everything about him. But now she was saying that there was something wrong with his semen.

Dave decided not to distress himself any further over the matter. He left a sample of his semen at a local clinic and awaited the report from his doctor.

"My angel was right as always," Dave said. "The lab tests came back that I was sterile, and I remembered the really severe case of mumps that I had had as a teenager. It was just as my angel had advised me: If I wanted to have children in my home, someone would have to grace me with them. So, I reasoned, what better children to have around me than the terrific kids of the woman whom I was truly beginning to love with all my heart and soul!"

Shortly before they were married, Dave told Tina that his guardian angel had picked her out for him years ago and had been shepherding him toward her corral ever since they met. Tina only smiled and said that with an angel guiding them, theirs should truly be a marriage made in Heaven.

Dave married Tina in December of 1987. Six-year-old Tammy was a junior bridesmaid and four-year-old Rodney walked a smooth course down the aisle as the ring bearer.

Dave said that he still receives intuitive hunches, and he is convinced that they come from his guardian angel. But the last time he heard her sweet angelic voice inside his head was when Tina was coming down the aisle on the arm of her father to stand beside him at the altar. "*Well done,*" he heard her say, "*well done!*"

Angels "Borrowed" a Pretty Blonde Lady to Bring the Steigers Together

In October of 1986, Brad Steiger received an invitation from his friend, Stan Kalson, the director of the International Holistic Center in Phoenix, to attend a public demonstration conducted by Dr. Caruso, a remarkable practitioner of polarity therapy who, although well into his eighties, was still actively engaged in the healing arts. Brad hadn't given Stan a firm commitment about whether or not he would attend, but since the demonstration was being held at a metaphysical center a short distance from his apartment, he decided at the last minute to go.

Brad took a seat in the front row so that Stan would be certain to see that his well-intentioned attempt to pry him away from nonstop work in his apartment had been successful.

Just before the evening's proceedings were to begin, an attractive blonde lady approached him and asked if he were Brad Steiger. When Brad acknowleged that he was, she introduced herself as Mary-Caroline Meadows and asked if the seat next to him was taken.

The pretty woman exuded a great deal of charm, so Brad was pleased to tell her that she was welcome to sit in the empty chair beside him. After only a few moments, Mary-Caroline turned to Brad and told him that she brought him greetings from their very dear mutual friend, Sherry Hansen.

Brad's charming new acquaintance suddenly had his complete attention. He had only met Sherry Hansen once, and he had thought her a beautiful, fascinating, and captivating woman. And even though the brief meeting had taken place more than four years before, Brad had not been able to get her out his mind. One reason for that fixation had been the peculiar fact that an image of a being with features resembling Sherry's had been placed in Brad's mind after a paranormal occurrence when he was just a boy of five.

"Is Sherry Hansen here in Phoenix?" Brad asked Mary-Caroline incredulously.

In 1982, Sherry had stopped by Brad's office in the company of her producer. At that time she had been on her way to Europe on business. She had read one of Brad's books and had wanted to meet him. Sherry was living at that time in Los Angeles, and Brad assumed that she still was.

"Why, yes, Sherry is here in Phoenix," Mary-Caroline said. "In fact, we take a class together. And last night in class, when I said that I would be seeing you tonight at Dr. Caruso's lecture, she said to be certain to say hello to you and to give you her love."

Brad was suddenly so excited to learn that Sherry Hansen was in Phoenix that his normally rational journalist's mind did not pause to wonder how Mary-Caroline Meadows, who was meeting him for the first time, could possibly have known that she would see him at the lecture that evening—especially since he hadn't known until minutes before the presentation began that he would be there. Brad's normal capacity for analysis had been completely suspended by his mental vision of the enchanting Sherry Hansen and the notion that she even thought enough about him to send her greetings with a friend.

Stan Kalson introduced his mentor, Dr. Caruso, and the energetic octogenarian began his demonstration. Brad observed with only a portion of his conscious attention. His memory was churning up some uncomfortable memories of his awkward first meeting with Sherry.

The moment that Sherry had stepped into his office in 1982, Brad had recognized her as the living embodiment of the fairy princess that he had seen in his childhood visions. But as fate would have it, Brad was so emotionally strung out at the time of the initial meeting that he held himself aloof from Sherry. Brad's marriage had disintegrated into bitter estrangement, and his acute embarrassment at the failure of the relationship caused him to transform his usual reserved nature into Mr. Freeze.

At the time that he met Sherry, Brad was the president of a small publishing company and recording studio, producing other people's books and cassette tapes, while striving to maintain his own career as an author, lecturer, and psychical researcher. Most evenings, after having worked on his duties for the company from ten to five, he would start work on his own writing projects. On many nights, he would often fall asleep at his typewriter and spend what remained of the night asleep on the floor beside his desk. Every day, Brad was forced to deal with the stresses arising from the financial problems of the company, the individual temperaments of the staff, the eccentricity of one of their principal backers, and the fickle demands of the marketplace.

When Sherry walked into his office that day, Brad maintained a cool, almost brusque demeanor, but inwardly he was screaming in frustration: "Dear God, why did you bring her into my life *now?*" It would have been unfair to Sherry to encourage any kind of relationship—even a platonic friendship—while he was so depressed. At this point his life, Brad had begun to believe that he was living under a curse.

What Brad did not yet realize is that when the angels really want to bring someone together with that special person, they will make it happen.

That night, as soon as Dr. Caruso's demonstration was completed and the reception in his honor had ended, Brad hurried back to his apartment to check the telephone book to verify that Sherry Hansen was living in Phoenix.

It was true. He found the listing: Rev. Sherry Hansen. Now all he had to do was to call her. Just pick up the telephone and dial her number. Maybe he could even say that he needed pastoral counseling.

It took Brad two weeks to muster the courage to call her. But as he sat alone in his apartment, night after night, he had a lot of time to think.

Just a few weeks before Mary-Caroline Meadows had brought him the welcome greetings from Sherry, Brad had experienced a significant dream about Sherry, a woman that he had met only once in the conscious state.

He had been visiting his childhood home in Iowa. His parents had suffered a house fire that had not destroyed their home but had caused them to move into town after a lifetime on the farm. As Brad walked around the acreage on which the house sat, he found the place where, as a boy, he had once found a magic circle in the grove. When Brad would stand in the middle of the circle, he would hear beautiful music and see the lovely, smiling face of a fairy princess who had auburn hair and unusually large blue-green eyes. At the same time, young Brad received an inner knowing that one day he would meet the fairy princess and together they would accomplish a special kind of mission.

That night in Iowa in his parents' home, he had a profound dream about Sherry Hansen, the lovely auburn-haired lady with the unusually large blue-green eyes who had walked into his office four years before. He was certain that she was the human representation of the fairy princess of his childhood visions. He was also certain that he would probably never see her again.

But now, thanks to her friend passing along her greetings, Brad knew that he still a chance to become better acquainted with this very special woman. The problem was, as more days went by and Brad had an opportunity to find out more about Sherry, the more nervous and reluctant he was to call her. Four years ago, she had left her resume when she visited his office. It made for rather intimidating reading.

Although she was an ordained Protestant minister, Sherry had also received national attention as a model, a writer-producer of television commercials, and as a publicist for some of the top acts in show business. If she hadn't developed a fever during a crucial shoot, everyone would know her as the "Excedrin P.M. Girl." If she had not been opposed to cigarette smoking, everyone would know her from the massive billboards depicting her as the "Marlboro Woman." She had appeared in small parts in a number of made-for-television movies, but acting was not really her thing. She even turned down an offer from Norman Lear, who wanted to build his first feature film around her after he had completed his popular run with the television series *All in the Family*.

Sherry had rejected opportunities that others would have "killed for" in order to remain true to her vision of elevating planetary consciousness. She had turned down offers to be an actress or a model to organize the Butterfly Center for Wholistic Education in Virginia Beach, Virginia, and to serve as a founding member of the Wholistic Healing Board through the Institutes of Health and Education in Washington, D.C.

Sherry was obviously a woman with a mission. And she was only a telephone number away from Brad.

Over and over Brad rehearsed how he would begin the conversation when he got up the nerve to call. When he finally made the call, he found himself speaking to a woman whose very voice transmitted vibrations of love, understanding, and deep wisdom.

But it still took him another three months to ask her out on a late-night coffee date.

In the meantime, they began to talk for hours, releasing veritable floodgates of communication. One night Sherry called Brad at one in the morning, and they talked until three. That was when they discovered that they were both night people.

Another night she called late to tell Brad of a remarkable vision that had come to her during a deep meditative experience. Although she found the imagery difficult to express in words, she had seen the two of them being transformed into living pyramids of light.

Brad confessed to Sherry that she had always been an enigma and mystery in his life. He admitted that he had flashed on her image a thousand times since they had met briefly four years before. Brad even got up the nerve to tell her about her resemblance to his fairy princess.

After more than three months of telephone conversations, they finally met at midnight for coffee in an all-night restaurant. Both of them wished that the night of conversation and perpetually poured cups of coffee would never end, but Brad had to leave the next morning for Los Angeles to give a lecture. The connection had been made, however, and on some deeper level of "knowing," the two of them perceived that it would be forever.

A few days after his return from Los Angeles, Brad received a call from Mary-Caroline Meadows, who in the weeks since their initial meeting had been away from Phoenix, conducting insightful research with dolphins. After they had chatted for a few minutes, Brad informed her that he was about to enter a business and research association with a good friend of hers. Naturally curious, Mary-Caroline asked who.

"Sherry Hansen."

There were several moments of silence. Finally, Mary-Caroline said that she didn't think she knew anyone named Sherry Hansen.

Brad was stunned. "Of course you do. The night that we met, you told me that you were bringing me greetings from our mutual dear friend, Sherry Hansen."

Mary-Caroline was silent for a few moments, then she repeated that she was certain that she didn't know anyone named Sherry Hansen.

Brad grew a bit impatient. "You told me that the two of you were taking a class together. Sherry asked you to say hello to me, to give me her love."

Keeping her voice pleasant, Mary-Caroline said, "Brad, I really do not know anyone named Sherry Hansen, so I could not have promised her that I would bring you greetings from her. Secondly, I have *taught* classes in the Phoenix area, but I have never *taken* a class from anyone in Phoenix."

Brad dropped the issue. But after he said good-bye to Mary-Caroline, he decided that he would solve the mystery of why Mary-Caroline had denied knowing Sherry, and he called Sherry at her office.

"I just had a call from your friend Mary-Caroline Meadows," he told her.

"My friend, *who?*" she asked.

"Mary-Caroline Meadows. Don't tell me you don't remember. An attractive, tall, blonde lady. You took a class with her in Phoenix just a few weeks ago."

Sherry was firm in her response. "I haven't taken a class *with* anyone or *from* anyone since I've been in Phoenix."

"Sherry," Brad began, becoming a little impatient with the whole business and deciding to come out with it, "it was because you asked Mary-Caroline to greet me at Dr. Caruso's lecture that I even knew you were in Phoenix. It was because of her relaying your message and your wishes of love that I called you."

"That is most interesting, Brad," Sherry responded a bit coolly, "because I will swear to you on all things that I consider holy that I do *not* know *anyone* by the name of Mary-Caroline Meadows—and I've never heard of any Dr. Caruso!"

By the time that Sherry and Brad had finished their conversation that afternoon, Brad had no question left in his mind: Sherry and Mary-Caroline definitely did not know each other.

And then, for the first time, it became clear to him. Mary-Caroline had been used by some unseen entity who had temporarily entered her body and her consciousness in order to bring Sherry and him together. In some remarkable way, angels had interacted physically in the flow of their lives. After all these years, they had brought Brad's fairy princess into his arms.

Sherry and Brad were married near the airport vortex in Sedona, Arizona, by the Reverend Jon Terrance Diegel on August 17, 1987, at midnight during the Harmonic Convergence. Jon's wife, Dr. Patricia Rochelle Diegel, was in attendance. The Diegels were two of Brad's oldest and dearest friends, who had always been supportive of all aspects of his research. Patricia and Jon accepted Sherry as their sister, as Brad had been their brother.

Patricia Rochelle, who passed away in 2005, had performed more than 50,000 psychic readings. She advised the newlyweds that they were not simply two entities coming together as one—they were the equal parts of a whole being. She also warned them that now that they had come together, forces of discord and chaos would strenuously seek to pull them apart, to break them up, to once again split the single entity in two.

The story of how the angels brought Brad and Sherry together has an interesting postscript:

About a year after their marriage, the Steigers were lecturing in New York City at a Whole Life Exposition. It was late at night. They were hungry—and nothing seemed to open except for a few all-night diners. At last they spotted a Chinese restaurant that appeared to be on the third floor of a building not far from their hotel.

There were only two other customers in the restaurant. One was a man who bore an uncanny resemblance to the actor and comedian Steve Martin. The other, his dinner companion, was Mary-Caroline Meadows.

Brad had not seen Mary-Caroline for nearly two years. Now, just to set his mind at peace forever, Brad would soon be able to detect if, in fact, Sherry and Mary-Caroline had ever met each other.

When, after cheerful introductions, Brad was unable to detect the slightest glimmer of recognition passing between the two women, he explained to Mary-Caroline what had occurred in his reality the night that she had sat beside him during Dr. Caruso's demonstration. She was astonished, and the story gave all four of them a marvelous, yet somewhat eerie feeling to know without question how subtly benevolent beings and angels of love can interact with humans in their lives.

Mary-Caroline said that she had absolutely no memory of having been "used" in such a manner to achieve such a high purpose, that of bringing two light workers together as one. But there was no question that her physical vehicle had been utilized to prompt Brad into contacting Sherry so that their mission—far too long delayed—could at last move forward.

Since that unusual evening in the Chinese restaurant, Mary-Caroline refers to herself as the Steigers' Cupid Unaware.

Seeing People Truly in Love Is the Angels' Greatest Joy

Although Marina was deeply in love with her boyfriend, she had grown tired of a long-distance relationship. She had lived in England for a year, and her boyfriend was in Canada.

"I told God that even though I was deeply in love with my boyfriend, I was going to split up with him if he couldn't come home with me to England," Marina said while she was visiting her boyfriend in Canada. "But I also told God that if it was His perfect will for my boyfriend and me to be together, if we were truly meant to share a life together, then I would trust Him and to find a way for us to be together."

Marina had a wonderful time with her boyfriend traveling all over Canada while they were waiting for his visa so they could go back to

England. However, the time came when she needed to return to England, and the visa had not yet arrived.

As Marina tells her story:

One night my boyfriend and I both at the very same time had the most intense feeling that we needed to ask God to intervene. We went to a nearby church to ask God for His intervention and His grace to bring the visa to us. We also asked that we would be granted some time to be alone with God in the church, and just as soon as we finished our prayer to God multitudes of people came in.

That day God showed us the true power of Love between two people in unity with Him. We had the presence of beautiful angels all around us. We were surrounded with the thickest atmosphere of love and peace, and we both ended up in tears together.

As we walked out of the church, we thanked God for the visa, even though we had no earthly proof of it have arrived. We knew that we got God's favor and that all would be done in His perfect timing.

On our way home we were both singing to God and just being a couple in love skipping in the snow, when my boyfriend told me that he would love to spend the rest of his life with me. The second we got to the front door, my boyfriend's visa was delivered. It was such a miracle and absolutely perfect timing!

Further, we needed to get back to England on the same flight. I asked God to let His perfect will to be done for us. Strangely, my flight was diverted though Amsterdam, but I knew all would be well because God doesn't do things half way.

I had learned in my life through a multitude of experiences that God is truly above everything, so I trusted Him to provide the most perfect way for my boyfriend and me to go home together. Even though flights were fully booked just before Christmas, we managed to find a flight for my boyfriend, going through Amsterdam, and he was given the very last seat available on that flight, which, absolutely amazingly, was the seat right next to mine!

God is truly awesome. He gave us everything we asked for in His perfect timing, which was totally and absolutely perfect! My boyfriend and I got engaged in Paris on my birthday, and we are now living a beautiful life together filled with more of God's perfect and amazing wonders.

The angels showed us that seeing two people in love and in unity with God at the center of that love relationship is what brings them the greatest joy.

20

A Very Special Night School Taught by Spirit Guides

As we read elsewhere in this book, the mystic Lori Jean Flory said that when she was a child the angels would come during the night and "attune" her. She would hear the tinkle of angelic bells, sense a change in the frequency or vibration of her bedroom, and then the benevolent beings would arrive to teach certain things so that they would be able to work together with her when she was an adult. On some occasions, they would rise with her spirit essence to other dimensions to provide her with instructions somewhere beyond the reality of her California childhood home.

As a child, Lori Jean admitted, the procedure was not really that much "fun," and she was sometimes confused by the process of being taken to other dimensions to attend night school with her angel instructors.

From an analysis of our questionnaire of mystical experiences, we have discovered thousands of men and women who have encountered spirit guides and angels since their early childhood. Interestingly, a considerable number of those who interacted with guardian angels and spirit teachers have mentioned attending some kind of other-dimensional classroom during the night and receiving extensive spiritual instruction.

Karen told us:

At first, two spirit guides would come to me and lift me from my physical body, but soon I was able to slip out of the body without their assistance. As soon as I was out of the body, I would receive instruction from spirit teachers. I suppose you could say it was like going to night school. During the day, I went to junior high. At night, my soul body was taken up to a higher plane to attend a spirit school.

I am often asked by those in whom I confide my youthful spirit instruction if such double schooling wasn't tiring. On the contrary, I used to awaken in the morning feeling completely refreshed. Now that I am in my thirties, I have developed my level of awareness so that I am aware of my guides' presence without leaving the physical body.

George said that he became aware of his spirit guides and his ability to leave the physical body and travel to Heaven after he had a terrible bout of illness when he was only twelve:

At first, it seemed, I was allowed simply to acquaint myself with the heavenly realms and to become aware of multidimensional levels of reality. Later, I remember clearly attending a class in a beautiful temple-like setting. Various spirit teachers came to instruct us. There were other boys and girls about my age. Some I have recognized when I have met them as we have grown older. A strange sense of recognition passes between us, and I know that they also remember me from angel school.

I regularly travel to the higher planes to meet with the spirits of friends who have passed on. I have been doing this for so long that it seems completely natural to me. When the time comes for me to make the final, ultimate projection to Heaven, I will already know my way around. I won't have to go through the period of adjustment that so many individuals have to go through when they leave their physical bodies behind in death.

Theodora wrote that she had been going through a lot of emotional trauma, raising four sons alone, becoming financially desperate, and beginning a new relationship that seemed uncertain:

Then one spring night in 1991, just as I was drifting off to sleep, something made me open my eyes—and there he was! I can still see him standing there in his dark brown robe, the hood closely draped around his shadowed face, a rope loosely knotted around his waist. He was about five-feet-eight, of slim to average build, and in the moonlight, his hand seemed olive-complexioned.

After an initial feeling of fear, I immediately became calm. He said nothing, but merely brought his hand very slowly close to mine so that the backs of our hands nearly touched. I think that our auras must have mingled somehow and that was the means of communication.

And then I remembered him—his soft brown eyes, his beautiful smile. I clearly recalled being taken by him to attend a classroom in the stars when I was just a child of seven or eight. I rejoiced in the glorious memory of attending that wondrous school of spiritual instruction taught by the angels.

I have a hard time finding words to describe all of this, but at that moment I was filled with a feeling of total and complete unconditional love. If there had been a gauge to measure my heart and spirit, I would have been at maximum capacity. The forgiveness and the absolute divine lovingness that he was conveying brought tears to my eyes—and I had the feeling that this was but one molecule of one grain of sand in an entire universe of love. I felt that if he were to turn up his love energy to full power, there could be no way in which my mind would ever be able to handle it. Then I fell asleep.

This visitation brought me back to my senses spiritually, and it seemed to have been a turning point in my life. In essence, I think that I was being told to "let go, and let God," and the memories of spiritual instruction received as a child in angel school returned full force to support me in my time of need.

Two Classmates of Angel School Find Each Other Later in Life

When Scott was seven years old, he almost died after being struck by an automobile. During his out-of-body journey to higher dimensions, he encountered a beautiful angel of light who told him that he was his guardian angel who would always be with him. Scott was informed that it was not yet his time to remain in the heavenly realms, so he was returned to his injured little body in the hospital.

But it wasn't long before little Scotty noticed that he could "hear" the unspoken thoughts of others. As sometimes occurs, he was returned to life with accelerated paranormal abilities.

"This can be very disconcerting to a seven-year-old," Scott recalled. "I was really frightened at first, but I soon learned to be very discreet about my new ability. Then, when I was eleven or so, I discovered that I was also picking up the emotional vibrations of others. This proved to be very difficult for me, because it took me quite a while to become truly aware of what was taking place."

One night, alone in his room, Scott's angel guide manifested before him in a glowing envelope of light and told him that while others around him might be spinning around in emotional and mental turmoil, he was to transmit a loving energy of tranquility and balance. His guardian angel also warned Scott that this task would not be an easy thing to accomplish on the Earth plane.

When he was thirteen, Scott was taken out of his body by his guardian angel and brought to a beautiful golden temple. "I was taught many beautiful things in this temple by hooded teachers, one of whom had a long, golden beard," Scott said. He continued:

There were a number of other children there that I could sense more as energy forms than as physical beings. Everything was explained to us students in terms of energy and vibrational patterns. We were told that there were many different levels of reality. As humans, we could only see one level at a time. When we recognized that we were multidimensional beings, we could perceive many different levels at the same time.

Good and evil, as we humans understood the concepts, did not truly exist. There were various levels of positive and negative energies, and whether we performed acts of "good" or "evil" depended upon our resonance to particular vibrational levels. Nothing would be negative (evil) forever. All energies would eventually be positive and pure and One.

One night when he was sixteen, as Scott absorbed these higher-level teachings in some other dimension of reality, he was suddenly able to see more of the celestial environment than ever before; and for the first time, he could clearly see the features of other human students seated near him. They all appeared to be teenagers, like himself.

When he awakened the next morning, one powerful thought reverberated within his consciousness mind—he was not alone. There were others like him. Scott remembered one student in particular—an attractive girl who had dark brown hair and green eyes. He vowed that one day he would find her.

Scott became increasingly popular among his friends, classmates, and teachers at the Ohio high school that he attended. He overheard teachers and peers alike talking about his "charisma" and the "optimistic energy" he exuded.

Scott became active in as many sports and extracurricular activities as his time would permit, in addition to helping out at his parents' neighborhood market. He was better at some pursuits than others, but that never seemed to trouble him. He told his friends who held back from joining clubs or trying out for sports not to be afraid to attempt different projects and activities, because there was really no such thing as failure. There is only the state of being and the opportunity for growth.

Scott dated only to fulfill social obligations at certain events on the high school calendar when it seemed appropriate to do so, but he had no romantic or emotional feelings for any of the girls he escorted on those special occasions. He knew that somewhere one of his fellow classmates in the angel night school was waiting for him.

For a quite a while, in spite of his dreams of finding her, Scott thought she might never show up. Then, one chilly day in November when he was twenty-nine, something caused him to turn around to face the person behind him at a bus stop in Akron—and there she was. Dark brown hair, bright green eyes, the same intense look that he remembered from those night classes when he was a teenager.

Although Scott was really quite a reserved person, he knew that this was the time to seize the moment. "I know you from somewhere," he said in a manner that he normally would have considered outrageously bold. "Somewhere really important. Almost heavenly, you could say."

She snapped out of her reverie, startled by a stranger speaking to her. He could read her expressions easily. She was almost ready to deal harshly with some fresh male chauvinist on the street, but after she actually took a focused look at him, she offered him a friendly smile.

"Why, yes," she laughed. "I believe that I do know you from ... *somewhere*. You are also very familiar to me. Was it high school or college?"

"You from Akron?" Scott asked.

"No. Chicago. I'm here on business for my company. I went to high school in a small town outside of Springfield, Illinois. I attended college at Northwestern in Evanston."

"Scratch high school and college, then," Scott said. "My name is Scott. Shouldn't we get off of the street corner and go somewhere nice and quiet and have a cup of coffee, maybe a little lunch, and talk about it?"

She said that her name was Sandy, and she agreed that they should do exactly that.

When he helped her off with her coat at the small, quiet restaurant he had selected for its lack of clientele at that particular hour of the day, he noticed that she wore a small, gold angel on a chain around her neck. Scott asked her if she believed in angels.

"Yes, most definitely."

As they were being seated at small table in the back of the restaurant, he asked Sandy in a soft voice if she had ever seen an angel.

She looked in his eyes for a long, silent moment. "Yes," she answered. "As a matter of fact, I have."

Sandy folded her napkin neatly in her lap and seemed to be somewhere else for a few moments. When she looked up again, she had tears in her eyes and she reached across the table for his hand. "And you, too, have seen angels, haven't you, Scott?"

It was apparent to Scott that a memory of having seen him at their angelic classroom in another dimension had suddenly returned to Sandy and flooded her with memories of those remarkable evenings spent in angel school.

Scott could not longer contain his feelings. "I've been waiting for you ... looking for you, hoping for you since I was sixteen," he told her.

"And I for you," she said softly, blinking back new tears. "I knew you were out there somewhere."

"I had prayed for years that she was out there waiting for me as I was waiting for her," Scott said, concluding his story. "I know that there are other angelically tutored kids out there who have now matured and are doing what they can to spread love and light to all the world. And I also know that new classes of kids are being taken up to the stars every night to receive spiritual instruction from their angels and guides."

Sandy and Scott now live and work in the Seattle area, conducting workshops and seminars and doing their best to create a loving reality in a world that is too often filled with negativity and chaos.

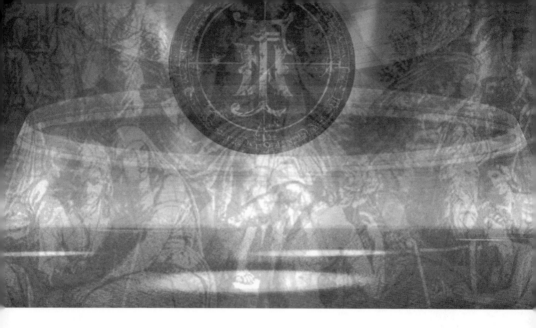

21

The Watchers and the Nephilim

What if, in addition to inspiring us, guiding us, teaching us, and forming our religions, the angels are also our creators?

Although some might consider it blasphemous even to consider such a theory, some researchers have suggested that a good number of us might carry within us the DNA of angelic beings. Of course, those researchers immediately clarify, our angelic progenitors wouldn't have been the ethereal benevolent beings, but rather the libidinous ones, the so-called fallen angels, who saw, according to Genesis, that "the daughters of men were fair" and mated with Earth women.

Scientists have often remarked that the laws of physics found in our universe are perfectly designed for our existence—too perfectly designed to have happened by accident or evolution. The science writer Marcus Chown recently observed that even the slightest deviations in the laws would prohibit the existence of stars and life. "If, for instance, the force of gravity were just a few percent weaker it could not squeeze and heat up the matter inside stars to the millions of degrees necessary to trigger sunlight-generating nuclear reactions. If gravity were only a few percent stronger, however, it would heat up stars, causing them to consume their fuel faster. They would not exist for the billions of years needed for evolution to produce intelligence."

The pioneering physicist Isaac Newton, whose discovery of the laws of gravity enhanced our understanding of the universe, said, "This most beautiful system could only proceed from the dominion of an intelligent and powerful being."

How is it that we are so fortunate to find ourselves in such a finely tuned universe? Edward Harrison, a British physicist, formerly of the Universe of Massachusetts at Amherst, theorized that our universe could be the outcome of an experiment carried out by a superior intelligence in another universe. At the most fundamental level, Harrison argues, our universe was designed for life, created by superior beings—which might as well be called angels. "Intelligent life takes over the universe-making business," Harrison says. "Consequently, the creation of the universe drops out of the religious sphere and becomes amenable to science."

In 2005 a group of researchers working at the Human Genome Project announced that they believe so-called non-coding sequences (97 percent) in human DNA is no less than the genetic code of an unknown extraterrestrial life form. Professor Sam Chang and Dr. Adnan Mussaelian said that their hypothesis is that "a higher extraterrestrial life form was engaged in creating new life and planting it on various planets.... We can't know their motives—whether it was a scientific experiment or a way of preparing new planets for colonization or [an] ongoing business of seedling life in the universe. If we think about it in our human terms, the extraterrestrial programmers were most probably working on one big code consisting of several projects."

In 1953 James Watson and Francis Crick made the seemingly impossible discovery of the double-helix structure of human DNA (an abbreviation for deoxyribonucleic acid). In recent years, scientists working to decode the molecule have discovered a complex language of three billion genetic "letters." Dr. Stephen Meyer, director of the Center for Science and Culture at the Discovery Institute in Seattle, expressed his opinion that one of the most extraordinary discoveries of the twentieth century was that a molecule of DNA—two-millionths of a millimeter thick—stores the detailed instructions for assembling proteins in the form of a four-character digit code. Although it boggles the brain, the amount of information in human DNA is equivalent to twelve complete sets of *The Encyclopaedia Britannica*—that is, 384 volumes that would stretch across 48 feet of library shelves. Some molecular biologists have speculated that a teaspoon of DNA could quite likely contain all the information to build the proteins for all the species or organisms that have ever lived on Earth.

Dr. Francis Collins was a self-assured atheist until, as a young doctor, he witnessed how the power of faith sustained his patients. Today, Dr. Collins is the director of the U.S. National Human Genome Research Institute and is highly regarded as the scientist who was in charge of the team that cracked the human genome. Unraveling the human genome, Dr. Collins said, allowed him to glimpse the workings of God. When he first had before him the "3.1-billion-letter instruction book" that conveys all kinds of information and all kinds of mystery about humankind, he felt a closeness to God, "having now perceived something that no human knew before but God knew all along."

On December 9, 2004, Professor Anthony Flew, an atheist, said that he couldn't explain how DNA could have been created and developed through evolution and that he now accepted the need for an intelligence to have been involved in the fashioning of the DNA code. "What I think the DNA material has done is to show that intelligence must have been involved in getting these extraordinary diverse elements together," Professor Flew said to Richard Denton of the Associated Press.

Dr. Francis Collins's research with the human genome has convinced him of a real possibility that God or some supernatural force outside nature created DNA. "It is not a logical problem," he said, "to admit that, occasionally, a supernatural force might stage an invasion."

The Supernatural Invasion of Earth

Another perspective on that supernatural invasion might be found in the book of Genesis 1:26–27:

Then God said, Let us make man in our image, in the image
of God he created him; male and female he created them. And
God blessed them, Be fruitful and multiply, and fill the earth,
and subdue it; and have dominion over the fish of the sea, and
over the fowl of the air, and over the cattle, and over all the wild
beasts that move upon the earth.

The Hebrew version of the Old Testament employs the word *Elohim* instead of *God* in Genesis. Elohim means many gods, rather than a
single deity. "Let us make man in our image," the Elohim say in 1:26,
"after our likeness."

Although most conventional biblical scholars insist that the word
Elohim is used to represent the many facets of God in his relationship
to Earth as its Creator, others have pointed out that the Hebrew language is carefully and efficiently constructed to denote gradations in
meaning by the structure and form of the words employed. Therefore,
some researchers affirm, the Elohim are members of a family, or even a
race of gods, much as the ancient Greek myths depict the Olympians to
be. Alternatively, the Elohim might be an extraterrestrial race of beings
thought by primitive humankind to be gods from the stars.

If we were to read the creation story in Genesis from the historical
perspective of our current awareness of DNA, the human genome, and
genetic engineering, the controversial account of the interaction
between the Sons of God and the fair daughters of men assumes a rather
different interpretation:

And it came to pass, when men began to multiply on the face
of the earth and daughters were born to them, that the sons of
God saw the daughters of men were fair; so they took them
wives of all whom they chose.... There were giants on the earth
in those days; and also after that, for the sons of God came in
unto the daughters of men, and they bore children to them, and
they became giants who in the olden days were men of renown.
(Genesis 6:1–4)

Of one type of angel it is written that "they neither marry nor are
given in marriage," which implies that they are essentially ethereal entities
whose number neither dies nor multiplies nor is dependent in any way
upon their ability to reproduce. The angels in Genesis 6:1–6, however, are
corporeal beings who engage in direct contact with a primitive species.

It seems clear that the ancient Israelites thought the Sons of God to be god-beings or angels, possessed of supernatural powers. If these particular Sons of God were physical or paraphysical entities, their "coming in unto" the daughters of men to produce "giants" could very likely refer to genetic manipulation, rather than actual sexual intercourse. If those fallen angels of Genesis should actually have been extraterrestrial scientists conducting experiments on female members of the developing strain of *Homo sapiens*, then rather than decadent heavenly beings sinning with Earth's daughters, they were scientists carrying out the directive of their superiors to provide nascent humankind with a genetic boost.

If the thought of angels or supernatural beings mating with or manipulating early humankind is offensive to some readers, there are a number of researchers who suggest that the genetic manipulation began long before "the daughters of man" with chimpanzees or other hominid species. Geneticists have estimated that the human-chimp lineages split somewhere between 4.6 and 6.2 million years ago, perhaps even earlier. A recent finding is that the X chromosomes of humans and chimps appeared to have diverged only about 1.2 million years ago. Females have two X chromosomes; males have one X and one Y chromosome.

One of the difficulties in hybridization is that the males are often sterile. In order to accomplish a new species, the angels, the Sons of God, may have had to utilize the female chimps for their program of creating humankind long before they fashioned the "fair daughters of man."

To further provide a possible answer to how modern humans may have emerged from early hominids, the astronomers Arden and Marjorie Meinel recently presented their theory that a burst of cosmic radiation profoundly mutated life on Earth and altered the course of human evolution. At a presentation at the University of San Diego, the host of the annual meeting of the Pacific Division of the American Association for the Advancement of Science on June 7, 2006, the Meinels explained how an examination of ice core data showed a significant surge in radiation roughly 40,000 years ago, about the time that modern humans emerged in Eurasia.

According to their hypothesis, the Cat's Nebula, discovered by William Herschel in 1786, emitted a burst of radiation approximately 200,000 years ago, around the time that Neanderthals began to appear.

Whether it was angels, genetic engineers from another world, or a mutating burst of radiation, one can argue for a cosmic or supernatural origin of humankind.

The Nephilim, Children of Angels, and Humans

The Hebrew word used to describe the giants of old—the men of great renown who were said to be the offspring of the sons of God and the daughters of men—is *nephilim*. Interestingly, the word used to denote human giants, as far as great stature was concerned, was *rephaim*. The Israelites found such giants among the Canaanite inhabitants of Palestine. Among these *rephaim* were the Anakims of Philisa and the Emims of Moab. Goliath was a Gittite, a man of great stature and bulk, but he was not a *nephilim*.

Information about the *nephilim* is derived largely from the apocryphal book of Enoch, which tells of an order of angels called "Watchers" or "The Sleepless Ones." The leader of the Watchers was called Semjaza (in other places, Azazel, the name of one of the Hebrews' principal demons), who led 200 Watchers down to Earth to take wives from among the daughters of men. It was from such a union that the *nephilim*, the giants or heroes of old, as well as the ancient practitioners of sorcery, were born.

The fallen angels taught their wives to cast various spells and to practice the arts of enchantment. They imparted to the women the lore of plants and the properties of certain roots. Semjaza did not neglect human men, for he taught them how to manufacture weapons and tools of destruction.

In Enochian magic, the practitioner employed words of power that allegedly had been passed down in an oral tradition from the times of Enoch. The actual evocation began with the chanting of the appropriate words, which varied from spirit to spirit. These words of power were said, by their very sounds, to exert a strong emotional effect. A famous example is: *Eca zodocare iad goho Torzodu odo kilale qaa! Zodacare od sodameranul Zodorje lape zodiredo ol noco mada dae iadapiel!* These words are supposedly from the Enochian language, believed by magicians and other occultists to pre-date Sanskrit. They were addressed to the angelic beings that the Magi believed would assist them in their magic, and they translate as follows: "Move, therefore, and show yourselves! Open the mysteries of your creation! Be friendly unto me, for I am servant of the same, your God, and I am a true worshipper of the Highest."

In all chanting, recitations, and litanies, the impact of a group is far more impressive than that of a single voice, and the Enochian practitioners always sought a group of individuals of like dedication. The power was heightened by a measured walking around the inside of a magic circle and dancing.

Again in the book of Enoch we read of what must certainly have been an ultimate lesson dealt to those fallen angels who had become embroiled with the daughters of men in such base designs that wickedness had become their mutual obsession: "Behold they committed crimes, laid aside their class, and intermingled with women. With them also they transgressed; married with them, and begot children. A great destruction therefore shall come upon the earth; a deluge, a great destruction, shall take place in one year."

The Great Flood: An Adjustment in the Experiment

In Genesis 6:5–6, we learn that the Creator is grieved in his heart that he had even made humans on the earth. Genesis 6:5: "And the Lord saw that the wickedness of man was great in the earth, and that every imagination of the thoughts of his heart was evil continually."

Perhaps an assessment was made that the experiment with the great majority of the apelike beings was not progressing as hoped. Perhaps large numbers remained at too low an animalistic level. The masses may not have developed the kind of cooperative spirit and compassionate soul desired by the angels. Only a few, the family of Noah, would be saved.

The Great Flood becomes a symbol of the time when the angels—or their superiors—coldly and dispassionately made the decision to eliminate great numbers of those primitive offshoots of humans and to preserve only the strain that would lead to *Homo sapiens*, modern man.

But the book of Enoch suggests that Noah himself was a very unusual individual, far different in appearance from his brothers, sisters, and friends.

In an article in the *British Medical Journal*, Professor Arnold Sosby analyzed the legend of Noah. He quoted ancient descriptions of Noah as a person with "a body white as snow, hair white as wool, and eyes that are like the rays of the sun." Such a description, Professor Sosby writes, indicates that Noah may have been an albino.

Professor Sosby's article also referred to passages in the Dead Sea Scrolls that told of Noah's mother, Bat-Enosh, being suspected of infidelity when the strange young baby was born. In the book of Enoch, Bat-Enosh tells her husband Lamech that the child is truly his son. "He is not the child of any stranger, nor of the watchers, nor of the sons of heaven," she insisted.

The Great Spiritual Warfare Between the Angels

Adherents of the monotheistic religions of Judaism, Islam, and Christianity believe that there exists a great warfare between the angels that was set in motion when Lucifer instigated a great revolt in Heaven before the Earth and humankind were formed. Armageddon, the final battle between the Angels of Light and the Angels of Darkness, shall occur one day (some say soon) when these warring factions meet on the plains of Megiddo.

Many researchers believe that such a great war between the forces of light and darkness raged in humankind's prehistory, and they supply evidence that someone once exercised weapons of formidable energy and power in the time before humankind was born.

Archaeologists have discovered strange areas in certain desert regions where it is apparent that temperatures once soared so high that large patches of sand melted into glass. Hill forts have been found with portions of their stone walls vitrified. Remains of ancient cities bear evidence of having been destroyed by what appears to have been extreme heat—far beyond that which could have been ignited by the torches of primitive human warriors. Even conventionally trained archaeologists who have encountered such anomalous finds have admitted that none of these catastrophes could have been caused by volcanoes, lightning, crashing comets, or conflagrations set by humankind.

Religious scriptures also lend credence to the theory that beings from other worlds may have prompted the destruction of Sodom and Gomorrah. The Russian scientist Matest M. Agrest has suggested that the cities were devastated by an ancient nuclear blast.

Moscow's Literary Gazette published an account of Dr. Agrest's theories as early as the 1960s, and Brad and Sherry Steiger were privileged to hear him discuss the matter in person a few years ago. In his view, simply stated, the two cities were fused together under the searing heat of a pre-Paleolithic atomic explosion.

In Genesis 19:1–28, we are informed that Lot is waiting by the community gate of Sodom when two angels approach him. Some scholars conclude that Lot must have made prior arrangements to meet these heavenly beings. After their meeting he escorts the entities to his home, where they are fed and lodged.

Such researchers as Professor Agrest maintain that if these angels were wholly spiritual beings, they would not have been interested in an evening meal, nor in a bed for the night.

Later, when the coarse men of Sodom pound on Lot's door and demand to "know" his visitors sexually, the angels appear to employ some kind of unusual weapon that instantly blinded the sodomists.

When Lot is informed by the heavenly representatives that Sodom will soon be destroyed, he chooses to remain in the city. Neither Lot nor other members of his family seem to take the warning seriously. However, when the morning sun rises, the angels urge Lot and his family to flee at once.

Those who subscribe to Professor Agrest's theory believe that a nuclear device had been triggered and the "angels" had been assigned to lead Lot and his family away from the blast area. They also point to the passage (Genesis 19:28) where Abraham, Lot's uncle, looks toward the cities of Sodom and Gomorrah in the dawning and sees the smoke of the blast going up "as the smoke of a furnace."

Other ancient texts mention flying machines, advanced technology, and awesome weapons wielded by the forces of light and darkness.

The sacred Hindu hymns collected in the Rig Veda constitute some of the oldest known religious documents, and they recount of the achievements of the Hindu pantheon of gods. Indra, a god-being who was honored when his name was turned into "India," became known as the "fort destroyer" because of his exploits in war. Indra was said to travel through the skies in a flying machine, the Vimana. This craft was equipped with awesome weapons capable of destroying a city. The effect of these weapons seems to have been like that of laser beams or some kind of nuclear devices.

Another ancient Indian text, the Mahabharata, tells of an attack on an enemy army:

> It was as if the elements had been unfurled. The sun spun around in the heavens. The world shuddered in fever, scorched by the terrible heat of this weapon. Elephants burst into flames.... The rivers boiled. Animals crumpled to the ground and died. The armies of the enemy were mowed down when the raging elements reached them. Forests collapsed in splintered rows. Horses and chariots were burned up.... The corpses of the fallen were mutilated by the terrible heat so that they looked other than human."

What Comes Next on the Angelic Agenda?

If the theory is true that the angels, a superior intelligence from another dimension or another universe, may be the creators of humankind, then we can rightfully wonder what is next on their agenda.

Professor Sam Chang and Dr. Adnan Mussaelian of the Human Genome Project, who presented us with their hypothesis that "a higher extraterrestrial life form" was engaged in creating life on our planet, remind us that since our DNA program was not written on Earth, there must be something more in the cosmic game plan. Although they do not claim to know exactly what that plan might be, they speculate that no programmers, whether from "Mars or Microsoft," would ever leave their work without the option for improvement or upgrade.

Science has known for some time that certain cosmic rays have the power to modify DNA. With this fact in mind, Chang and Mussaelian speculate:

The extraterrestrial programmers may use just one flash of the right energy from somewhere in the Universe to instruct the basic code to ... jump-start the working of our whole DNA. That would change us forever. Some of us within months, some of us within generations. The change would be not too much physical (except no more cancers, diseases and short life), but it will catapult us intellectually. Suddenly, we will be comparable to coexistence of Neanderthals with Cro-Magnons. The old will be replaced, giving birth to a new cycle. The complete program is elegant, very clever, self-organizing, auto-executing, auto-developing and auto-correcting software for a highly advanced biological computer with built-in connection to the ageless energy and wisdom of the Universe. [We have] the potential [to become] super-intelligent super-beings with a long and healthy life.

Chang and Mussaelian give notice that sooner or later we must accept the previously unbelievable notion that every life on Earth carries a genetic code for its extraterrestrial cousin and that evolution is not what we thought it was. Such a discovery may well shake the very roots of humanity and alter our concept of God and of our own power over our destiny. "With the right paradigm," the scientists say, "we may discover one day that all forms of life and the whole Universe is just one huge intellectual exercise in thoughts expressed mathematically, by Design, by Creator."

22

Majestic, but Not Magical: Spiritual Hazards of Seeking to Command Angels

We believe that benevolent beings are everywhere present and are waiting to make contact with those individuals who have learned to quiet their mind, body, and spirit and who have achieved an attitude of openness and receptivity that will enable them to hear the words of guidance and special teachings offered by their spirit guide or guardian angel.

In recent years, with the advent of a series of successful books on angels, images of heavenly beings have appeared everywhere. And as a complement to the great number of books, angel stores with shelves upon shelves of angel figures, angel candles, and even special angel scents to attract the heavenly beings sprang up in shopping malls throughout North America. The more conventional members of the clergy were astonished. For decades, angels had received attention only during the Christmas holiday when their role in announcing the birth of Jesus was acknowledged. Now, to the awe of serious students of holy scriptures, angels had become a national fad—one that was treading dangerously near angel worship.

While many of the most popular angel titles offered inspirational accounts of benevolent beings, certain angel experts emerged who promised a very special kind of angelic contact. These alleged angel communicators guaranteed intimacy with benevolent beings and implied that angels were some kind of magical servants who would carry out the bidding of those humans who learned the proper prayers (or spells) to command them. Some authors went so far as to lead their readers to believe that the heavenly messengers might be commanded to reveal winning lottery tickets and the names of the fastest horses at the race track. Other self-styled angelic experts hinted that the wondrous beings of Light could even be commanded to carry out acts of personal revenge on one's enemies.

We cannot imagine a true angelic being permitting itself to be transformed into a money machine or an assassin—however, we readily acknowledge that the fallen angels would willingly appear to obey any would-be magicians just long enough to ensnare their souls. It seems that understanding just how we humans are to regard benevolent beings is a problem that has been with us for many centuries. We must always remember the ancient admonition that while angels are powerful and majestic, they are not magical beings and they are not to be worshipped.

Various scriptures state firmly that true benevolent beings will immediately discourage any humans from attempting to bow their knees to them. On the other hand, the fallen angels, the demons, are motivated by their own selfish goals and delight in corrupting humans. They encourage mortals to express greed and to seek the acquisition of material, rather than spiritual, treasures. As a general spiritual law, these negative entities cannot achieve power over humans unless they are somehow invited into a person's private space—or unless they are attracted to an individual by that person's negativity or vulnerability.

Those humans who would seek to command these powers and principalities are cautioned to do so at their own risk.

Magic and Angels

The problem of discerning between the good angels and the bad angels probably began with the advent of magic in Paleolithic times, at least 50,000 years ago. In the earliest of societies, the roles of priest and magician were often combined into a man or a woman who had the ability to enter a trance state and commune with the entities who dwelt in nature and the spirits who lived in the unseen world. Our word *magic* comes from the Greek *magein*, denoting the science and religion of the priests of Zoroaster, who were the Magi, "Wise Ones."

The four main principles behind early magic remained constant throughout the evolution of magical practices:

1. A representation of a person or thing can be made to affect the person or thing that it depicts.

2. Once objects have been in touch with each other they continue to influence one another even at great distances.

3. An unseen world of spirit forces may be invoked to fulfill the magician's will.

4. As above, so it is below; as within, so it is without. There is nothing in Heaven or in Earth that is not also in humankind.

The desire to use supernatural entities to wreak havoc upon one's enemy or to acquire material wealth and power was very much in play during the time of the ancient Egyptians and Persians. The Greeks and Hebrews adapted many of the rituals and incantations, transforming the gods of the earlier cultures into the demons of their own time. This process of deity transmutation was continued into medieval times when the earlier gods of the Middle East became devils, the ancient mysteries and fertility rites became orgies, and the orders of worship for the old hierarchy of gods and goddesses became patterns for sorcery.

The deity most often invoked by the dark sorcerers of medieval times was Satanas, a direct descendant of the Egyptian Set and an alias for the Persians' Ahriman, the Muslims' Iblis, the Hebrews' Asmodeus and Beelzebub, and Pan, the goat-footed nature god of the Greeks, who later became the image of Satan that persists in the common mind to this day. In addition to Satan, there were many other ancient gods who had been transformed into demons who could be ordered to do the bidding of the black magicians of the Middle Ages: Moloch, who devours children; Belial, who foments rebellion; Astarte and Astaroth, who seduce men and women into debauchery; Baphomet, who plots murders, and so on.

Alchemists Seek Angelic Power to Change Base Metals into Gold

By the twelfth century, alchemy, built on the magical systems of the Spanish Moors and the Jewish Kabballah, had begun to achieve popularity among the intellectuals of Europe. The essence of alchemy lay in the belief that certain incantations and rituals could convince or command angelic beings to change base metals into precious ones.

Zosimus of Panapolis, a self-appointed apologist of alchemy, cited a passage in the biblical book of Genesis as the origin of the arcane art: "The sons of God saw that the daughters of men were fair." To this scriptural reference, Zosimus added the tradition that in reward for their favors, the "sons of God," who were believed to be fallen angels, endowed these women with the knowledge of how to make jewels, colorful garments, and perfumes with which to enhance their earthly charms.

The seven principal angels whose favor the alchemist sought to obtain were Michael, who was believed to transmute base metals into gold and to dissolve any enmity directed toward the alchemist; Gabriel, who fashioned silver and foresaw the future; Samuel, who protected against physical harm; and Raphael, Sachiel, Ansel, and Cassiel, who could create various gems and guard the alchemist from attack by demons. However, members of the clergy were skeptical that the alchemists were truly calling upon angels, rather than demons in disguise, and they recalled the words of the church father Tertullian (c. 160–c. 240), who confirmed earlier beliefs that the "sons of God" referred to in Genesis were evil perverters of humans who bequeathed their wisdom to mortals with the sole intention of seducing them to mundane pleasures.

Words of Power That Permit Mastery over Angels and Demons

The essence of Abramelin Magic is found in *The Sacred Magic of Abramelin the Mage*. Dated 1458, the work claims to be much older and translated originally from Hebrew. The text reveals to the adept that the universe is teeming with hordes of angels and demons who interact with human beings on many levels. All the vast array of phenomena on Earth are produced by the demonic entities, who are under the control of the angels. Humans are somewhere midway between the angelic and the demonic intelligences on the spiritual scale, and each human entity has both a guardian angel and a malevolent demon that hover near him or her from birth until death.

Abramelin Magick provides instruction to the initiates of the "Magic of Light," which will enable them to achieve mastery over the demons and place them under their control. Abramelin learned how to accomplish such a difficult task by undergoing a process of spiritual cleansing and the development of a powerful will. In addition to spiritual and mental exercises, Abramelin discovered words of power that can be arranged in magic squares and written on parchment. With the proper application of these magical squares, the magus can command the demons and order them to assist him in the acquisition of earthly knowledge and power. By applying such magic words, Abramelin magicians can gain the love of anyone they desire, discover hidden treasures, become invisible, invoke spirits to appear, fly through the air and travel great distances in a matter of minutes, and shapeshift into different animal or human forms.

Magi and the Seven Great Archangels

In the Europe of the Middle Ages, those who bore the title of *magi* contended that angelic beings could be summoned to assist in the practice of "white" magic. There were seven major planetary spirits, or Archangels, that the magi were interested in contacting: Raphael, Gabriel, Canael, Michael, Zadkiel, Haniel, and Zaphkiel.

One of the original sources of such instruction allegedly came from a great Egyptian magi and master of the occult, Hermes-Thoth, who described the revelation he had been given when he received a shimmering vision of a perfectly formed, colossal man of great beauty. The being identified itself to Hermes as Pymander, the thought of the All-Powerful, who had come to give him strength because of his love of justice and his desire to seek the truth.

Pymander told Hermes that he might make a wish and it would be granted to him. Hermes-Thoth asked for a ray of the entity's divine knowledge. Pymander granted the wish, and from the All-Powerful came seven spirits who moved in seven circles; and in the circles were all the beings that composed the universe. The action of the seven spirits in their circles is called Fate, and these circles themselves are enclosed in the divine Thought that permeates them eternally.

Hermes was told that God had committed to the seven spirits the governing of the elements; however, because God created humans in His own image and had given them power over terrestrial nature, God would grant the ability to command the seven spirits to those humans who could learn to conquer the duality of their earthly nature. God would allow such adepts to penetrate the most profound mysteries of nature. Assisting these magi in their work on Earth would be the seven superior spirits of the Egyptian system, acting as intermediaries between God and humans. These seven spirits were the same beings that the Brahmans of ancient India called the seven Devas, that in Persia were called the seven Amaschapands, that in Chaldea were called the seven Great Angels, and that in Jewish Kabbalism are called the seven Archangels.

Later, various magi sought to reconcile the Christian hierarchy of celestial spirits with the traditions of Hermes by classifying the angels into three hierarchies, each subdivided into three orders: The First Hierarchy: Seraphim, Cherubim, and Thrones; the Second Hierarchy: Dominions, Powers, and Authorities (or Virtues); and the Third Hierarchy: Principalities, Archangels, and Angels. These spirits are more perfect in essence than man, and they are here to help humankind. They work out the pattern of ordeals that each human being must pass through, and they give an account of all human actions to God after human spirits pass from the physical plane. They cannot, however, interfere in any way with human free will, which always must make the choice between good and evil. In their capacity to help, though, these angels can be called upon to assist the magi in various ways.

These archangels are the entities the magi evoke in their ceremonies. Accompanying the concept of the planetary spirits, or archangels, was something the Egyptians called *hekau*, or *word of power*. The word of power, when spoken, released a vibration capable of evoking spirits. The most powerful *hekau* for calling up a specific spirit in ceremonial magic is that spirit's name.

"To name is to define," decreed Count Cagliostro, a famous occultist of the eighteenth century. To the magi of the Middle Ages, to know the name of a spirit was to be able to command its presence and its obedience.

In contemporary times, too many people learn too late that it is spiritually hazardous to attempt to command the presence of an angel, for in most cases, it will not be an angelic being who responds but an astral masquerader, a spirit parasite.

The Human Soul Is the Prize in a Great Spiritual Warfare

Theologians of Judaism, Christianity, and Islam remind their followers that as mortal beings they are in the midst of a great spiritual warfare between the angels of light who serve God and the fallen angels who serve the forces of darkness—and that their very souls may be the prize for the victors.

In the teachings of most world religious traditions, demons are spiritual entities without physical bodies that roam the earth seeking to torment any human who may attract them by signs of spiritual and physical weaknesses or by attempts at working magic. According to these ancient traditions, demons have supernatural powers; they are numerous; and they are organized. They can inflict sickness and mental disorders on their victims. They can possess and control humans and animals. Demons lie and deceive and teach false and misleading doctrines of spirituality. They oppose all teachings and actions that seek to serve the good and God.

Since the angels of darkness are such skilled deceivers, it is very difficult to discern with unfailing accuracy the true nature of any spirit. Many spiritual teachers advise their students that the good spirits will never try to interfere with the free will of humans or seek to possess their bodies. On the other hand, the evil spirits greatly desire the physical host body of a human being. In fact, they must have such a vehicle if they are to experience earthly pleasures.

There are numerous admonitions in the New Testament cautioning conjurers of any manifesting entity to test it to determine its true motives; for example: "Test the spirits to see whether they are of God" (1 John 4:1).

While such a passage is easily quoted, its admonition is much more difficult to put in to practice when we are warned in 2 Corinthians 11:14: "Even Satan disguises himself as an angel of light."

According to some spiritual teachers, a test of alleged heavenly beings might contain these elements:

1. Did the being tell you that it has appeared because you are a chosen person from a special group of evolved humans?

2. Does the being encourage you to pray to it or to worship it?

3. Does it promise to reward you with material wealth in exchange for your devotion?

4. Does it begin to issue short-term prophecies that all come true?

5. Does it perform apparent miracles for your benefit?

6. Does it issue revelations that upon closer scrutiny are filled with half-truths, lies, and bigotry?

The Fallen Angels Have Always Hated Humans

In the traditions of Judaism, Christianity, and Islam, the animosity between demons (the fallen angels) and the human race can be traced to the very moment when God granted his earthly creations of dust and clay the priceless gift of free will. In the Judeo-Christian Bible and in the Qur'anic traditions we find references to the jealousy that afflicted certain angels regarding the attention that God displayed toward his human creation. In the Qur'an (17:61–64), Iblis (Satan), the leader of the rebellious angels, refuses to bow to a creature that God has created of clay, and he threatens to make existence miserable for the descendents of the being that the Creator has honored above them. The epistle writer Paul seems to give good counsel when he warns that humans not only engage in spiritual warfare with those of flesh and blood who serve evil, "but against the principalities, against the powers, against the world rulers of this present darkness, against the spiritual hosts of wickedness in the *heavenly* places" (Ephesians 6:12).

Although Buddhism generally rejects a cosmological dualism between good and bad, angels and demons, there is an aspect within the traditional lives of the Buddha that echoes the jealousy motif of various entities toward humans. Mara, who tempted the Awakened One on the night of his enlightenment, is said to be an *asura* or a Deva (a being of light) who was jealous of the power that was about to be bestowed on a human, for to become a Buddha would be to achieve spiritual status greater than they. Tibetan Buddhism borrows its demons from Hinduism and adds a number of indigenous entities who are ambivalent toward the inhabitants of the Himalayas, sometimes appearing as fierce and malevolent creatures, other times manifesting as teachers of enlightenment.

Elaine Was Ensnared by a Being from the Dark Side

Elaine found herself ensnared with one of the "astral tramps" that assume the guise of angels in order to seduce and deceive their human victims. She was fortunate enough to undergo an awakening process with her true guardian spirit, who managed to free her from the malevolent being who had deceived her.

Elaine's mystical initiation occurred when she had a spontaneous out-of-body experience: "I stood at my bedroom window and 'saw' through walls. It was a few moments before I realized that my physical body was still asleep on the bed."

She had never before heard of such things. She was so amazed that she told many of her friends and family about the experience, hoping that someone could explain it to her. They either looked at her peculiarly, dismissed it as a dream, or urged her to pray and to read her Bible before falling asleep.

But Elaine's search for answers had been set in motion. Cautiously at first, because of her strict Baptist upbringing, she began to read some books about metaphysics and to practice meditation.

Then *someone* began to flash back answers to her mental questions.

Before long this *someone* had taken on a personality. He was Elaine's image of the Ideal. He was infinitely patient and possessed of keen, yet compassionate, humor.

When her husband, Lowell, who was in the military service, sent for her to join him in his overseas assignment, Elaine's "companion" became more vivid. He had revealed his name as Dominion (affectionately, Dom), and her general feeling of well-being greatly increased. She could cure people's minor illnesses overnight, and she was imbued with seemingly endless energy to accomplish whatever goal she wished to achieve. She became immensely popular with the other wives in the military community. She was in demand for all the parties and gatherings. She had never before enjoyed the attention and the envy of other women.

By the time she and her husband returned to the United States, Elaine had discovered the Ouija board, and she now believed herself to be completely awakened. Dom was taking a more active role in her life, and he was encouraging her to explore the deeper mysteries of the universe. He told her to seek out certain occult practices and to try her hand at them.

"My consciousness leaped ahead in time, speeding, out of control," Elaine said. "I saw other dimensions and the creatures in them. I understood their needs, their problems. I felt their misery, as well as their joy. Many times I was visited by astral forms. I even became aware of the children in the astral world who were my students."

At the same time, she was working a full-time, nine-to-five job. She was filled with incredible energy, and she felt Dom urging her on to explore even further into the in-between dimensions. Sleep didn't matter. Food didn't matter. Her family didn't matter. What did matter was exploring the astral worlds.

Eventually, however, Elaine's hold on the material world began to slip. "The two dimensions became one—with my consent, of course," she recalled. "I felt that I had the ability to bring the subjective and objective worlds into focus, thus giving deeper meaning to both."

Elaine's daughter Becky began to work the Ouija board with her. "But Becky never got drawn into this other dimension," Elaine said. "Her objective life stayed objective. She had some inner protection that kept her free from distortion. She is the strongest person spiritually I know."

When her daughter withdrew from working the board with her, Elaine no longer had the younger woman's spiritual balance to ground her. "The Gateway between dimensions broadened, and I could no longer control the entities who chose to traffic between dimensions," Elaine admitted. "For a period of a week, demonic entities forced themselves through and tried to possess my husband and my son through me."

As Elaine sunk into greater mental and spiritual confusion, she became more aware of the true identity of the being who had been responsible for directing her mad whirl through other dimensions. Dominion had assumed the role of her spiritual companion, her guardian, and he had deceived her into going on a psychic power trip.

Now he revealed himself to Elaine as a truly malevolent entity, and he took great satisfaction in having forced her to play his game. He taunted her and said that she was in his power and must now obey his every command. Elaine tried to reject him, pitting her will against his. In spite of all of her energy being directed against him, Dom seemed to grow even stronger, literally feeding off her energy, while she grew more exhausted.

At the moment when she thought she would surely perish, Elaine prayed and cried out for her true guardian spirit. She told us:

> He manifested and dissolved the blackness around me. Knowledge of my complete Self returned to me, and I knew what the blackness was and that the malevolent entity had been drawing power from my lower self, the self that contained all the negativity that I had ever collected. And then my spirit guide set me free to float in a timelessness in which there was no past, present, or future. There was nothing to press me or make demands of me. I was my Original Self—before life and after life.

> I called out into the darkness, and out of nothing came a magnificent light, my true guide; and I realized that he had never really left me during my experience with the malevolent being that had manipulated my lower self. In the years since my awakening, I know that my true spiritual guide will always be there for me.

Discernment, Discipline, and Devoted Study

We believe that every sincere seeker who is willing to practice discernment, discipline, and devoted study may receive inspiration and guidance from angelic beings. And if you should truly believe that you have made contact with a heavenly being, remember the admonition of scripture to test the spirits. Don't forget that the astral masqueraders who take such great delight in deceiving humans are always out there, waiting patiently to ensnare the innocent, the unwary, and the unprepared.

Angelic and Other Heavenly Resources

Books

Ali, Ahmed (translator). *The Qur'an*. New York: Book-of-the-Month Club, 1992.

Alper, Matthew. *The "God" Part of the Brain*. New Hartford, NY: Rogue Press, 2001.

Anderson, Joan Wester. *In the Arms of Angels: True Stories of Heavenly Guardians*. Chicago: Loyola Press, 2004.

Anderson, Joan Wester. *Where Angels Walk*. New York: Ballantine Books, 1993.

Atwater, P.M.H. *Beyond the Light*. New York: Avon, 1997.

Bach, Marcus. *The Inner Ecstasy*. New York, Cleveland: World Publishing, 1969.

Bamberger, Bernard J. *Fallen Angels*. New York: Jewish Publication Society, Barnes & Noble, 1995.

Bennett, Hal Zina. *Spirit Animals and the Wheel of Life*. Charlottesville, VA: Hampton Roads Publishing Company, 2000.

Brandon, S.G.F. *Religion in Ancient History*. New York: Charles Scribner's Sons, 1969.

Burkhardt, Frederic, and Fredson Bowers (editors). *The Works of William James: Essays in Psychical Research*. Cambridge, MA: Harvard University Press, 1986.

Burnham, Sophy. *A Book of Angels*. New York: Fawcett Columbine, 1995.

Caron, M., and S. Hutin (translated by Helen R. Lane). *The Alchemists*. New York: Grove Press, 1961.

Carrington, Hereward. *The Case for Psychic Survival*. New York: The Citadel Press, 1957.

Carter, John Ross, and Mahinda Palihawadana (translators). *Buddhism: The Dhammapada*. New York: Book-of-the-Month Club, 1992.

Crim, Keith (general editor). *The Perennial Dictionary of World Religions*. San Francisco: HarperSanFrancisco, 1989.

De Givry, Emile Grillot (translated by J. Courtenay Locke). *Illustrated Anthology of Sorcery, Magic and Alchemy*. New York: Causeway Books, 1973.

Downing, Barry. *The Bible and Flying Saucers*. New York: Lippincott, 1968; Avon, 1970; Marlowe, 1997.

Drake, W. Raymond. *Gods and Spacemen in the Ancient West*. New York: New American Library, 1974.

Ensley, Eddie. *Visions: The Soul's Path to the Sacred*. New Orleans: Loyola Press, 2001.

Goldman, Karen. *Angel Encounters: Real Stories of Angelic Intervention*. New York: Simon & Schuster, 1995.

Harner, Michael. *The Way of the Shaman*. New York: Bantam Books, 1982.

Harpur, James, and Jennifer Westwood. *The Atlas of Legendary Places*. New York: Konecky & Konecky, 1997.

Hastings, Arthur. *With the Tongues of Men and Angels: A Study of Channeling*. New York: Holt, Rinehart, and Winston, 1991.

Hirschfelder, Arlene, and Paulette Molin. *The Encyclopedia of Native American Religions*. New York: MJF Books, 1992.

Humphrey, Nicholas. *Science, Miracles, and the Search for Supernatural Consolation*. New York: Basic Books, 1996.

Ingpen, Robert, and Philip Wilkinson. *Encyclopedia of Mysterious Places*. New York: Barnes & Noble, 1999.

James, William. *Varieties of Religious Experience*. Garden City, NY: Masterworks Program, 1971.

Jewish Publication Society Translation. *The Tanakh*. New York: Book-of-the-Month Club, 1992.

Kinnaman, Gary. *Angels Dark and Light*. Ann Arbor, MI: Servant Publications, 1994.

Kübler-Ross, Elisabeth. *On Death and Dying*. New York: Macmillan, 1969.

Larousse Dictionary of Beliefs and Religions. New York: Larousse, 1994.

Lewis, C.S. *Miracles*. New York: Macmillan, 1970.

Lissner, Ivar. *Man, God, and Magic*. New York: G.P. Putnam's Sons, 1961.

Meyer, Marvin, and Richard Smith, editors. *Ancient Christian Magic*. San Francisco: HarperSanFrancisco, 1994.

Montgomery, John Warwick. *Powers and Principalities*. Minneapolis: Dimension Books, 1975.

Moody, Raymond A., Jr. *Life after Life*. New York: Bantam Books, 1981.

Moolenburg, H.C. *Meetings with Angels*. New York: Barnes & Noble, 1995.

Morse, Melvin. *Parting Visions: Uses and Meaning of Pre-Death*. New York: Villard Books, 1994.

Newberg, Andrew, Eugene G. D'Aquili, and Vince Rause. *Why God Won't Go Away: Brain Science and the Biology of Belief*. New York: Ballantine, 2001.

Oesterreich, Traugott Konstantin. *Possession, Demoniacal and Other: Among Primitive Races in Antiquity, the Middle Ages, and Modern Times*. New Hyde Park, NY: University Books, 1966.

Otto, Rudolf. *The Idea of the Holy*. New York: Galaxy Books, 1958.

Pelikan, Jaroslav (editor). *Christianity: The Apocrypha and the New Testament*. New York: Book-of-the-Month Club, 1992.

Pelikan, Jaroslav (translated by Ralph T.H. Griffith). *Hinduism: The Rig Veda*. New York: Book-of-the-Month Club, 1992.

Ring, Kenneth. *Life at Death*. New York: Coward, McCann and Geoghegan, 1980.

Seligmann, Kurt. *The History of Magic*. New York: Meridian Books, 1960.

Shklovski, I.S., and Carl Sagan. *Intelligent Life in the Universe*. New York: Dell Books, 1968.

Sitchin, Zecharia. *The 12th Planet*. New York: Avon, 1978.

Smith, Huston. *Why Religion Matters: The Future of Faith in an Age of Disbelief*. San Francisco: Harper San Francisco, 2001.

Sullivan, Lawrence E. (editor). *Death, Afterlife, and the Soul.* New York: Macmillan, 1989.

Suzuki, D.T. *Mysticism, Christian and Buddhist.* New York: Perennial, 1971.

Tart, Charles T. *Altered States of Consciousness.* New York: John Wiley & Sons, 1969.

Underhill, Evelyn. *Mysticism.* New York: Dutton, 1961.

Unterman, Alan. *Dictionary of Jewish Lore and Legend.* New York: Thames and Hudson, 1991.

Van Dusen, Wilson. *The Presence of Other Worlds: The Findings of Emanuel Swedenborg.* New York: Harper & Row, 1974.

Villoldo, Aberto, and Stanley Krippner. *Healing States.* New York: Fireside, Simon & Schuster, 1987.

White, John. *A Practical Guide to Death and Dying.* Wheaton, IL: Theosophical Publishing House, 1988.

Willis-Brandon, Carla. *One Last Hug Before I Go: The Mystery and Meaning of Deathbed Visions.* Deerfield Beach, FL: Health Communications, 2000.

Wilson, Andrew (editor). *World Scripture: A Comparative Anthology of Sacred Texts.* New York: Paragon House, 1995.

Zaehner, R.C. (editor). *Encyclopedia of the World's Religions.* New York: Barnes & Noble, 1997.

Movies

In our opinion, angels have not been very well treated in motion pictures. We don't mean to suggest that some of Hollywood's attempts to portray angelic beings have not been good entertainment—indeed, some are considered classic films—but the manner in which benevolent beings have been portrayed in many storylines has been inaccurate, insensitive, and in some instances, insulting. However, one aspect of Hollywood's approach to the subject of angels that must be lauded is that, by and large, most of the films are ecumenical in tone and are largely absent the dictates or the dogma of any particular religious faith. Television has been kinder. For all those who enjoy a good deal of sentiment with their inspiration, several seasons of *Touched by an Angel* are available on DVD. *Highway to Heaven*, Michael Landon's take on portraying an angel, also made for a popular series and is available on DVD.

Almost an Angel (1990): This film is *almost* about an angel, and we have reservations about including it. However, we mentioned Paul Hogan's near-death experience that inspired this motion picture within the text of the book, so we decided that such firsthand research on his part had to count for something.

Hogan plays Terry Dean, a small-time crook who is hit by a car while saving a young girl's life. During a near-death experience, Dean has a vision that he had become an angel and that he must begin performing good deeds to perform penance for his past life as a thief. Although he soon discovers that he really has no "angel powers," he begins to use his innate skills and abilities to make good things happen.

Director: John Cornell. **Writing credits:** Paul Hogan. **Cast members include:** Paul Hogan, Elias Koteas, Linda Kozlowski, Doreen Lang.

Angels in the Outfield (1951): A young reporter (Janet Leigh) attributes the losing streak suffered by the Pittsburgh Pirates baseball team directly to the manager's (Paul Douglas) obscene and abusive language and his crude manner. After the reporter gets on his case, Guffy McGovern, the Pirates' manager, begins to hear the voice of an angel admonishing him to mend his ways. If he does, the angel promises, the Pirates will start winning. As the tough guy begins to soften, an orphan girl (Donna Corcoran), who has been devoutly praying for the Pirates, begins to see angels moving among the team members on the field.

Angels in the Outfield was remade in 1994 starring Danny Glover, Brenda Fricker, Tony Danza, Christopher Lloyd, Ben Johnson, and Joseph Gordon-Levitt. Directed by William Dear, the storyline was updated, and this time it was a boy who was praying for the California Angels to win the pennant. His entreaties are answered by heavenly angels who are assigned to play ball with the California Angels.

Director: Clarence Brown. **Writing credits:** Richard Conlin, story; Dorothy Kingsley, screenplay. **Cast members include:** Keenan Wynn, Lewis Stone, Spring Byington, Bruce Bennett.

The Bishop's Wife (1947): This film starring Cary Grant as Dudley, the handsome angel who comes to Earth on a mission to help a troubled bishop rediscover the true meaning of his calling, has become a Christmas classic. Although the Hollywood promotion machine teased potential audiences with the prospect of a romantic triangle among Dudley, the bishop's wife Julia (Loretta Young), and the bishop (David Niven), there are no double entendres and no offensive scenes. Grant carries off the role of a charming but purposeful angel, with the aplomb for which he was so rightly noted as an actor. This motion picture offers one of Hollywood's better characterizations of how an angel might conduct the successful accomplishment of his heavenly assignment: reminding a bishop that truly serving God does not mean conducting fundraisers to build bigger churches.

The film was remade as *The Preacher's Wife* (1996) by director Penny Marshall, with Denzel Washington as Dudley, Courtney B. Vance as the "preacher" (downgraded from bishop), and Whitney Houston as his choir director wife. The movie had audiences asking why anyone thought that the Christmas classic had to be remade in the first place. The capable cast, in addition to Washington, Vance, and Houston, included Gregory Hines, Loretta Devine, Jenifer Lewis, and Lionel Richie. However, the critical consensus is that the original is a far superior film.

Director: Henry Koster, who won the Academy Award for best director. **Writing credits:** Robert E. Sherwood, Leonardo Bercovici, and Robert Nathan. **Cast members include:** Cary Grant, Loretta Young, and David Niven, along with a roster of Hollywood's greatest character actors, including Monty Woolley, James Gleason, Gladys Cooper, Sara Haden, and Elsa Lanchester.

Date with an Angel (1987): A young man who is set to walk down the aisle wakes up after his bachelor party to discover an angel with a broken wing in his swimming pool. After an extended comedy of misunderstandings and misjudgments, the fellow falls in the love with the angel, who makes the great sacrifice of becoming human for him.

> **Director:** Tom McLoughlin. **Writing credits:** Tom McLoughlin. **Cast members include:** Michael E. Knight, as the young man; Phoebe Cates, as his human intended; and Emmanuelle Beart, as the angel.

Dogma (1999): Ben Affleck and Matt Damon are two exiled angels, Bartleby and Loki, who have been living in Wisconsin but now wish to return to heaven. The two renegades set out for New Jersey, where they believe they have found a loophole in spiritual law that will allow them to be redeemed. However, the Voice of God reveals that if the plan of Bartleby and Loki should succeed, such an action would unravel the very fabric of the universe and negate all of existence, and the Voice calls upon the last descendant of Jesus, who is an abortion clinic worker; the Thirteenth Apostle, a wise-cracking African American; and two joint-smoking, foul-talking prophets to halt the scheme of the mischievous angels. This motley crew of crusaders must also avoid the destructive powers of the demon Azrael, who would like to see Bartleby and Loki succeed as an act of revenge against God. For those moviegoers who feared the movie was about Catholic Church dogma, nothing could be further from the reality of the film. Some critics greeted the film with reviews condemning it as "blasphemous," while others deplored the waste of a great cast in a poorly directed, crudely written film. There were those reviewers, however, who saw in *Dogma* a perception of angels that was unique in motion pictures and emphasized the conflict that began in Heaven long before Adam was created.

> **Director:** Kevin Smith. **Writing credits:** Kevin Smith. **Cast members include:** Ben Affleck, Matt Damon, Linda Fiorentino, Chris Rock, Alan Rickman, Jason Lee, Salma Hayek, Janeane Garofalo, George Carlin, and Kevin Smith.

A Guy Named Joe (1943): The marvelous actor Spencer Tracy is Pete Sandridge, a daring but reckless World War II fighter pilot who dies in combat and returns as a guardian angel (spirit guide) for a young pilot named Ted Randall (Van Johnson). As if adjusting to existence as an angel guide weren't difficult enough, Pete has to stand by as a spirit and watch Randall fall in love with his girlfriend, Dorinda (Irene Dunne). This motion picture—with its powerful themes of unconditional love, friendship, and a spirit's ascension to a higher dimension—became one of the most popular movies of the World War II era. Although the main character is named Pete, the title comes from the credo of the American servicemen that any stand-up guy was called Joe.

In 1989 director Steven Spielberg, who had been a great admirer of the 1943 film, remade *A Guy Named Joe* as *Always*. Pete (Richard Dreyfuss) now became a daredevil pilot fighting fires rather than enemy aircraft, and his spirit returns to watch over Ted (Brad Johnson) as he develops his skills as a firefighter. Holly Hunter is Dorinda, Pete's girlfriend, who falls in love with Ted. Audrey Hepburn, in her last film role, plays the heavenly angel who escorts Pete back to Earth and to his role as an unseen tutor for Ted.

Director: Victor Fleming. **Writing credits:** David Boehm, Frederick Hazlitt Brennan, Chandler Sprague, and Dalton Trumbo. **Cast members include:** Spencer Tracy, Van Johnson, Irene Dunne, Ward Bond, James Gleason, Lionel Barrymore, Barry Nelson, Don DeFore.

Heaven Only Knows (1947): Because of the initial resistance of audiences to a religious fantasy about an angel, the film was withdrawn, retitled, and rereleased in the same year as *Montana Mike*. Interestingly, the story played well both in small Bible Belt towns strictly as a Western, *Montana Mike*, and in larger venues under its original title, *Heaven Only Knows*, as a religious film. The plot has actor Brian Donlevy, famous for his tough-guy, often villainous roles, as a Montana saloon owner and ruthless killer, causing a heavenly uproar of great consequence when it is discovered that when he was born the angels neglected to make an entry for him in the Book of Life. Because of this oversight, the Book of Life and the Book of Destiny cannot be balanced, and an angel (Robert Cummings) is assigned to visit the tough cattle town and put things right.

Director: Albert S. Rogell. **Writing credits:** Art Arthur, Ernest Haycox. **Cast members include:** Brian Donlevy, Robert Cummings,

Jorja Curtright, Marjorie Reynolds, Bill Goodwin, John Litel, Stuart Erwin.

The Heavenly Kid (1985): Following the popular Hollywood theme that humans become angels after their death, this film says that certain people have to stay in the lower realms for a while and learn to look in their hearts before they can ascend to Heaven. When Bobby dies in an automobile accident, he is informed that he cannot walk through the heavenly gates until he has put in some time as a teenager's guardian angel.

Director: Cary Medoway. **Writing credits:** Cary Medoway and Martin Copeland. **Cast members include:** Lewis Smith, Jason Gedrick, Jane Kaczmarek, Richard Mulligan.

It's a Wonderful Life (1946): There is no question that this classic film is the best-known Hollywood presentation of an angel interacting with his human charge. One may quibble about whether humans become angels after an afterlife process spent earning that status, but only a viewer with the hardest of hearts will not be reaching for a tissue in the film's closing moments when the Christmas tree ornament tinkles and the little daughter in George Bailey's arms reminds her daddy (and all of us) that "teacher says" that whenever a bell rings, an angel is getting its wings.

The compassionate businessman George Bailey (James Stewart), who becomes increasingly frustrated with the crooked and dishonest dealings of his town's more worldly citizens until he falls into despair, was director Frank Capra's spokesperson for the restoration of solid values into American life. World War II had recently ended, and Capra, famous for his comedic view of life, was now becoming depressed by what he saw as the deterioration of family values and an increasing apathy toward God, goodness, freedom and the American way. Although Capra's cinematic wish to remind the film's viewers of what was truly important in life was an initial box office failure, it went on to win the hearts of several generations of film audiences. In June 2006 the American Film Institute named *It's a Wonderful Life* Hollywood's most inspirational film. The motion picture became a Christmas classic in the 1970s, and both black and white and colorized DVDs are available.

Director: Frank Capra. **Writing credits:** Philip Van Doren Stern, Frances Goodrich. **Cast members include:** James Stewart, Donna Reed, Lionel Barrymore, Thomas Mitchell, Henry Travers, Beulah Bondi, Frank Faylen, Ward Bond, Gloria Grahame.

Michael (1966): Two reporters track down reports that the Archangel Michael has left Heaven and is living with an elderly woman in Iowa. While the jaded tabloid reporters are shocked to find that the story leads are true, they are even more astonished to find that Michael, very large wings and all, is also a chain smoker who loves to drink beer, speaks occasionally in colorful language, and has what appears to be a very strong libido. While the portrayal of Michael is no doubt considered blasphemous at worst and disillusioning at best, John Travolta, as the archangel, and an excellent supporting cast manage to make the drive from Iowa to Chicago a life-altering quest for the participants.

Director: Nora Ephron. **Writing credits:** Peter Dexter, Jim Quinlan. **Cast members include:** John Travolta, Andie MacDowell, William Hurt, Bob Hoskins, Robert Pastorelli, Jean Stapleton, Teri Garr, Wallace Langham.

The Prophecy (1995); The Prophecy II (1998): These films deal with the war in Heaven with a dash of the Watchers and the Nephilim thrown in for good measure. Christopher Walken appears in both films as the Archangel Gabriel, and the way he sneeringly refers to humans as "God's monkeys" insinuates the resentment that some angels feel over God having presented humans to them as his greatest achievement. In the first of the films, Gabriel comes to Earth to collect a soul that has been decreed to end the stalemate that has occurred in yet another war in Heaven. It is up to a former priest and a little girl to stop him, but woe to anyone who gets in Gabe's way.

The second film takes place after Gabriel has been blocked in Heaven and returns to Earth determined to annihilate the human species that he has resented for so many millennia. The climactic battle in this film occurs not on the plains of Megiddo but in the sacred grounds of Eden.

Director, 1995: Gregory Widen. **Writing credits:** Gregory Wilden. **Cast members include:** Christopher Walken, Elias Koteas, Virginia Madsen, Eric Stoltz, Viggo Mortensen, Amanda Plummer, Adam Goldberg, Mariah "Shining Dove" Snyder.

Director, 1998: Greg Spence. **Writing credits:** Gregory Widen, Matt Greenberg. **Cast members include:** Christopher Walken, Russell Wong, Jennifer Beals, Brittany Murphy, Eric Roberts, Glenn Danzig, Steve Hynter.

Wings of Desire/Der Himmel uber Berlin (1987); Faraway, So Close!/In weiter Ferne, so nah! (1993): Many people have found Wim Wender's film about Damiel and Cassiel, two angels who have spent their entire existence watching over humans, to be very touching. The angels move about Berlin, invisible to all but children, observing, collecting, and preserving. As Damiel and Cassiel walk through the streets unnoticed, they cannot help overhearing the inner thoughts, daydreams, and fantasies of the men, women, and children whom they pass. Cassiel is content to spend eternity following the same endless process of being a watcher, overseeing human activities. Damiel, however, is growing restless with the eternal role of an observer. The more he savors the sights, sounds, and smells of human existence, the more he would like to feel the emotions of a man or a woman and to be able to touch someone's life. Eventually Damiel begins to fall in love with a mortal.

Director (1987): Wim Wenders. **Writing credits:** Peter Handke, Richard Reitinger. **Cast members include:** Bruno Ganz, Otto Sander, Solveig Dommartin, Curt Bois, Peter Falk.

The convincing portrayal of an invisible angelic presence forever watching over humans became so successful with international audiences that Wender was encouraged to film a sequel in 1993, *In weiter Ferne, so nah! (Faraway, So Close!)*, which continued to follow the paths of Damiel and Cassiel as they moved unseen through streets, apartments, and subways in Berlin.

Director (1993): Wim Wenders. **Writing credits:** Richard Reitinger, Wim Wenders. **Cast members include:** Bruno Ganz, Otto Sander, Nastassja Kinski, Aline Krajewski, Peter Falk.

In 1998 Brad Silberling was given the assignment of remaking *Wings of Desire* and transplanting the watchful angels from Berlin to Los Angeles. Wim Wenders and Peter Handke adapted the concepts of their screenplays from *Wings of Desire* and *Faraway, So Close!* for *City of Angels*, but since it was now an American film set in Los Angeles, the angels spent a lot of time at the beach—and, strangely enough, hanging out at the library. We also learn that in sunny California, there are a number of former angels who have chosen to give up their immortality for a taste of mortal pleasures.

When a doctor (Meg Ryan) catches a glimpse of an angel (Nicholas Cage) in the operating room, the angel feels his heart light being turned on. Cage, an Academy Award winner, has created many fine performances. Unfortunately, the manner in which he manifests behind and around the doctor and stares longingly at her reminds one of a vampire stalking his victim rather than a lovesick angel contemplating the embrace of a mortal woman.

Cast members include: Meg Ryan, Nicholas Cage, Andre Braugher, Dennis Franz, Robin Bartlett, Colm Feore, Joanna Merlin.

Index

abir, 14
Abraham, 211
Abramelin Magic, 218
Afrika Korps, 46
Agrest, Matest M., 211
Ahriman, 216
alchemy, 15, 217
Alexander, Hartley Burr, 108–9
al-jinn, 17, 143
Amaschapands, 219
American Indian Ceremonial Dances (Collier), 104
Anakims of Philisa, 208
Ancient Egypt, 1
angel "night school"
    recollections of, 196–99
    two classmates find each other later in life, 199–202
angel wings, sound and sight of
    angel with flaming sword scares away apartment building thugs, 21–23
    car accident victims comforted by praying angel, 23–24
    dying friend sees guardian angel's wings, 24–25
    woman avoids traffic accident, 20–21
angelic communication, guidelines for, 164–66
angelic presence
    angel saves hiker stuck on Yellowstone cliff, 97
    experiences with angel guide, 94–96
angelic visions

    appearances of glowing light, 3
    blinding white light, 3
    brain chemistry, 3
angel(s). *See also* guardian angel(s); hooded angels; shamanism; other angel and angelic entries
    and Abramelin Magic, 218
    and alchemy, 217
    benevolent spirit teachers from other dimensions, 7
    derivation of word, 14
    description of, 2
    encouragement of, 167
    fallen angels, 8
    God's heavenly messengers, 4
    guardian angels, 4–5
    guides, 95–96
    Magi and archangels, 218–20
    and magic, 216–17
    mysterious Watchers, 7
    nature spirits, 6–7
    popularity of, 214–16
    songs, 166–67
    sons of God, 7
    space brothers and sisters, 7–8
    spirit guides, 5–6
    spirits of the dead who earn their wings, 6
    supernatural figures, 8–12
    vs. devils, 158
angels and their sacred places
    discovering one's own sacred place, 120–22
    glowing angels zig-zagging at sacred Peruvian lake, 117–18

man finds hope with Apaches in Tierra Blanca, 113–15

multidimensional phenomena, 118–19

white horse as sign from deceased son, 116–17

angels and UFOs, 118–19
alien angel from childhood years returns to save woman from sniper shot, 136

angel calls boy "son," 137

contactees, 7

hooded beings alter woman's state of consciousness, 140–41

man reminded of when he was pulled away from semi truck as a five-year-old, 142

possibility of guardian angels and spirit guides flying them, 139–40

space brothers and sisters, 137–38

theory that Jesus Christ will return in space vehicle, 138–39

UFO phenomena, 117–18

youngster sees alien angels, 135–36

angels as creators
future agenda for angels, 212–13

Genesis, Book of, 205–8

great flood, 209–10

nephilim, 208–9

spiritual warfare between angels, 210–12

theories on, 203–5

angels of darkness, 210, 220–21

angels of death, 17

angels of light, 210, 220–21

Angels (third hierarchy), 219

angels who appear human-like, 137–38
angelic man visits lonely couple on Christmas Eve, 73–74

angelic nurse tells accident victim he "can't leave just yet," 70–73

hitchhiker expresses thanks and provides peace, 78–79

Jesus appears as homeless man and cures dying baby, 79–81

man's search for missing object results in woman's discovery of earring she didn't know was missing, 75–78

son learns recently deceased father is in good hands, 69–70

young girl with beaming smile in restroom, 74–75

angels who bring men and women together
God and angels show Brit and Canadian that they belong together, 193–95

man told that woman was "the one" after years of being told otherwise about other women, 181–86

Steigers brought together by angel "borrowing" persona of woman, 186–93

angels who heal
artist with cancer is cured after angel appears through her five-year-old, 172–73

dead teenage girl brought back to life by four angels, 175–78

teenage girl with incurable disease is cured after hearing beautiful angelsong, 169–72

teenage son cured after mother prays with reassuring stranger, 178–80

toddler's brain surgery reveals that growth is noncancerous, 168–69

woman with pain after spinal surgery healed by angel with seashell, 174

angels who intervened in crisis situations
abusive father changes his ways, 57–58

getting in touch the gentle way, 65–68

guide mountain climbers survive blinding snowstorm, 62–65

passerby finds badly injured motorist after accident, 59–60

soldier protected behind enemy lines, 55–57

violin-playing angel saves boy's life, 60–62

angels who leave evidence of their visits
angel figure on fireplace brick, 52–54

"beautiful man" leaves blankets and money, 49–51

man gives his last dollars to starving man, 47–49

money from heaven, 51–52

soldier receives water in desert, 45–47

angels who provided comfort following death of family member, 2

angels who warned of imminent danger, 2–3

angiris, 17

Ansel, 217
Apocalypse, 143
apsaras, 17
archangels, 218–20
Archangels (third hierarchy), 219
Armageddon, 143, 210
Asmodeus, 216
Astaroth, 217
Astarte, 217
asura, 222
asuras, 17
Aurobindo, Sri, 159
Authorities, 219
Azazcl, 208
Azrael, 15

Baphomet, 217
Barachiel, 15
Bat-Enosh, 210
Beelzebub, 216
Belial, 143, 217
benevolent being of light, 2
Benevolent Outcome, 66–68
benevolent spirit teachers from other
    dimensions, 7
Bernhardt, Clarisa, 163–67
Bible, 11, 19
The Blue Danube, 61–62
bne Elohim, 14, 18
bodhisattva, 15
bright moon, 9
British Commandos, 45
Brooks, Philip, 19
Bryant, M., 74–78
Buddha, 222
Buddhism, 15

Cagliostro, Count, 220
Canael, 218
Candler, Nancy, 20–21
Caruso, Dr., 186, 187, 191–92, 193
Cassiel, 217
Cat's Nebula, 207
cave artists, 106
Cayce, Edgar, 143
Chamuel, 15

Chang, Sam, 204, 212–13
channels, 5–6
Cherubim, 219
chimpanzees, 207
Ching, Diane, 128–30
Choueke, Esmond, 60
Chown, Marcus, 203–4
Christian mystics, 15
Christianity, 6, 14, 15–16
Church of Jesus Christ of Latter-day
    Saints, 158
Clarence (fictional angel), 6
clouds, 9
Collier, John, 104
Collins, Francis, 205
The Council of Creators (Shapiro), 66
Crick, Francis, 204
Crofts, Eric, 130–31
Crofts, Mary, 130–31
curandera, 102

Daephrenocles, 95, 97, 98–99
Daniel, 11, 18
daughters of men, 206, 207, 209
deceased relatives as guardian angels, 10,
    123–24
    appear during night, 128
    deceased fiancé warns against one
        prospective marriage and approves
        of another, 131–34
    grandfather looks after mother's son
        stationed in Iraq, 130–31
    grandmother warns grandson to avoid
        gas station that was soon to be
        robbed, 126–27
    great uncle comforts plane crash vic-
        tim at fish pond, 128–30
    late wife sends sign through license
        plate and billboards, 124–26
demons, 220
Devas, 6, 16–17, 219, 222
Diegel, Patricia Rochelle, 192
Diegel, Rev. Jon Terrance, 192
DNA, 204–5, 206, 212–13
Dominions, 219
Drake, W. Raymond, 140
Draun, Sandor (Shony) Alex, 60–62

Eastern Orthodox Christians, 15
Eduardo, Don, 121–22
electronic voice phenomenon (EPV), 54
Elijah (spirit teacher), 148
Elohim, 14, 18, 206
elves, 6
Emims of Moab, 208
End Times, 142–44
Enoch, Book of, 208–9, 210
evil spirits, 17
Ezekiel, 11, 18

face of religious figures, 9
fair daughters of man, 206, 207
fairies, 6
fallen angels, 8, 208–9, 215–16, 220–21,
    221–22
Fate, 219
Fatima, Portugal, 10
First Ranger Battalion, 45
Flew, Anthony, 205
flood, 209–10
Flory, Lori Jean, 35, 94–96, 97, 98–99, 196
footsteps, 9
Franco-Cantabrian cave artists, 106
Fryzel, Mike, 60

Gabriel, 15, 17, 19, 217, 218
garudas, 17
Genesis, Book of, 205–8, 211
The Gentle Way (Moore), 66–68
ghosts, 9
glowing lights, 144–45
gods and goddesses, 7
God's heavenly messengers, 4
Goliath, 208
Grana, Stephanie, 59–60
Great Angels, 219
great flood, 209–10
Great Spirit, 115

guardian angel(s), 4–5. See also deceased
    relatives as guardian angels; invisible
    guardian angels
  blessings from, 35
  dog as, 106–8
  driver asleep at wheel protected, 30–31
  getting in touch the gentle way, 65–68
  motorcyclist avoids injuries during
    accident, 34–35
  percentage who have seen, 2
  soldier protected behind enemy lines,
    55–57
  traffic stops to prevent further colli-
    sions during accident, 31–32
  visualizing one's, 25–29
  woman brought back from the Dark
    Side, 222–25
  woman in labor safely arrives at hospi-
    tal during snowstorm, 32–33
Gunderson, Sarah, 175–78
Gunderson, Thor, 175

Haniel, 15, 218
Hansen, Eleanor, 40–42
Hansen, George, 40–42
Hansen, Sherry. See Steiger, Sherry
    Hansen
Harricharan, John and Mardai, 124–26
Harrison, Edward, 204
Healing States (Villoldo and Krippner),
    121–22
hekau, 220
Hermes-Thoth, 218–19
Herschel, William, 207
hierarchies, 219
Hinduism, 16–17
Holy Ones, 7
hooded angels
  abusive biker's girlfriend assisted by,
    151
  assists counselor during guidance ses-
    sions, 147–48
  effects of stroke on mother disappear,
    149–50
  "I am" concept, 161
  injured diver's health dramatically
    improves, 151–52

man's head and neck pain disappears, 156–58

as master librarians, 162

mission of, 155

repeated presence of, prior to awakening, 159–62

Steiger, Brad, 148

teenager cured of allergies, 146–47

teenager cured of strep, 148–49

Human Genome Project, 204, 212

"I am" concept, 144–45, 161

Iblis, 17–18, 216, 221

image noted only by witnesses singled out for communication, 10

Indra, 212

invisible guardian angels. *See also* deceased relatives as guardian angels; guardian angel(s)

    child copes with abusive family, 37–38

    child warned of rattlesnake in berry bushes, 38–39

    driver urged to put shoulder belt on just before accident, 42

    nun on side of road, 43–44

    seen only with one's heart, 36–37

    stranded motorists pushing car warned to jump in ditch to avoid oncoming car, 39–42

Iraq war, 130–31

Islam, 6, 14, 17–18

Israfel, 15

Israfil, 17

It's a Wonderful Life, 6

Iza' il, 17

Jedidiah, 147

Jegudiel, 15

Jehudiel, 15

Jeremial, 15

Jesus, 80–81

Jophiel, 15

Jorgensen, Alf and Marta, 85

Judaism, 6, 14, 18–19

Kalson, Stan, 186, 187

Kaul, Dave, 59–60

Krippner, Stanley, 121–22

Kübler-Ross, Elisabeth, 86–87

lamassu, 11

Lamech, 210

leaf, 99–100

League of Seekers, 156

ley lines, 119

light, 10

light beings, 142–44

linear time, 104

lipika, 17

Lissner, Ivar, 104, 105–6

Little Butterfly (Priscilla Garduno Wolf), 102, 172

Lot, 211

lower-spirit worlds, 10

Lowery, Jimmy, 52

Lucifer, 210

Magi, 218–20

magic, 216–17

Magic of Light, 218

Mahabharata, 212

mal' ach, 14

malaikah, 17

Malik, 15

Man, God, and Magic (Lissner), 105–6

Marino, Sal and Benedette, 85

materialization of holy figures, 9

Meadows, Mary-Caroline, 186–87, 189, 190–92, 193

Medicine people, 102–4

Medicine power, 108–9

Meinel, Arden and Marjorie, 207

Mesopotamia, 1, 11

messenger, 14

Meyer, Stephen, 204–5

Michael (archangel), 15, 19, 35, 99–101, 217, 218

"mighty," 14

miracles, 115
mist, 9
Mohr, James, 126–27
Moloch, 217
moon, 9
Moore, Tom T., 65–68
Moorhead, Lee, 151–52
Moses, 18, 19
multidimensional beings, 9
Munkar, 15, 17
Mussaelian, Adnan, 204, 212–13
mysterious Watchers, 7

Nakir, 15, 17
Native Americans, 108–9
nature spirits, 6–7
near-death experiences
    angel helps transition from death to
      life, 86–89
    core of, 89
    decision made for man to complete
      divine mission amidst bright light, 83
    family reunion in Heaven, 83–86
    presence of angels, 11
    Steiger, Sherry, series of, 90–93
    as teaching, revelatory experience, 89
    tunnel and bright light, 82
Nebuchadnezzar, 18
nephilim, 208–9
New Jerusalem, 92–93
Newton, Isaac, 204
Noah, 209–10

Obbieuth, 15
O' Grady, Scott, 55–57
Other Side, 5, 90, 96, 105
Ouija board, 223, 224
out-of-body phenomena, 10, 96

Paleolithic Age, 1
Palmer, Rev. B. W., 8–12
Pan, 216–17
Paul (apostle), 69, 222
Phanuel, 15

Phares, Darlene, 78–79
picture on wall, 9
powers, 14
Powers (second hierarchy), 219
Principalities, 219
Protestant Christians, 15–16
Purcell, Tom, 87–89
Pymander, 219

radiation, 207–8
Raguel, 15
Raphael, 15, 19, 166–67, 217, 218
Raziel, 15
religious figures magnified, 9
Remiel, 15
Rig Veda, 212
Roman Catholics, 15, 16
Rommel, Erwin, 46

Sachiel, 217
sacred places. See angels and their sacred
  places
Samuel, 217
Sandalphon, 15
Sariel, 15
Satan, 217, 221
Satanas, 216
Selaphiel, 15
Semjaza, 208
Seraphim, 219
Set, 216
shaft of light, 9
Shaitan, 17–18
shamanism. See also under angel(s)
    definition, 104–5
    spirit guides, 5–6
    spirit helpers, 105
    totem animal, 105–6
    vision quest, 108–9
    Wakan Tanka spirits, 102–4
Shamsiel, 15
Shapiro, Robert, 66
Silver Cloud, 109
Sister Wolf, 172
skies open up, 9
Smith, Joseph, 158

Sodom and Gomorrah, 211
solid object, 9
songs, angelic, 166–67
sons of God, 7, 14, 206–7
Sosby, Arnold, 210
space brothers and sisters, 7–8, 137–38, 139
spirit entities, 9
spirit guides, 2, 5–6, 25–29, 105
spirit teacher, 152–55
spiritual presence, 9
spiritual warfare, 220–21
Spotted Horse, Pete, 103
Sri Aurobindo, 159
Stardancer, 115
Steiger, Brad
    discovering one's own sacred place,
        120–22
    glowing angels zig-zagging at sacred
        Peruvian lake, 117–18
    and hooded angel, 148
    meets former batallion ranger, 45, 47
    meets future wife Sherry, 186–93
    multidimensional phenomena, 118–19
    recalls childhood near-death experi-
        ence, 93
    Silver Cloud, 109
    white horse as sign from wife's
        deceased son, 116
Steiger Questionnaire of Mystical, Para-
    normal and UFO Experiences, 2, 128, 147
Steiger, Sherry Hansen
    glowing angels zig-zagging at sacred
        Peruvian lake, 117–18
    meets future husband Brad, 187–93
    multidimensional phenomena, 118–19
    series of near-death experiences, 90–93
    white horse as sign from deceased son,
        116–17
Stewart, James, 6
sudden vanishment, 10
supernatural figures, 8–12
supernatural invasion of Earth, 203–13
supernatural light, 10
swan, 100–101

telepathic communication, 164–66
Tertullian, 217
test (of angels), 16

third eye, 96
Thrones, 219
time, shaman vs. linear, 104–5
totem animal, 105–6
totemism, 109–12
touch, 9
Trujillo, Matilde Fernandez, 106
trumpeter swan, 100–101

UFOs. See angels and UFOs
Uriel, 15, 19

Vaca, Marina Sanzuez, 174
Van Tassel, George, 139
Villoldo, Alberto, 121–22
Vimana, 212
violin, 60–62
Virgin Mary, 9
Virtues, 219
vision quest, 108–12
visualization technique, 152–55
voices, 9
Voltaire, 138

Wagner, Stephen, 51–52
Wakan Tanka spirits, 102–4
Watchers, 7, 208
Watson, James, 204
West, Julian, 156
White Eagle, Paul, 103
white horse, 116–17
Williams, David, 166
wings. See angel wings, sound and sight of
Winnebago tribe, 109
Wolf, Priscilla Garduno, 79–81, 102–4,
    105, 106, 113–15, 172–73
Wolfman Dan, 115
word of power, 220
World War II, 45–47
The World's Rim: Great Mysteries of the
    North American Indians (Alexander), 108

Y

Yahweh, 18
Yun, Chang, 128–30

Z

Zadkiel, 15, 218
Zaphkiel, 218
Zechariah, 18
Zoroastrianism, 18
Zosimus of Panapolis, 217